THE LONG ROAD TO ARMAGEDDON

THE LONG ROAD TO ARMAGEDDON

MARVIN MOORE

Pacific Press®
Publishing Association
Nampa, Idaho | Oshawa, Ontario, Canada
www.pacificpress.com

Cover design by Steve Lanto
Cover design resources from iStockphoto

The author assumes full responsibility for the accuracy of all facts and quotations as cited in this book.

Additional copies of this book are available by calling toll-free 1-800-765-6955 or by visiting http://www.AdventistBookCenter.com.

Library of Congress Cataloging-in-Publication Data
Names: Moore, Marvin, 1937- author.
Title: The long road to Armageddon / Marvin Moore.
Description: Nampa : Pacific Press Publishing Association, 2017.
Identifiers: LCCN 2017003883 | ISBN 9780816362622 (pbk.)
Subjects: LCSH: Good and evil—Biblical teaching. | Good and evil—Religious aspects—
    Christianity. | Spiritual warfare. | Devil—Christianity. | Jesus Christ. | Armageddon. | End
    of the world. | General Conference of Seventh-day Adventists—Doctrines.
Classification: LCC BS680.G6 M66 2017 | DDC 236/.9—dc23 LC record available at
    https://lccn.loc.gov/2017003883

ISBN 978-0-8163-6262-2

March 2017

What This Book Is About

When I began writing this book, I had in mind to title it *Armageddon*. However, I soon realized that this title would be quite misleading. The real theme of this book is the conflict between good and evil—what Adventists have always referred to as *the great controversy*. In this book, I have used insights about this conflict from both the Bible and Ellen White's writings. Ellen White wrote a whole series of books on this theme, titled The Conflict of the Ages—five books that cover the history of good and evil from Lucifer's rebellion in heaven to his destruction in the lake of fire and the re-creation of our planet into the eternal home of the redeemed.[1]

In this one book, I obviously can't cover the great-controversy theme in the detail that Ellen White did in her five books, as each of which is two or three times longer than mine. So I've focused most of my attention on three critical points in the conflict between good and evil, with a couple of chapters inserted between each of these critical points. The three critical points are (1) Lucifer's fall from heaven and his subsequent entanglement of the human race in his rebellion; (2) Christ's victory over Satan during Christ's life on earth; and (3) the final crisis that will reach its climax with the battle of Armageddon. Also, I have divided discussion about the battle of Armageddon into two parts. Part 1 deals with the battle before the second coming of Christ, which will bring the history of sin on earth to an end; and part 2 examines the battle at the end of the millennium, which will bring the universal conflict between good and evil to a close.

I'm convinced that the world we live in is entering the beginning stages of that final crisis and that we need to be preparing spiritually for what lies ahead. I hope that what I've written here will help you understand your role and the role of your church in today's world.

I hope that you are as blessed by reading this book as I have been in writing it!

---

1. The five books in The Conflict of the Ages are titled *Patriarchs and Prophets, Prophets and Kings, The Desire of Ages, The Acts of the Apostles,* and *The Great Controversy.*

Contents

CHAPTER 1

What the Kingdom of Light Is Like

Take an imaginary trip with me back in time, back before Christ and the Cross, back before Adam and Eve, back before Lucifer's rebellion in heaven, and back even before the Trinity had created angels. It was just the three of Them. And They were lonesome. They had each other, to be sure, and we can only faintly imagine what the love that flowed between Them was like. It must have been profound.

Yet, it wasn't enough! They wanted more beings whom They could love and who could love Them.

If you and I want someone to love, we go in search of that someone, and we keep searching till we find him or her (or keep hoping we will). But the Trinity had just the three of Them. There weren't any other "someones" out there whom They could find to love. So They created them—huge numbers of them! If the biblical math is anywhere close to correct, the Trinity may have created as many as 150 trillion angels.* God the Father, Son, and Holy Spirit must have been truly lonesome!

Of course, They couldn't just create all of these angels and then put them out there to get along as best they could. Every society of intelligent beings needs a government to organize their interactions. Back in the late 1700s, James Madison, one of the founders of the American republic, said that "if men were angels, no government would be necessary."[1] That's actually not correct. Every society needs a government with laws and the authority to enforce them, and

---

* In Revelation 5:11, John said that he "heard the voice of many angels, numbering thousands upon thousands, and ten thousand times ten thousand" (see also Daniel 7:10). If you multiply 10,000 times 10,000, you get 100 million. Then keep in mind that a third of the angels that the Trinity created joined Lucifer in his rebellion (Revelation 12:3, 4), so the 100 million that John saw in vision represented only two-thirds of the original number. This means that the Trinity actually created 150 million angels. And this doesn't take into account the additional "thousands upon thousands" of angels that John said he also saw in his vision. He didn't give us a mathematical formula for calculating them into the equation, but if we multiply the 150 million by 1,000 twice, we get 150 trillion.

that's as true of heaven's perfect society as it is of any of our imperfect societies on Earth. I'm choosing to call heaven's government the Kingdom of Light.

So here's a question I would like you to consider with me: what was the nature of this Kingdom of Light that the Trinity established? It's important to understand that I'm not asking you what heaven is like, though what I discuss in this chapter will certainly help to answer that question as well. But the topic of this chapter is the *nature* of the government that God established when He created the angels.

The society that made up the Kingdom of Light had laws and the authority to enforce them, but in addition it had two other qualities that we don't find in earthly societies. Those two qualities were love and freedom. So here are the four major qualities of the Kingdom of Light that we will be discussing in this chapter: love, law, authority, and freedom.

Love

Now imagine 150 trillion people on planet Earth. There would be standing room only! But let's just suppose that our world was as large as the sun and could comfortably accommodate 150 trillion people. What would that society be like? With 7.5 billion people in today's world, we have a hard enough time getting along. The idea of 150 trillion of us bunched up on one planet is beyond frightening! How did all those angels manage to get along in peace and harmony?

The answer is God's law of love. Jesus said that the greatest commandment is to "love the Lord your God with all your heart and with all your soul and with all your mind" and that the second greatest commandment is to "love your neighbor as yourself" (Matthew 22:37, 39). These laws apply just as much in heaven as they do here on Earth, for "God is love" (1 John 4:8), and every intelligent being He creates is loving.

Unfortunately, on our planet, we're all infected with selfishness, and the majority of people operate on that principle most of the time. It's frankly hard for us to imagine an entire society that operates on the law of love all the time with no exceptions. Some of us *try* to operate according to that law, but we have trouble doing it. We have many kinds of jealousies and hatreds and anger issues. Even the church is infected with these traits!

Let's consider that law of love for a moment. Does it mean that the angels always agreed on everything all the time? Absolutely not! While none of us has ever been in heaven, the mere fact that the most loving people on this planet often have strong disagreements tells me that it's the same with the angels in heaven. Love doesn't mean that everyone has to see eye to eye. In fact, what a boring society that would be! Love means that we disagree respectfully. The apostle Paul had that in mind when he wrote to the Christians in Ephesus, "I urge you to . . . be completely humble and gentle; be patient, bearing with one another in love. Make every effort to keep the unity of the Spirit through the bond of peace" (Ephesians 4:1–3).

Notice, however, that Paul had to *urge* these believers to be humble, gentle, patient, and to bear with one another in love. That's because it wasn't happening in the church back then to the extent that it should have, nor is it today. We live in a world that's dominated by the Kingdom of Darkness, where selfishness still has a hold on everyone, even those of us in the church. But what Paul had to *urge* upon the Christians in Ephesus came naturally to the angels in the Kingdom of Light prior to Lucifer's rebellion. In fact, just as we find it difficult to imagine a heaven where humility, gentleness, patience, and forbearance are as natural a part of the culture as water flowing downhill, so the angels would have found it impossible to imagine a culture where these qualities did not exist. What to us is inspired counsel—because we need it so much in our sinful society—would have seemed absurd to them. Urging people to be humble, patient, gentle, and kind? Why would anyone have to say *that*?

Love was the dominant characteristic in the Kingdom of Light, which the Trinity created. However, three other characteristics were also very important. Law is the one we'll examine next.

Law

I've already mentioned law in connection with God's law of love, but there's more about law that we need to look at.

Law is the foundation of government. The purpose of government is to bring about a stable society; and to achieve that, a government has to create laws that people are required to obey.

We humans have two kinds of laws. One kind of law keeps us organized and safe from harm, such as traffic laws and building codes. One-way streets keep traffic moving more smoothly, and building codes keep structures from collapsing. The second kind of law is moral law, which protects our lives and our property from criminals who would steal from us and injure or kill us. Moral law is our concern here. Moral law can work only where created beings have two mental characteristics: a high level of intelligence and a moral sense. So let's examine each of these in a bit more detail.

Intelligence. Animals have consciousness and the limited intelligence they need to observe the world around them and take care of their basic needs for survival. The intelligence of angels and humans is of a much higher order. God has given us the ability to process abstract ideas, such as philosophy, mathematics, and music. We can investigate, understand concepts, and create extremely complex technology; none of which animals can do. The scientific age, which began about five hundred years ago, has produced amazing tools for communication, travel, and everyday living. Telephones, fax machines, and the Internet have transformed the way we communicate, and these tools are bringing dramatic changes even to the developing parts of the world.* Cars have made it possible for us to travel at ground speeds of eighty to one hundred miles per hour or more on freeways,† and airplanes have surpassed the speed of sound in the air. Running water, electricity, and air conditioning have made life far more comfortable; and advances in medical technology have at least doubled the life span of people in the developed parts of the world.

That's what our intelligence has made possible.

Moral sense. Animals have an instinctive desire to protect themselves, which is why lions and tigers will growl when they feel threatened and why they don't hesitate to attack and injure or kill if the threat intensifies. We humans have the same instinctive desire for self-protection, but the moral part of our nature tells us intuitively that it's wrong to steal and kill and rape. An important part of our moral sense is the guilt we feel when we violate it. Even if we feel compelled to injure or kill another human being to protect ourselves from harm, we'll probably feel guilty for doing so. While I can't get into the minds of animals, I think they don't feel guilty when they attack and kill because they don't have our innate moral sense.

Unfortunately, the advances in science and technology that I mentioned a moment ago haven't improved our moral consciousness. To the contrary, they've enabled us to produce weapons that can maim and kill a few people with a gun to a million people with a nuclear bomb or two. Photography and the Internet have combined to produce a massive and global pornography industry. And the food industry is producing a generation of people whose medical problems are crippling our health-care system. Clearly, advances in

---

* My wife, Lois, and I have traveled extensively in India during the past few years, especially in the rural parts of the country, and there's hardly a village we've been in where cell phone service was not available.

† Some states in the western United States have speed limits of eighty or eighty-five miles per hour. Some European nations don't have speed limits, and drivers on freeways there often travel at one hundred miles per hour or more.

science and technology don't necessarily lead to improved morals.

Our perceptions of right and wrong can also vary widely. Christians believe it's sinful to engage in sex outside of marriage, and violations of that principle can cause intense guilt. However, millions of people in today's world play around with multiple sexual partners and don't give it a second thought. Then there's the Islamic State of Iraq and Syria (ISIS) and Boko Haram in Africa who believe it's their moral duty to impose their version of religion on everyone else and who don't hesitate to maim and kill those who get in their way. And they can be horribly brutal about it, such as burning people alive in locked cages or throwing them off of roofs. Both groups have kidnapped women and girls and raped them. Their moral sense is horribly distorted. While human beings are born with a moral aspect to their mental and emotional natures, there's no such thing as a "God spot" in the brain that instinctively guides everyone's understanding of morality. We learn about moral values through the interaction between our intellectual and moral natures and what we're taught, especially as children. And, of course, the Bible provides us with the world's most accurate source of moral instruction.

Fortunately, we don't have to guess at what constitutes right and wrong. God has given us His law, the Ten Commandments, which expresses the fundamental principles of good moral thinking and behavior; the rest of the Bible elaborates on that law, especially the life and teachings of Jesus.

A third characteristic of the Kingdom of Light is authority.

Authority

How did you feel the last time you looked in your rearview mirror and saw those flashing red-and-blue lights? If you're like me, your heart jumped momentarily into your throat; you said, "Oh, no!" and you glanced down at your speedometer to see how fast you had been driving. That's how we who live in the Kingdom of Darkness often react to authority. We tense up around it, because we're afraid of it. There are times, of course, when we welcome authority. If you should call 9-1-1 when you spot someone prowling around your house at midnight, you would be relieved when the police arrived. But even then the Kingdom of Darkness would be afflicting you, as evidenced by your fear that a burglar was about to break into your house. Nobody in heaven's Kingdom of Light would have to worry about burglars, and they don't have to be afraid of authority.

Every government has to place some people in authority over others in order to enforce the laws that the government has legislated or proclaimed. Without authority, our earthly societies would descend into anarchy. The Bible recognizes the need for authority. When God brought the children of Israel out of Egypt, He organized them into a nation with Moses as the chief executive officer. Moses' father-in-law, Jethro, further advised Moses to organize the people into groups of thousands, hundreds, fifties, and tens, with a leader over each group. These leaders had the authority to judge and resolve disputes, and they also had the option of referring more difficult cases to a higher authority (Exodus 18:13–26).

I propose that authority relationships also exist in heaven's Kingdom of Light. God the Father is the supreme authority, and second in command under Him is Michael, whom we know as Christ.* Other angels were placed in authority under Michael. The angel with the highest authority under Michael was an angel named Lucifer, who was given authority over other angels under him.

How do we know that authority relationships exist in the Kingdom of Light?

Several texts in the Bible suggest it. Revelation 12:7 says, "There was war in heaven. Michael and his angels fought against the dragon, and the dragon and his angels fought back." I have much more to say about this war in later chapters. For now, I want to call your attention to the fact that Michael is a leader who has angels under Him, and the dragon, Satan, is a leader who has other angels under him. Were there other leaders below them in this war? The Bible doesn't answer that question, but it's difficult to imagine that there wouldn't have been. Our armies on this earth have privates with sergeants over them who have lieutenants over them who have captains over them who have majors over them who have colonels over them who have generals over them. Then there are one, two, three, four, and five-star generals who have ascending lines of authority. While significant differences surely must exist between earthly and heavenly armies, any battle that lacks careful organization and well-defined authority relationships is doomed to failure. It seems reasonable to conclude that this would be as true of heaven's armies as it is of our earthly ones.

Revelation 12 provides us with one other evidence of authority in heaven. On Earth, wars happen when one nation challenges the authority of another nation. Often it's a group of nations challenging the authority of another group of nations, such as in World Wars I and II. Revelation says that the au-

* I will discuss the reasons for understanding the biblical Michael to be Christ in chapter 2.

thority of Michael and His angels prevailed over the authority of the dragon and his angels so that "the great dragon," Satan, "was hurled to the earth, and his angels with him" (Revelation 12:9). In other words, the Kingdom of Darkness challenged the authority of God's Kingdom of Light. The Kingdom of Light prevailed, and the Kingdom of Darkness lost.

A couple of texts in the Old Testament also indicate that there are authority relationships in heaven. Shortly before the Israelites conquered Jericho, Joshua was confronted by a warrior whom he didn't recognize. Startled, Joshua asked,

> "Are you for us or for our enemies?"
> "Neither," he replied, "but as commander of the army of the LORD I have now come" (Joshua 5:13, 14).

So again, we see that God's army in heaven has a commander with authority, and Daniel informs us that this commander, whom Daniel calls a "Prince," has a "host" of others under Him (Daniel 8:11).

In chapter 1 of the book *Patriarchs and Prophets*, Ellen White gives a detailed account of Lucifer's rebellion, and among other things she makes it clear that before his fall he had authority over certain angels. She wrote, for example, that Lucifer "was beloved and reverenced by the heavenly host, [and] *angels delighted to execute his commands.*"[2] A page later she wrote that Lucifer took advantage of "the loving, loyal trust reposed in him by *the holy beings under his command.*"[3] A couple of pages after that she wrote that "Lucifer, 'the light bearer,' . . . became Satan, 'the adversary' of God and holy beings and *the destroyer of those whom Heaven had committed to his guidance and guardianship.*"[4] This last statement suggests that Lucifer had not only authority ("command") over certain of heaven's angels but that he was also their advisor, their counselor, and their protector. In her book *The Story of Redemption*, Ellen White said that in preparation for the war against Satan and his angels Christ's angels "were marshaled in companies, each division with a higher commanding angel at its head."[5]

It seems evident from both Scripture and Ellen White that authority is another significant characteristic of life in the Kingdom of Light. The importance of this characteristic will become obvious in chapter 3 and beyond.

Freedom

A fourth characteristic of the Kingdom of Light is freedom. The intelligent beings God created can think for themselves, draw conclusions based on what they know, and act on those conclusions. And this includes the freedom to ask questions, debate the meaning of evidence, and disagree with the conclusions of others.

In 1988, Zondervan published a book by Philip Yancey, titled *Disappointment With God: Three Questions No One Asks Aloud.* Yancey's title suggests a marvelous truth about God: He gives us the freedom to question *Him.* He allows us to challenge *His* actions and laws and disagree with *Him*! Does this sound heretical to you? It shouldn't. Have you ever had an experience in which God's leading seemed mysterious and even frightening? Have you ever asked, "God, why is such and such happening to me?" We all have, which means that we're questioning God. Habakkuk posed the agonizing question, "How long, O LORD, must I call for help, but you do not listen?" (Habakkuk 1:2). And the psalmist cried out, "O LORD! Why do you sleep? . . . Why do you hide your face and forget our misery and oppression?" (Psalm 44:23, 24).

Our God gives us the freedom to question Him!

I will discuss the Kingdom of Darkness in chapters 3 and 4, but here I will say that this freedom to question God and disagree with Him lies at the foundation of Lucifer's rebellion. Some people ask why God didn't create Lucifer so that he could *not* rebel and so that he could *not* sin and lead others to sin with him. Think of the human suffering this would have prevented!

God has, in fact, created millions and billions of just such creatures. We call them "animals." Animals have varying degrees of intelligence, from earthworms that probably aren't even conscious (at least not in any sense that we would consider to be consciousness) to dogs, dolphins, and elephants, which are among the most intelligent creatures in the animal kingdom. Yet none of these higher animals even come close to having the intelligence that God has given to angels and humans. We humans have the abilities to reason and reflect and debate and ask questions. So before asking why God didn't create Lucifer in such a way that he couldn't rebel, we have to ask ourselves whether we would want our abilities to reason and reflect and debate and ask questions taken away from us. I'm sure everyone reading this book would say an emphatic *No!*

In order for God to give us intelligence yet forbid us the freedom to ask questions and challenge His decisions, He would have had to set up a dictatorship akin to that of the Inquisition, North Korea, or ISIS. The unfortunate people who live under these types of government have the intelligence to question the ruling political and religious leadership, but those who do so risk imprisonment, torture, and possibly execution. Once God created beings with the level of intelligence that angels and humans have, He had to give us the freedom to openly ask questions, challenge evidence, and seek answers. He had to give us the freedom to question *Him* and to receive answers that can satisfy our intelligence and our ability to reason from cause to effect.*

God gave the intelligent beings He created the freedom to question even His *moral* laws. These laws are based on the principle of love. David said, "Oh, how I love your law! . . . My heart is set on keeping your decrees to the very end" (Psalm 119:97, 112).

But when God created us, He gave us the freedom to reject His *moral* laws. Rejection of God's moral laws is, in fact, the foundation of the Kingdom of Darkness.

Putting it all together

Love, law, authority, and freedom—these are some of the important characteristics of the Kingdom of Light, and love lies at the foundation of them all. Without love, authority can be harsh and cruel, moral law becomes simply a bunch of rules and regulations, and the freedom to think and act for one's self is nonexistent. So love is the critical factor that makes the Kingdom of Light function.

The question is, how does one get that love—a love that permeates all of society so that everybody is just as concerned about the well-being of their neighbors as they are about their own?

The truth is that you and I cannot conjure up that kind of love on our own. There are, of course, non-Christians who have very loving families, who are thoughtful, patient, kind, and tolerant, and have all of the other positive qualities that it takes to make up a civilized society. This is what I call earthly love, because most people are capable of experiencing it to one degree or another. I suspect that even some terrorists love their families in this way. Unfortunately, there's also plenty of jealousy, anger, hatred, and sexual abuse in our world, and often it's mixed right in with our earthly human love. A person can be loving and kind in his family relationships yet be a bear to live with at work—or vice versa.

---

* Note that I said we need to receive answers that *can* satisfy our reason, and not that *will* satisfy our reason. Lucifer asked profound questions about God, and the answers God gave Him *could* have satisfied his intelligence, but they *did not* satisfy him. But more on that in chapter 3.

So how does one get the heavenly love on which the Kingdom of Light operates? You and I can't create it within ourselves. We can't just decide, *That's the way I'm going to be. That's how I'm going to think and feel.* We need supernatural help to make us those kinds of people. Shortly before He left this planet, Jesus explained how we get it. He told His disciples that He would soon be going away, but He assured them and us, "I will not leave you as orphans; I will come to you" (John 14:18). How would He do that? Through the Holy Spirit who "lives with you and will be in you" (verse 17).

When God created us, He arranged for the Third Member of the Godhead to touch our brains[6] and implant that heavenly form of love in our minds. As long as our thoughts and feelings are under the influence of the Holy Spirit's touch, we are attuned to heaven's love. We love the Three Members of the Trinity. We love heaven's laws. We love heaven's authority. And our minds and hearts are attuned to freely choose to love and serve both God and each other. This is what God meant when He said through the prophet Jeremiah, "I will put my law in their minds and write it on their hearts" (Jeremiah 31:33). If God's law isn't written on our minds and hearts, it's just a bunch of rules and regulations, which is legalism.

These are some of the ways the Kingdom of Light operates.

---

1. No. 51 in *The Federalist Papers* (New York: Mentor Books, 1961), 322.

2. Ellen G. White, *Patriarchs and Prophets* (Mountain View, CA: Pacific Press® Pub. Assn., 1958), 37; emphasis added.

3. Ibid., 38; emphasis added.

4. Ibid., 40; emphasis added.

5. Ellen G. White, *The Story of Redemption* (Washington, DC: Review and Herald® Pub. Assn., 1947), 17.

6. Human intelligence arises from the chemical reactions within our physical brains. Ellen White made the insightful comment that "the brain nerves which communicate with the entire system are the only medium through which Heaven can communicate to man and affect his inmost life." Ellen G. White, *Testimonies for the Church*, vol. 2 (Mountain View, CA: Pacific Press® Pub. Assn., 1948), 347.

CHAPTER 2

Michael

S eventh-day Adventists have historically identified the biblical Michael as
Christ, and I agree with that conclusion. However, it's one of our interpretations of Scripture that many non-Adventist Christians disagree with.
For this reason, and because it isn't one of our key doctrines, I avoid saying
much about it in *Signs of the Times.*® Occasionally, the author of an article will
mention it, and sometimes I have allowed it. Following one such occurrence, I
received a strongly worded e-mail from a reader who gave me twenty reasons
why, in his view, it's heresy to identify Michael as Christ. I responded with a
fairly extended explanation of the biblical reasons why Seventh-day Adventists
believe that Michael *is* Christ, and he kindly wrote back and thanked me for the
response, though I don't think I convinced him.

The purpose of this chapter is to share my explanation with you, because
it will be helpful for you to understand it before we get into a discussion of
the Kingdom of Darkness in the next chapter.

Revelation 12:7–9 is the biblical text that forms the foundation for our
belief that Michael is Christ: "And there was war in heaven. Michael and his
angels fought against the dragon, and the dragon and his angels fought back.
But he was not strong enough, and they lost their place in heaven. The great
dragon was hurled down—that ancient serpent called the devil, or Satan,
who leads the whole world astray. He was hurled to the earth, and his angels
with him." Revelation identifies the dragon as Satan, but it identifies Michael
only as the leader of heaven's army—their general—and that He is Satan's
adversary.

Jude, the biblical book that immediately precedes Revelation, adds a
significant clue to Michael's identity: "The archangel Michael, when he was
disputing with the devil about the body of Moses, did not dare to bring a slan-
derous accusation against him, but said, 'The Lord rebuke you!' " (verse 9).
In this verse, Michael is once again in conflict with Satan, and He's called
"the archangel."

In 1 Thessalonians 4, Paul added another piece to the puzzle of Michael
the archangel. He said that at Christ's second coming "the Lord himself will

come down from heaven, with a loud command, *with the voice of the archangel* and with the trumpet call of God" (verse 16; emphasis added).

At first glance, Paul seems to be referring to three distinct heavenly beings in this verse: the Lord, the archangel, and God. However, I propose that each of these is a reference to Jesus Christ. "The Lord" is clearly a reference to Jesus, for Paul often referred to Him as "Lord,"* and the context is Christ's second coming. Who is the "God" who will sound a trumpet? Seventh-day Adventists agree with most other Christians that Jesus is fully divine, and therefore it would be appropriate to identify Him as "God" in this verse. Then notice that the voice of the archangel occurs in connection with the trumpet call. Perhaps there will be a literal trumpet that sounds at Christ's second coming (see 1 Corinthians 15:51, 52). However, the reference to a trumpet may well be symbolic. In Old Testament times, the sounding of a trumpet was typically used as either a call to war (Numbers 10:9) or a call to worship (verses 2–4, 10). The call to war is especially appropriate here, because Revelation 19:11–21 describes Christ at His second coming as a warrior riding on a white horse. Thus, it seems reasonable to understand "the trumpet call of God" in 1 Thessalonians 4:16 to be the trumpet call of Christ in His role as a warrior. If we understand Christ to also be the archangel, as I am suggesting, then all three of the Persons referred to in verse 16 are Christ.

Those who reject the idea that Michael is Christ primarily do so because they believe that applying the title *archangel* to Him suggests that, as an angel, He is a created being and therefore not fully divine. The strongest evidence in support of this view is the first chapter of Hebrews, which makes it crystal clear that Christ is not an angel, because He is much more than an angel. Hebrews 1:4, for example, states that Christ "became as much superior to the angels as the name he has inherited is superior to theirs." And verses 7 and 8 declare,

> In speaking of the angels he [the psalmist] says,
>
> "He makes his angels winds,
>   his servants flames of fire."
>
> But about the Son he says,
>
> "Your throne, O God, will last for ever and ever."

---

* See, e.g., Romans 5:1; 1 Corinthians 1:2; Ephesians 1:17.

So how can Adventists say that the archangel Michael is Christ when the Bible states so clearly that Christ is a Divine Being, the Second Member of the Godhead, and not a created angel? This is a good question, and I will respond with what I believe is a good answer.

During World War II, the German field marshal Erwin Rommel was popularly known as the "Desert Fox." Nobody in his right mind would claim that Rommel was literally a fox. We all understand that the word *fox*, when used of Rommel, was a nickname—a title, and not a statement about the kind of being he was. Foxes are popularly thought of as sly, cunning creatures, and it was this characteristic that gave Rommel the title "Desert Fox." In the same way, if Michael is Christ, then the word *archangel* is a title and not a description of His nature. The question we need to answer is whether there is sufficient biblical evidence to support the idea that Michael the archangel is in fact the Divine Son of God—Jesus Christ—who holds the *title* Archangel. The pages that follow will provide this evidence.

Several texts in the Old Testament speak of "the angel of the Lord," and the context makes it abundantly clear that this angel of the Lord is in fact a Divine Being and not a mere angel. The best evidence for this is found in Exodus 3, which tells the story of Moses at the burning bush. Verse 2 says that "the angel of the LORD appeared to him [Moses] in flames of fire from within a bush." Notice carefully just who it was that appeared to Moses: "the *angel* of the LORD." So who exactly was this angel of the Lord? We get a clue from what the angel said as Moses approached the bush: "Take off your sandals, for the place where you are standing is holy ground" (verse 5). So what would make the ground holy? The presence of Deity, of course. So this angel of the Lord was a Divine Being!

This conclusion is thoroughly confirmed in the conversation between Moses and the angel of the Lord that followed. In verse 6, the Being in the bush said, "I am the God of your father, the God of Abraham, the God of Isaac and the God of Jacob." This is the same word for God that's used in Genesis 1:1: "In the beginning God created the heavens and the earth." So the "angel of the LORD" that appeared to Moses was the God who created the universe!

This conclusion is further confirmed by what transpired next. The "angel" told Moses to return to Egypt and deliver his people from their slavery. He also instructed Moses to tell the leaders of the Israelites that God had sent him. Moses replied, "Suppose I go to the Israelites and say to them, 'The God of your fathers has sent me to you,' and they ask me, 'What is his name?' Then what shall I tell them?" (Exodus 3:13).

The angel's response is very significant for our study: "God said to Moses, 'I AM WHO I AM. This is what you are to say to the Israelites, "I AM has sent me to you" ' " (verse 14).

The Hebrew word translated "I AM" in our English Bibles is *YHWH* (pronounced *Yahweh*), which is the verb "to be";* the idea is that the angel of the Lord is self-existent. Only God is self-existent, and the notion that the angel of the Lord is indeed a Divine Being is confirmed by His name *YHWH*, which is translated "Jehovah" everywhere else in the Bible. Jehovah, of course, is God in the highest sense, which means that the angel of the Lord is also God in the highest sense. Obviously, God is much more than an angel, so the term "angel of the LORD," which is applied to Him in verse 3, is a title and not a description of His nature. Another strong evidence in support of understanding Michael as a Divine Being is found in the fifth chapter of Joshua. Joshua was the leader of the Israelites as they conquered Canaan. The people had crossed the Jordan River only a short time before, and Joshua was away from the camp, praying about the upcoming conquest of the land.† Suddenly, he "saw a man standing in front of him with a drawn sword in his hand" (Joshua 5:13). Startled, Joshua asked,

"Are you for us or for our enemies?"

"Neither," he replied, "but as commander of the army of the LORD I have now come" (verses 13, 14).

This is extremely significant, because in Revelation Michael is the commander of the Lord's army.

So Michael and the man who appeared to Joshua are one and the same Person. The Bible writer then says that

Joshua fell facedown to the ground in reverence, and asked him, "What message does my Lord have for his servant?"

The commander of the LORD's army replied, "Take off your sandals, for the place where you are standing is holy." And Joshua did so (verses 14, 15).

Moses, in the story of the burning bush, is the only other person in the

---

* This is why it's translated "I AM" in verse 14.

† On page 487 of *Patriarchs and Prophets*, Ellen White said that Joshua had gone away from the camp to meditate.

Bible who was ordered to take off his shoes because he was standing on holy ground. The presence of Deity is what made the ground holy. We've just seen that the Being who talked to Moses was none other than Jehovah, who is God in the highest sense. Therefore, the conclusion is inevitable that the commander of the Lord's army who appeared to Joshua was also a Divine Being, because He ordered Joshua to remove the sandals from his feet. And He was also the commander of the Lord's army, whom Revelation identifies by the name Michael.

That being the case, we are left with just one question: Which member of the Trinity appeared to Joshua? Was it God the Father, Jesus Christ, or the Holy Spirit? My conclusion is that it was Jesus Christ; and I have a very good reason.

In Revelation 19:11, John saw "heaven standing open and there before me was a white horse, whose rider is called Faithful and True. With justice he judges and makes war." Verse 14 says that "the armies of heaven were following him, riding on white horses." Who is the rider on a white horse who's leading the armies of heaven to battle? Verse 13 answers that question. It says that the rider's name is "the Word of God," and verse 16 adds the information that His name is also "KING OF KINGS AND LORD OF LORDS." That's Jesus! Please note that Jesus is the leader of heaven's army here in Revelation 19, just as Michael is in Revelation 12:7. How much more evidence do we need to establish the fact that Michael is Christ?

CHAPTER 3

How the Kingdom
of Darkness Began—Part 1

S eventh-day Adventists have two sources of information that we accept
as inspired and on which we base our teachings. The primary source is
the Bible. It's the foundation of our twenty-eight fundamental beliefs.* If
you read through those beliefs, you'll find only Bible texts to support them—
never a quote from Ellen White. However, we do believe that Ellen White
was inspired by God in what she wrote, and therefore, for us, her writings
constitute a secondary and reliable source of information about divine things.

I have divided the description of the Kingdom of Darkness into two sec-
tions, partly because the topic is too extensive for one chapter and partly to
distinguish between what the Bible says about it and what Ellen White says.
The Bible provides us with a basic summary of Satan's rebellion in heaven,
and that's what I will consider in this chapter. In the next chapter, "How the
Kingdom of Darkness Began—Part 2," we'll consider what Ellen White had
to say on the subject.

Three primary texts in the Bible describe Satan's fall from heaven:
Revelation 12:7–9; Ezekiel 28:11–17; and Isaiah 14:12–14. Let's consider
them in that order.

Revelation 12:7–9

I discussed this passage briefly in the previous chapter. Here we'll take a
more detailed look. Again, this is what these verses say: "There was war in
heaven. Michael and his angels fought against the dragon, and the dragon
and his angels fought back. But he was not strong enough, and they lost their
place in heaven. The great dragon was hurled down—that ancient serpent
called the devil, or Satan, who leads the whole world astray. He was hurled
to the earth, and his angels with him."

On our planet, war happens when two countries take up arms against each

---

* To read the Bible-based fundamental beliefs, see the Beliefs page of the Seventh-day
Adventist Church's Web site at https://www.adventist.org/en/beliefs/.

other. It has happened time and time again throughout history. Sometimes war is simply a grab for power and territory. World War II is a good example. Hitler wanted to bring Europe, and ultimately the world, under German domination. At other times, the motive is more "noble." Each side is sure that its cause is just and that the other side is to blame for the conflict. We see this today in the conflict between Israel and Hamas. The leaders on each side exchange bitter accusations. Anger and hatred build up. Sometimes other countries put forth efforts toward mediation, but eventually the antagonism spills over into war. Bullets fly, and bombs drop. It's the international version of the schoolyard fight between two bullies.

The Bible says that war broke out in heaven.

However, this wasn't a war between two bullies. It was a grab for power, as we will see when we've reviewed everything the Bible says about Satan and his fall from heaven.

War in heaven?

Heaven is where God's throne is located. It's supposed to be a perfect place. Who would have thought that war would break out in heaven, of all places? But it did. A bitter fight broke out; God's side won, and the rebels were forced out.

The two generals in this war were Michael and the dragon. Revelation tells us that the word *dragon* is a symbol for the devil, or Satan (Revelation 12:9). We refer to the dragon as Lucifer prior to the time when he was cast out of heaven. But Michael and Lucifer weren't the only ones involved in this war. Each had angels on his side. This is stated specifically in Revelation 12:7, and it is also evident from verse 4, which says that the dragon's tail "swept a third of the stars out of the sky and flung them to the earth." Seventh-day Adventists and other conservative commentators understand this to mean that one-third of heaven's angels joined Lucifer in his rebellion. In chapter 1, I mentioned that Lucifer may have had as many as fifty trillion angels on his side and Michael as many as one hundred trillion on His side. Ellen White said that "a vast number of the angels" sided with Lucifer.[1]

The question is, why would Michael (Christ) initiate the war? Isn't He "the Prince of Peace" (Isaiah 9:6)? In order to answer that question, we need to ask another one: who *initiated* the conflict that led to this war? The answer to that question is that Lucifer did. This will become evident as we consider Ezekiel's and Isaiah's descriptions of Lucifer's fall from heaven. The situation in heaven became so tense that something had to happen. The Trinity told Lucifer that his rebellious attitude could no longer be tolerated in heaven and that he and his angels would have to leave. They refused, so Michael and His angels used force to expel them. Satan and his angels resisted, and war broke out.

Now here's another important question: what prompted the angels in Lucifer's army to join him? Obviously, God wouldn't have ordered them to follow Lucifer, and common sense tells us that Lucifer wouldn't have been able to force them to join him. After all, as I pointed out in chapter 1, a basic principle of the Kingdom of Light is freedom—freedom to think; draw conclusions; and believe those conclusions, even if they disagree with God's conclusions. Therefore, even though the Bible doesn't say so, we can reasonably conclude that Lucifer *persuaded* this vast number of angels to join him in his rebellion against God and His law. Lucifer must have had what seemed at the time to be extremely compelling reasons for his beliefs!

It's now time to examine Ezekiel and Isaiah to find out what prompted this rebellion.

Ezekiel 28:11–17

This passage from Ezekiel and the one from Isaiah that follows have several things in common. For example, although we understand Ezekiel and Isaiah as describing Lucifer in these verses, both passages are actually in the context of dirges the respective prophets uttered against two of the well-known kings of their day. Ezekiel rebuked the king of Tyre, and Isaiah rebuked the king of Babylon.

Ezekiel's lament against the king of Tyre begins with the following words:

> In the pride of your heart
>   you say, "I am a god;
> I sit on the throne of a god
>   in the heart of the seas."
> But you are a man and not a god,
>   though you think you are as wise as a god (Ezekiel 28:2).

There's nothing particularly unusual about an earthly king considering himself to be divine. The pharaohs and the caesars also made this claim. However, verses 11–19 describe a being who is much more than an earthly monarch. Commenting on Ezekiel's words, *The Seventh-day Adventist Bible Commentary* states,

Though presented as a dirge upon the king of Tyrus, [this passage] can hardly be limited in its application to the Tyrian prince. The imagery so far transcends such a local reference that designations such as "extreme irony" fail to answer the problems created if a wholly local application is given to the passage. . . .

It thus appears simpler to consider the passage as digressing from the prophecy upon the king of Tyre to present a history of him who was indeed the real king of Tyrus, Satan himself. So understood, this passage provides us with a history of the origin, initial position, and downfall of the angel who later became known as the devil and Satan. Apart from this passage and the one in Isa. 14:12-14, we would be left without a reasonably complete account of the origin, primeval state, and causes of the fall of this prince of evil.[2]

So let's examine Ezekiel 28:11–19. The passage divides into two parts. Verses 11–15a describe Lucifer in heaven prior to his fall,* and verses 15b–19 describe his fall.

Lucifer in heaven prior to his fall. The passage begins with Ezekiel saying that "the word of the LORD came to me: 'Son of man, take up a lament concerning the king of Tyre and say to him, "This is what the Sovereign LORD says" ' " (verses 11, 12).

Ezekiel then goes on to quote what God said. His first statement is that the king of Tyre was "the model of perfection, full of wisdom and perfect in beauty" (verse 12). The description of the king of Tyre as "the model of perfection" seems a bit extravagant for an earthly king—even for Solomon during the early part of his reign, though it could have been said that Solomon was "full of wisdom and perfect in beauty." But all of these comments would certainly apply to Lucifer before his fall.

In the first part of verse 13, Ezekiel said, "You were in Eden, the garden of God." This is a very definite clue that Ezekiel is describing more than an earthly king. Eden hadn't existed on earth for thousands of years prior to the time of Ezekiel, so it would be impossible for the king of Tyre to have been there. And the only biblical record of Lucifer being in Eden is after his fall, by which time he had become Satan, the serpent. How could it be said that Lucifer in heaven was "in Eden, the garden of God"? *The Seventh-day Adventist Bible Commentary* notes that here the word *Eden* is "to be taken in

---

* Ezekiel didn't use the name *Lucifer*. That name comes from Isaiah, which we will examine in a moment.

its larger sense as the dwelling place of God."[3] Given everything that's said about Lucifer in verses 11–15 this seems like a reasonable conclusion.

The second part of verse 13 describes Lucifer's adornment:

> Every precious stone adorned you:
> ruby, topaz and emerald,
> chrysolite, onyx and jasper,
> sapphire, turquoise and beryl.
> Your settings and mountings were made of gold;
> on the day you were created they were prepared.

Lucifer was quite obviously a very beautiful angel!

Verse 14 makes three statements that can be applied only to Lucifer before his fall and not to the king of Tyre. In the first statement, God said, "You were anointed as a guardian cherub, for so I ordained you." In the second statement, He said, "You were on the holy mount of God." And in the third statement, He said, "You walked among the fiery stones."

Let's begin with "You were anointed as a guardian cherub." What do these words mean?

When God gave Moses the instructions for constructing the wilderness sanctuary, He told him to place two golden cherubim facing each other on the mercy seat that covered the top of the ark of the covenant (Exodus 25:17–20). This ark represented God's throne in heaven. In fact, God's own presence, sometimes called the Shekinah,* appeared between the two cherubim. So Ezekiel's statement that God had ordained Lucifer as a guardian cherub means that Lucifer stood in God's presence in heaven, and no doubt next to His throne. Obviously, this could not be said of the earthly king of Tyre.

Next Ezekiel said that Lucifer had been "on the holy mount of God" (verse 14). In the Old Testament, Mount Zion is the same as Mount Moriah, where Abraham offered his son Isaac as a sacrifice. It's also the mountain on which the temples were built, both by Solomon and by the Jews after their return from Babylon. However, Ezekiel was not saying that Lucifer had been on the earthly Mount Zion. The "holy mount of God" that Lucifer had been

---

* The word *Shekinah* does not appear in the Bible. We get it from the Jewish writings after the destruction of the temple in A.D. 70. Ellen White used the word on page 349 of *Patriarchs and Prophets*; she took a paragraph to describe it.

on was the "mountain" in heaven where God's throne is located.*

What about the "fiery stones" that Lucifer walked on? In the vision of God's throne that Daniel describes in Daniel 7:9, 10, he said that "a river of fire was flowing, coming out from before him [God, the Ancient of Days]" (verse 10). John, writing in Revelation, saw a "sea of glass mixed with fire," and standing beside the sea† were "those who had been victorious over the beast and his image and over the number of his name" (Revelation 15:2). John saw this same sea of glass in his vision recorded in Revelation 4:6, and he said that it was "before the throne." Thus, whether it's a river of fire, a sea of fire, or stones of fire, it's obvious that God's throne has fire in front of and perhaps around it. Ezekiel and Revelation also tell us that created beings can stand and walk on that fire. And Ezekiel informs us that Lucifer is one of those who stood in the presence of God and walked on the fire.

In Ezekiel 28:15, Ezekiel gives us another important piece of information about Lucifer. The New International Version says of Lucifer that "you were *blameless* in your ways from the day you were created till wickedness was found in you" (emphasis added). The King James Version and the New King James Version say that Lucifer was *perfect* in his ways. Some people wonder why God created the devil. He didn't; He created a perfect being. It was only some time later that sin *was found* in him. Lucifer created his own sin by the choices he made as an individual with the freedom to choose, including the freedom to make wrong moral choices.

Notice also that Lucifer was perfect from the day he was *created*. While it's true that every person on Earth is a created being, we don't normally speak of people being *created*, except for Adam and Eve. From Cain and Abel to the present, human beings have been *born*. However, Ezekiel said that Lucifer was *created*. So far as we know, angels don't have our human reproductive ability, which means that God created each of them individually. So Ezekiel's statement that Lucifer was *created* is significant evidence that he was speaking of more than the king of Tyre, who was *born*. Note also that Ezekiel said this guardian cherub was blameless—that is, perfect. This could hardly have been said about the king of Tyre.

---

* Commenting on this "holy mount of God," the *Seventh-day Adventist Bible Commentary* says, "Holy Mountain. Here representing the seat of God's government, heaven itself, figuratively represented as a mountain." Vol. 4, 676.

† The NIV and RSV say that those who were victorious over the beast were standing *beside* the sea. The KJV, NKJV, and NASB say that they were standing *on* the sea. It's often the case that prepositions in the Greek can be correctly translated with more than one preposition in today's languages, including English.

Lucifer's fall from heaven. Beginning in verse 16 and continuing through verse 19, Ezekiel describes the fall of the king of Tyre, which we understand to be the fall of Lucifer.

> Through your widespread trade
> you were filled with violence,
> and you sinned.
> So I drove you in disgrace from the mount of God,
> and I expelled you, O guardian cherub,
> from among the fiery stones (verse 16).

The first statement in this quote suggests that Lucifer engaged in some form of commercial work while in heaven—his "widespread trade." We have no other inspired information to suggest what that might mean. It could apply more to the king of Tyre than to Lucifer prior to the time he was cast out of heaven. However, the next statement clearly applies to Lucifer. Ezekiel said that God expelled the "guardian cherub" from "the mount of God" and from "among the fiery stones." The significance of the words "I drove you in disgrace from the mount of God, and I expelled you," is that they harmonize so well with Revelation 12:7–9, which says that as a result of the war between Michael and Satan, Satan and his angels were cast out of heaven and hurled to the earth. This harmony between the statement in Revelation and Ezekiel's statement is another reason why it's reasonable to understand Ezekiel as describing Lucifer before and after his fall and not just the king of Tyre.

Verse 17 is the final statement from Ezekiel 28 that I will consider here. It says,

> Your heart became proud
> on account of your beauty,
> and you corrupted your wisdom
> because of your splendor.

We read a few verses previously that Lucifer was covered with precious stones that were set in gold. He must have been a gorgeous being, and that's because God loves beauty. Think of all the beauty we see in our world even in its marred condition—flowers, snow-capped mountains, sunsets, tropical fish, handsome men and gorgeous women, to name a few things. Many of us covet good looks and are jealous of people whom we perceive to be more attractive than ourselves. Personal beauty is a dangerous thing. It can easily lead us to become conceited and proud. And, according to Ezekiel, that's exactly what happened to Lucifer. His "heart became proud on account of . . . [his] beauty," and he "corrupted . . . [his] wisdom because of . . . [his] splendor."

Isaiah 14:12–15

Conservative Bible scholars generally agree that, like the passage we just examined in Ezekiel, Isaiah 14:12–14 describes Lucifer's rebellion in heaven prior to the time he was cast out and that verses 15–17 describe his fate after he was cast out. Seventh-day Adventists agree with that conclusion.

However, like Ezekiel's description of Lucifer prior to his fall, the immediate context of Isaiah's words is also a dirge against an earthly king; in this case, the king of Babylon (verses 3, 4). Nevertheless, we apply them to Lucifer for the same reasons we applied Ezekiel's words to Lucifer even though they were a dirge against the king of Tyre. The interpretation that the real protagonist in these verses is Lucifer dates back to the early Christian era. Most Christian interpreters at that time understood the passage that way.[4] I'll begin by quoting Isaiah 14:12–15:

> How you have fallen from heaven,
>   O morning star [KJV, NKJV: Lucifer], son of the dawn! . . .
> You said in your heart,
>   "I will ascend to heaven;
> I will raise my throne
>   above the stars of God;
> I will sit enthroned on the mount of assembly,
>   on the utmost heights of the sacred mountain.
> I will ascend above the tops of the clouds;
>   I will make myself like the Most High."
> But you are brought down to the grave [Hebrew: *sheol*],
>   to the depths of the pit.

In the discussion about Ezekiel, I said that when we came to Isaiah I would explain the origin and meaning of the word *Lucifer*. The King James Version translates the first line of verse 12, "How art thou fallen from heaven, O *Lucifer*, son of the morning!" (emphasis added). Notice, however, that where the King James Version says "Lucifer," the New International Version says "morning star." The Hebrew word is *helel*, which means "shining one." *The*

Seventh-day Adventist Bible Commentary notes that in Bible times *helel* was "commonly applied to the planet Venus as a morning star because of its unrivaled brilliance."[5] This is why most modern versions of the Bible translate *helel* as "morning star" (NIV), "star of the morning" (NASB), or "Day Star" (RSV). Our English word *Lucifer* comes from the Latin word *lucifero*, which means "light bearer" (*luc* = "light"; *fero* = "bearer"). The Vulgate, the Latin version of the Bible, translates *helel* as *lucifero*, and from there, it came into early English translations as "Lucifer."

Now let's examine verses 12–15. Note that, though this opening line sounds like it could be a question, it is punctuated as an astonished exclamation: "How you have fallen from heaven, O morning star, son of the dawn!" Think of it as expressing this idea: "How awful, Lucifer, that you have fallen from heaven!" Nearly all versions of the Bible punctuate Isaiah's words as an exclamation.* However, if we understand it as a question ("Lucifer, what happened? Why did you fall from heaven?"), the idea is also appropriate. The reference to Lucifer falling from heaven harmonizes with what John said in Revelation 12:9 about Satan and his angels being cast out of heaven as a result of the war between Satan and Michael.

Then Isaiah gives the reason why Lucifer fell from heaven: he was aspiring to a higher position in God's government than the one he already had been given. Note the following statements by Lucifer:

- *"I will raise my throne above the stars of God."* A throne is a symbol of governmental authority. In prophetic language, stars symbolize God's holy created beings, either angels or humans.† So in saying that he wanted to raise his throne above the stars of God, Lucifer meant that he wanted greater governmental authority over the angels than God had given him.
- *"I will sit enthroned on the mount of the assembly."* Again, Lucifer aspired to dominion—to "sit enthroned." This time he wanted to rule "on the mount of the assembly." Commenting on Lucifer's words, *The Seventh-day Adventist Bible Commentary* points out that "in heathen mythology the gods held their council meetings on a high mountain, where they determined the affairs of earth. The literal 'king of Babylon' . . . would thus presume to usurp the control of the gods—

---

* See, e.g., KJV, NKJV, NASB, RSV, Living Bible, AMP, and the Spanish Reina de Valera.

† See, e.g., Daniel 8:10 and 12:3 where stars represent God's people and Revelation 1:20 and 12:4 where stars represent angels.

that is, supreme authority—over the affairs of earth. As king of mystical Babylon . . . Satan would similarly aspire to control the councils of heaven, that is, to rule the universe of God."[6] In other words, Isaiah was describing Lucifer's ambition to have God's position of authority over the angels.

- *"I will make myself like the Most High."* Lucifer now comes right out and says it: He wants to be like God. He wants to make himself—that is, exalt himself—to occupy God's position!

But Isaiah says that Lucifer was instead "brought down to the grave, to the depths of the pit." The Hebrew word *bowr*, which means "pit," sometimes refers to "the grave" (see Job 33:18; Psalms 30:3; 69:15). This doesn't mean that Lucifer and his angels were immediately destroyed after they were banished from heaven. The Bible is very clear that Satan is still very active in our world. Rather, Isaiah is describing the horrible extent of Lucifer's fall, which will result in his final destruction (Revelation 20:10).

Putting it all together

Each of the passages we've considered in Revelation, Ezekiel, and Isaiah adds to our understanding; and by putting them all together, we get a much more complete picture of what happened in heaven. I will summarize the contribution of each source.

Revelation
- Lucifer won as many as a third of the angels to his side.
- A serious conflict broke out between Lucifer's angels and the angels who were loyal to God.
- A showdown finally came, and war broke out between the two sides. War is the effort to use force to achieve one's objectives. However, Revelation doesn't tell us how that force was exercised or the nature of the weapons that were used.
- Satan (Lucifer) was the leader—the general—of the rebellion, and Michael (Christ) was the general leading the forces that were loyal to God.
- Michael and his army won the war, and Satan and his angels were cast out of heaven to earth.

Ezekiel
- Lucifer was a created angel, not a divine being.
- He was a very beautiful angel, as he was adorned with many precious jewels set in gold.
- He was created a blameless, perfect being.
- He stood on the holy mountain in God's very presence as a guardian cherub.
- He became proud of his beauty.
- God expelled him from heaven to earth.

Isaiah
- Lucifer was assigned to a particular position, but he aspired to a higher position.
- He wanted to rule over the rest of the angels (stars) in heaven.
- He wanted to be like God.
- God brought him down to the grave.

A common thread runs through each of these passages. They all say that Lucifer began life in heaven and that God cast him out. And by combining the evidence from these three sources, we get a much more complete understanding of what actually happened in heaven. Lucifer tried to take over God's position in heaven. He wanted to rule over the angels. As I pointed out in the previous chapter, he did get a large number of the angels to join his side. However, he didn't *force* them to join him. He *persuaded* them to join him. The fact that as many as a third of the angels did join him gave him a reason to believe that he would succeed in his ambition to take over Christ's position. It's no wonder that all three sources agree on the fate of Lucifer and his angels: Revelation says they were cast out of heaven to earth; Ezekiel says that God cast the guardian cherub "from the mount of God," "from among the fiery stones"; and Isaiah says that Lucifer was "brought down to the grave, to the depths of the pit."

I will draw one final conclusion from these three passages. Today we understand what Isaiah almost certainly did not—that the Godhead consists of three Persons, not just one. So here's a question for you to ponder: Was Lucifer aspiring to take over the position of all Three Members of the Godhead or just one? And if it was just one, whose was it? I propose that Lucifer coveted only Christ's position, not that of the Father or the Holy Spirit. I will explain why.

I believe there's a reason why Michael—that is, Jesus, the Second Member of the Trinity—is given the title *Archangel*. I can't prove this from the Bible, but I believe it's correct. When the Godhead decided to create intelligent beings such as angels and humans, They recognized that there would be a vast difference between the intelligence and power of the beings They would create and Their own intelligence and power. This difference would be so great that it would be impossible for these created beings to understand divinity. So They agreed that one of the members of the Godhead would assume the form of an angel and at least *appear* as one of them. This would make it possible for created beings to *see* the character of the Godhead lived out among them.* And the Second Member of the Godhead is the One who took this position. He assumed the role of an angel.† However, Lucifer, with his beauty and the high position God had given him, could tell no difference between himself and Christ. He may even have been more highly adorned than Christ. Yet Christ held greater authority over the angels than Lucifer did, and Christ attended council meetings with the Godhead from which Lucifer was excluded. All of this aroused Lucifer's jealousy, and he challenged Christ's position as a member of the Trinity. He challenged Christ's position as God.

Thus, when Isaiah says that Lucifer wanted to "make . . . [himself] like the Most High," I propose that it was Christ's role in the Godhead that he aspired to, not that of the Father or the Holy Spirit. That's why, when war broke out in heaven, it was Michael, Christ, against whom Lucifer and his angels fought. This conclusion will become much more evident in the next chapter.

---

1. White, *Patriarchs and Prophets*, 331.

2. Francis D. Nichol, ed., *The Seventh-day Adventist Bible Commentary*, vol. 4 (Washington, DC: Review and Herald® Pub. Assn., 1955), 675.

3. Ibid.

4. Ibid., 170.

5. Ibid.

6. Ibid., 171.

---

* This was one of the reasons why Jesus came to our world as a human being—to live out the character of God among us. That's why, when Philip asked Jesus to "show us the Father," Jesus replied, "Don't you know me, Philip, even after I have been among you such a long time? Anyone who has seen me has seen the Father" (John 14:8, 9).

† Whether Michael actually became an angel as well as being divine or whether He only appeared as an angel without actually being one, we do not know. However, either way would be theologically acceptable, given the fact that Jesus was both fully human and fully divine while on Earth.

CHAPTER 4

How the Kingdom
of Darkness Began–Part 2

I sometimes wonder what heaven will be like. The Bible gives us a few glimpses of the new earth: there won't be any pain, suffering, or death (Revelation 21:4); we'll build houses and plant vineyards (Isaiah 65:17, 21); and there won't be any wild animals to contend with (verse 25). We also know there will be a tree of life and that we'll enjoy eating its fruit at least once a month. Revelation even suggests that we'll eat the leaves! (Revelation 22:2). But we have almost no information about the place where we'll spend the millennium. We do know that it's the home of God (the Trinity) and the angels, and we know that it's free of sin and evil. Yet one of the great puzzles of Christian theology is how and why evil originated in heaven.

I pointed out in chapter 1 that God gave angels and humans intelligence—the ability to reason and reflect and debate and ask questions, including the ability to question Him. He also gave us another quality—emotions, which make it possible for us to experience feelings such as joy and sadness, love and anger, and peace and fear. Furthermore, our emotions and our intelligence interact. What we *know* can influence how we *feel*, and how we *feel* can influence what we *think* and *believe*. For example, if I'm informed that I got a job I applied for (an intellectual fact), I'll feel glad (an emotional response).

How evil originated

Now here's a concept that's critical for understanding the origin of evil: our minds—our intellectual powers—are supposed to be in charge of our feelings. But it's possible for our feelings to override what our intellect tells us is true. Thus, if someone else gets the job I interviewed for, my disappointed feelings may cause me to believe that the prospective employer has something against me personally; but if I would reflect for a moment, I would realize that this conclusion has no basis in fact. My feelings are overriding my intellect.

You'll also recall that in chapter 1 I shared with you four characteristics of God's Kingdom of Light: love, law, authority, and freedom. Sin arose through Lucifer's distortion of each of these characteristics. Let's focus on freedom for a moment.

Genuine freedom means that we can ask questions, including questions about God and His decisions and actions, without any fear of retaliation. And Lucifer asked questions about the Second Member of the Godhead. Ellen White told us exactly what that question was: " 'Why,' questioned this mighty angel, 'should Christ have the supremacy? Why is He honored above Lucifer?' "[1] Please note that this is a perfectly reasonable question: "God, is there a reason Michael has authority over me? Can You explain why He can attend Your divine counsels and I can't?" The answer was very simple: Christ (Michael) had supremacy over Lucifer and was honored above Lucifer because Christ was deity whereas Lucifer was a created being. The Bible makes it very clear that Christ is a Divine Being: "In the beginning was the Word, and the Word was with God, and the Word was God" (John 1:1). Ellen White said that "before the entrance of evil . . . Christ the Word, the Only Begotten of God, was one with the eternal Father,—one in nature, in character, and in purpose,—the only being in all the universe that could enter into all the counsels and purposes of God."[2]

The problem was not with Lucifer's question. The problem was with his motive in asking it. Pride motivated Lucifer's question. Ezekiel stated it plainly:

> Your heart became proud
> on account of your beauty,
> and you corrupted your wisdom
> because of your splendor (Ezekiel 28:17).

Lucifer asked why Christ had a position superior to his because he was jealous of Christ and coveted His higher position of authority over the angels. As Isaiah said, Lucifer wanted to be "like the Most High" (Isaiah 14:14). Ellen White said that by "coveting the glory with which the infinite Father had invested His Son, this prince of angels aspired to power that was the prerogative of Christ alone."[3] She also said that Lucifer and his fellow angels "rebelled against the authority of the Son," and "Satan was jealous of Jesus."[4]

I previously pointed out that God intends for our intellect and reason to be in control of our emotions. But according to Ezekiel, Lucifer reversed those two. Pride in his beauty (emotion) caused him to corrupt his wisdom (intellect).

Paul gave counsel on this issue to the Christians in Rome. He said, "By the grace given me I say to every one of you: Do not think of yourself more highly than you ought, but rather think of yourself with sober judgment" (Romans 12:3). Imagining that you are important can feel really good. But that's emotional thinking, which is exactly what Lucifer allowed himself to do. Paul counseled, "But rather think of yourself with sober judgment." In other words, use your head. Let your intellect be in charge of your estimation of yourself. Don't allow your emotions to override your better judgment.

That's critically wise advice for every one of us today.

Unfortunately, Lucifer was not content to just mull over his feelings in his own mind. He "went forth to diffuse the spirit of discontent among the angels."[5] Lucifer's challenge to Christ's authority "aroused a feeling of apprehension when observed by those [angels] who considered that the glory of God should be supreme. In heavenly council the angels pleaded with Lucifer. The Son of God [Michael] presented before him the greatness, the goodness, and the justice of the Creator, and the sacred, unchanging nature of His law."[6] However, Lucifer rejected the counsel.

> The warning, given in infinite love and mercy, only aroused a spirit of re-sistance. Lucifer allowed his jealousy of Christ to prevail, and [he] became the more determined.
>
> To dispute the supremacy of the Son of God, thus impeaching the wisdom and love of the Creator [God the Father] had become the purpose of this prince of angels.[7]

In chapter 2, I pointed out the biblical evidence that Michael is Christ, and in chapter 3, I drew the tentative conclusion that in his ambition to be "like the Most High" (Isaiah 14:14) Lucifer aspired to have Christ's position, not that of God the Father. Ellen White confirmed this when she wrote that Lucifer allowed his jealousy of Christ to prevail and became the more determined to dispute the supremacy of Christ,[8] and she repeated the point numerous times in several of her accounts of the origin of evil.[9] Furthermore, Lucifer didn't just challenge Christ's position himself. He tried to get as many of the angels as possible to side with him.

God intervenes

Lucifer's jealous challenge to Christ's position and authority finally developed to the point that God the Father stepped in to clarify who Christ really is. "The King of the universe summoned the heavenly hosts before Him, that in their presence He might set forth the true position of His Son and show the relation He sustained to all created beings. . . . About the throne gathered the holy angels, a vast, unnumbered throng."[10]

We have no idea what God's throne room looks like, but it must be huge, because Daniel saw "thousands upon thousands" and "ten thousand times ten thousand angels" gathered before God's throne (Daniel 7:10; see also John's description in Revelation 5:11). God explained to these angels that

> the Son of God shared the Father's throne, and the glory of the eternal, self-existent one encircled both. . . . Before the assembled inhabitants of heaven the King declared that none but Christ, the Only Begotten Son of God, could fully enter into His purposes, and to Him it was committed to execute the mighty counsels of His will. The Son of God had wrought the Father's will in the creation of all the hosts of heaven; and to Him, as well as to God, their homage and allegiance were due.[11]

Imagine that you're Lucifer listening to these words as you stand among this huge gathering of angels. You've challenged Christ's position and claimed equality with Him. How would you feel? What would be going through your mind? "The angels joyfully acknowledged the supremacy of Christ, and prostrating themselves before Him, poured out their love and adoration. Lucifer bowed with them, but in his heart there was a strange, fierce conflict. Truth, justice, and loyalty were struggling against envy and jealousy."[12] Put yourself in Lucifer's place for a moment: the very ones whose loyalty you had sought are giving their heartfelt allegiance to your enemy. Yet God the Father has spoken. He has revealed who Michael really is, whom you had thought all along was simply another angel such as yourself. And you're faced with a choice: believe God the Father, or follow your own instincts.

Have you ever experienced a conflict like that—your desires pulling you one way, and God's revealed will pulling you another? The answer is, of course! We all have, if we take our relationship with God and Christ seriously. We can understand exactly what was going through Lucifer's mind!

Ellen White went on to write that "the influence of the holy angels seemed for a time to carry him [Lucifer] with them. As songs of praise ascended in melodious strains, swelled by thousands of glad voices, the spirit of evil seemed vanquished; unutterable love thrilled his entire being; his soul went out, in harmony with the sinless worshipers, in love to the Father and the Son." Unfortunately, Lucifer was again "filled with pride in his own glory. His desire for supremacy returned, and envy of Christ was once more indulged. . . . [Christ] shared the Father's counsels, while Lucifer did not thus enter into the purposes of God. 'Why,' questioned this mighty angel, 'should Christ have the supremacy? Why is He honored above Lucifer?' "[13]

The real issue

The critical point here is Lucifer's emotions. He had become proud of his beauty and the high position he held as the guardian cherub who stood next to God's throne. After all, *he, Lucifer,* went on important errands for Almighty God, the Ancient of Days, and the Creator of all that exists! He, Lucifer, was the guardian cherub who stood beside God on His throne! *He, Lucifer,* was gorgeously decorated with many jewels that were set in gold! How his chest must have swelled at the thought. How he must have strutted as he looked at his reflection in the sea of glass!

Pride is an emotion, and rightly used it's a good emotion. Completing a difficult task feels good, and it should. Creating a beautiful piece of art feels good, and it should! Success feels good, and it should. These are all powerful motives. Lucifer surely had this good kind of pride during the years—perhaps centuries or even millennia—prior to his fall. And it was OK. God created us to have these satisfying feelings about our accomplishments.

But then Lucifer observed that Michael had privileges that went beyond his. All the angels worshiped Michael. Michael attended the councils of the Godhead. Michael had greater authority over the angels than Lucifer did. Michael even had the authority to give orders to Lucifer! Yet Michael appeared to be an angel like the other angels. At first, Lucifer probably felt a twinge of resentment: *Who is* He *to boss* me *around?* With each order that Michael gave him, Lucifer's resentment increased. Then he began comparing his own appearance and his own position with that of Michael, and he came to the conclusion that he was, indeed, greater than Michael. In fact, since humility is one of Christ's most defining characteristics (Philippians 2:5–11; John 13:2–17), it's entirely possible that His appearance was more simple than Lucifer's. And jealousy set in.

Now please pay careful attention to what was taking place. Ellen White said that God the Father had explained very clearly why Christ had a higher position than Lucifer. This means that Lucifer had the *information* he needed to understand why Christ held a position superior to his own. And "the influence of the holy angels seemed for a time to carry him with them. . . . The spirit of evil seemed vanquished; unutterable love filled his entire being; his soul went out, in harmony with the sinless worshipers, in love to the Father and the

Son."[14] Not only did Lucifer *understand* Christ's role, for a time he even *rejoiced* in it. Yet "in his heart there was a strange, fierce conflict. Truth, justice, and loyalty were struggling against envy and jealousy. . . . But again he was filled with pride in his own glory. His desire for supremacy returned, and envy of Christ was once more indulged."[15] So Lucifer had a choice to make: whether to follow what he *knew* to be true or to follow his *feelings*. Unfortunately, as we all know, he chose to follow his evil feelings.

Lucifer intensifies his rebellion

Having chosen to follow his feelings rather than what he knew to be true, Lucifer left

> his place in the immediate presence of the Father, [and] went forth to dif-
> fuse the spirit of discontent among the angels. . . . The exaltation of the Son
> of God as equal with the Father was represented as an injustice to Lucifer,
> who, it was claimed, was also entitled to reverence and honor. If this prince
> of angels could but attain to his true, exalted position, great good would
> accrue to the entire host of heaven; for it was his object to secure freedom
> for all. But now even the liberty which they had hitherto enjoyed was at an
> end; for an absolute Ruler had been appointed them, and to His authority
> all must pay homage.[16]

Notice the intensification of Lucifer's feelings.

Apparently, prior to the grand meeting that God the Father called to ex-plain the true role of His Son, the angels had not fully understood who Christ was. God had to explain that to them, and Lucifer disputed the explanation. Also prior to God's clarification, Lucifer ostensibly had just *talked* about his dissatisfaction with Christ's authority; but after God had spoken, Lucifer began turning toward out-and-out *rebellion*. At first, however, he made a point not to come across that way to his fellow angels.

> He worked with mysterious secrecy, and for a time concealed his real pur-
> pose under an appearance of reverence for God. . . .
> . . . Claiming for himself perfect loyalty to God. . . . While secretly foment-
> ing discord and rebellion, he with consummate craft caused it to appear as
> his sole purpose to promote loyalty and to preserve harmony and peace.[17]

Unfortunately, "many of the angels were . . . blinded by Lucifer's deceptions."[18]

Fortunately, not all the angels were taken in by Lucifer's crafty falsehoods. "The loyal angels could see only terrible consequences from this dissension, and with earnest entreaty they counseled the disaffected ones to renounce their purpose and prove themselves loyal to God by fidelity to His government."[19]

The angels weren't the only ones seeking to draw Lucifer back from his rebellion. "Such efforts as infinite love and wisdom only could devise* were made to convince him of his error. His disaffection was proved to be without a cause, and *he was made to see* what would be the result of persisting in revolt. Lucifer was convinced that he was in the wrong. He saw that . . . the divine statutes are just, and that he ought to acknowledge them as such before all heaven."[20]

"Lucifer himself had not at first been acquainted with the real nature of his feelings."[21] That happens to all of us. In a sudden flash of insight, we recognize where we've been selfish or angry or jealous. Suddenly, we *understand* something we didn't know before. And now we have a choice to make. Will we follow our new insight, which we *know* to be the right choice, or will we follow our *feelings*? Unfortunately, Lucifer chose to follow his feelings.

By this time, he had gained a great following among heaven's angels—as much as a third of the "vast, unnumbered throng" that Ellen White spoke about.[22] Revelation 12:4 suggests that about a third of the angels sided with Lucifer, and that was enough to convince him that if he persisted, he could win. He declared to his loyal followers that if they would

> stand firmly with him, . . . they could yet gain all that they desired. . . .
>
> . . . God's government included not only the inhabitants of heaven, but of all the worlds that He had created; and Lucifer had concluded that if he could carry the angels of heaven with him in rebellion, he could carry also all the worlds.[23]

Lucifer truly had great ambitions!

At this point, Lucifer had "fully committed himself to the great controversy against his Maker," and he declared that "he would never again acknowledge the supremacy of Christ."[24]

The loyal angels warned Lucifer and his followers that "He who had cre-

---

* The Holy Spirit is the member of the Godhead who convicts us and guides us into all truth (John 16:8, 13), and I suggest that the truth He especially convicts us of and guides us into is the truth about ourselves. Therefore, it's most likely that the Third Member of the Godhead had an important role in convicting Lucifer of his error.

ated them could overthrow their power and signally punish their rebellious daring."[25] We have to wonder how Lucifer could be so foolish as to think that he could successfully oppose the great God of heaven, the Almighty, the Ancient of Days, in whose presence he had stood and whose commands he had carried out. But he refused to bend. Such is the power of determined emotion that refuses to listen to logic and reason.

That's a characteristic of desire and emotion that we also must watch out for. We may think that we wouldn't allow our emotions to so easily overpower what we know to be true. But day after day, each of us is faced with choices, often very small ones that seem insignificant. But as we yield to our desires instead of our knowledge in these minor situations, we gradually establish a pattern. Yielding to desire becomes easier each time; and when the big choice comes, we yield once again. That's what happened to Lucifer and his followers.

Love, law, and authority

I pointed out in chapter 1 that it's easy for us humans, in our broken way of thinking, to be afraid of authority. That's partly because authority is so often abused in our world. On a national and global scale, think Hitler, North Korea, and ISIS. On a domestic scale, think spousal and child abuse. When an authority figure commands us, do we tremble on the inside, perhaps cower in fear or lash out in anger (a response that's also triggered by fear)? Or are we able to stand our ground? Or turn that around. Do you have a commanding presence and use it to get your way from timid people? Either way, you're allowing your emotions to rule your behavior instead of following what you know to be right.

How do you suppose the loyal angels in heaven feel about authority? I can assure you they aren't afraid of it. To the contrary, I believe they welcome it! I'm quite certain they learned to appreciate it even more following the chaos that Lucifer's rebellion caused in heaven when he rebelled against Christ's authority. Paul was a strong supporter of governmental authority. He advised the Christians in Rome to "submit . . . to the governing authorities. . . . The authorities that exist have been established by God" (Romans 13:1). The only time the Bible gives us permission to disobey governmental authority is when it conflicts with our duty to obey God (Acts 5:29; 4:20).

The primary purpose of authority is to enforce laws. This includes the authority of government officials to require that citizens obey the laws of the land; the authority of companies to require that employees obey their policies; and the authority of parents to require that their children obey the family's rules. Respect for authority is one of the keys to a well-ordered, peaceful society.

God has established laws in heaven, and He uses His authority to enforce them. God also delegates to some of the angels the authority to enforce His laws. He especially delegated this authority to Lucifer prior to his fall. I pointed out in chapter 1 that Ellen White spoke about angels being "under his [Lucifer's] command," and that the "angels delighted to execute his commands."[26] This, in fact, may be what got Lucifer in trouble in the first place. He enjoyed the authority he had over the other angels, and he resented the fact that Christ, who as far as he was concerned was just another angel like himself, had greater authority over the angels than he (Lucifer) did. In fact, Christ had authority over Lucifer—and Lucifer *really* resented that! And that's where his rebellion against God and His laws began.

Lucifer's rebellion

It's important to understand that Lucifer rebelled against more than a written moral code. God's law is based on love; a principle that involves the entire being—mental, physical, emotional, and spiritual. It's what a person *is*, not just how he or she *behaves*. That's what Jesus meant when He said that the first commandment is to "love the Lord your God with all your heart and with all your soul and with all your mind and with all your strength . . . [and] your neighbor as yourself" (Mark 12:30, 31).

Love has to do with our attitudes. It's a way of thinking and feeling. It's a mind-set. In God's system of law, loving actions arise from a loving mind-set. Speaking through Jeremiah, God said that He would write His laws on the *minds* and *hearts* of His people (Jeremiah 31:33). Anyone who has gone through the second or third grade can *read* the Ten Commandments, but that doesn't mean he or she will *appreciate* them and *want* to obey them. It's reasonable to assume that God created Lucifer with the law of love written on his mind and heart. So when Lucifer became jealous of Christ, he violated his own mind, his own heart, and his own emotions; in doing that, he violated the most fundamental principle of God's laws.

One of the arguments Lucifer made in his effort to win the angels to his side was that "though laws might be necessary for the inhabitants of the worlds, angels, being more exalted, needed no such restraint, for their own wisdom was a sufficient guide. They were not beings that could bring dishonor to God; all their thoughts were holy; it was no more possible for them than for God Himself to err."[27]

44

That's a very interesting argument. It's the same one we suggest when we ask why God didn't make intelligent beings in such a way that they couldn't sin. We may *wish* He had made the angels and us that way. But Lucifer said that God *did* make the angels that way. That's a very subtle lie—and a very dangerous one—because it implants in the minds of intelligent beings the idea that they don't have to guard their minds and emotions. They can do anything they want, because anything they want to do is OK. Lucifer treated God's laws as though they were a mere external moral code. He failed to realize that his jealousy of Christ was itself a violation of the principle of love that lies at the foundation of God's law. There's no such thing as obedience to a divine law if the mind and heart aren't in it.

Authority in the Kingdom of Light is founded on love. The kingdom's citizens have to appreciate its authority relationships and submit to them gladly. And their appreciation has to be given freely. God can, and does at times, enforce His laws as an external moral code that controls behavior (such as the Flood, Sodom and Gomorrah, and Egypt's armies in the Red Sea), but He absolutely refuses to force His intelligent creatures to love His laws and His authority. They have to *choose* that part. But He gives them the freedom not to choose to love His laws and authority. Lucifer made that choice, and all over our world, human beings are still making it.

Fortunately, God has made it possible for sinful human beings to once again love His laws and His authority. However, we can't just snap our fingers one day and say, "You know, I think I'll love God's laws. I think I'll welcome His authority." In our natural state, we humans find God's laws to be very distasteful. It takes a supernatural act on God's part to *help* us love His laws. We call this supernatural act "conversion." I'll have much more to say about this in future chapters.

Summary of the Kingdom of Darkness in heaven

In chapter 1, I described four characteristics of the Kingdom of Light: love, law, authority, and freedom. In this chapter, I have described a characteristic of our human nature: emotions. This is also a characteristic of God Himself and of all the intelligent beings He created. Even animals have emotions.

In establishing his Kingdom of Darkness, Lucifer violated all of these characteristics. Our emotions are supposed to be under the control of reason, but Lucifer allowed his pride to dictate his attitude toward Michael. In doing this, he violated the foundational principle of God's law, which is love. God made it very clear to all of the angels that Michael held a higher position than any of the angels, but pride caused Lucifer to reject that declaration and rebel against God's authority. We will see this pattern repeated time and again throughout the history of the conflict between the Kingdom of Light and the Kingdom of Darkness, which will end with Armageddon.

However, before we continue with the story of this conflict, we need to spend a few moments reflecting on God's creation of our world.

1. White, *Patriarchs and Prophets*, 37.

2. Ellen G. White, *The Great Controversy* (Mountain View, CA: Pacific Press® Pub. Assn., 1911), 493.

3. White, *Patriarchs and Prophets*, 35.

4. Ellen G. White, *Early Writings* (Washington, DC: Review and Herald® Pub. Assn., 1945), 145.

5. White, *Patriarchs and Prophets*, 37.

6. Ibid., 35, 36.

7. Ibid., 36.

8. Ibid.

9. See especially *Patriarchs and Prophets*, chap. 1; *The Great Controversy*, 492–504; and *Early Writings*, 145–147.

10. Ibid.

11. Ibid.

12. Ibid., 36, 37.

13. Ibid., 37.

14. Ibid.

15. Ibid., 36, 37.

16. Ibid., 37.

17. Ibid., 37, 38.

18. Ibid., 38.

19. Ibid., 39.

20. Ibid.; emphasis added.

21. Ibid., 39.

22. Ibid., 36.

23. Ibid., 39, 41.

24. Ibid., 40.

25. Ibid.

26. Ibid., 38, 37.

27. Ibid., 37.

CHAPTER 5

The Creation
of the World

One hundred trillion angels, or however many there actually were, weren't enough for God. He wanted more—many more intelligent beings whom He could love. So He created humans. But before He could do that, He had to create a planet on which they could live. And He accomplished the feat in six literal days! I don't have to tell you the story (I'm assuming you've heard it many times).* My purpose in this chapter is to reflect on the *meaning* of Creation.

It's easy for those of us in conservative Christian circles to say that "God is the Creator" without pausing to reflect on all that this statement implies. So let's reflect.

When people in Bible times referred to "the heavens," they had no idea of the vastness of the universe. They thought of it in terms of what they could see: the sun during the day and the moon and thousands of stars in the night sky. Some Bible students have suggested that people in Bible times thought the sky consisted of a dome made out of some solid substance, such as bronze, and that the sun, moon, and stars consisted of holes in the dome that allowed the light from God's throne room to shine through. The ancients actually did not think of the sky in quite those terms,† but the idea does suggest the limited view of the universe that they held. How could it be otherwise? We can understand nature only by the way we perceive it with our five senses, including whatever scientific instruments have been created to extend the reach of our senses. But the ancients had no such instruments. They were limited to what they could see with their eyes and hear with their ears.

---

* If you aren't familiar with the biblical account of Creation, you can read about it in the first two chapters of Genesis.

† The idea of the sky being some solid substance may have come from a statement in Deuteronomy 28:23 where Moses, listing the curses that would come on Israel if they refused to obey God, said, "The sky over your head will be bronze, the ground beneath you iron." Moses was almost certainly speaking metaphorically.

Fast-forward two or three millennia. Telescopes were invented in 1608. When Galileo heard about it a year later, he developed one of his own, used it, and discovered that some of those stars shining out there were actually planets—huge worlds like the one on which he lived. Suddenly, the human concept of the universe changed drastically. Yet that was only a start. As telescopes became more and more powerful, astronomers and other scientists came to realize that most of those tiny specks in the night sky were actually stars like our sun. They also realized that planet Earth was located in a cluster of stars that they called a *galaxy*. And they discovered that our world is near one edge of that galaxy and that what humans had called the Milky Way was what we see when we look through that galaxy to the far side. That's about where our human understanding of the universe stood at the beginning of the twentieth century.

But then came spaceships, which put a telescope called Hubble into orbit around our planet, and suddenly the astronomers' view of the universe exploded. We now know that there are *billions* of galaxies in the universe and that the farthest galaxy from ours is 13.4 billion light-years away from us! When we pause to remember that light travels at a speed of 186,000 *miles per second*, the distance from Earth to the farthest reaches of the universe is far beyond our imagination's ability to comprehend.

But that isn't the end of the story. Other scientists discovered that all matter is made up of minute atoms, which are so tiny that only the most powerful microscopes can actually "see" them. And atoms consist of neutrons and protons that whirl around inside them. Inorganic matter is made up of innumerable atoms; and organic matter consists of cells, which are made up of millions of atoms all working together like miniature factories.

The planets and stars are made up of these tiny atoms; and living things, from the tiniest amoeba to the largest elephant, are made up of cells that work together to keep the living organism alive and functioning.

Now stop to think about the implication of this: *God made those tiny atoms and clustered them together to create planets, suns, and galaxies. He flung those galaxies into outer space in what we call the universe. God also created cells and put them together to make amoebas, elephants, and humans that are alive.*

I cannot wrap my mind around these ideas! The wisdom and power of our Creator God is awesome, and that's an understatement if there ever was one! But we can understand enough that we can fall on our knees, and with the four living creatures around God's throne, we can cry: "Holy, holy, holy is the Lord God almighty, who was, and is, and is to come" (Revelation 4:8).

With the twenty-four elders, we can, in our imaginations, bow before God and sing,

"You are worthy, our Lord and God,
to receive glory and honor and power,
for you created all things,
and by your will they were created
and have their being" (verse 11).

Then God created human beings!

God's crowning act of creation was the first two humans—Adam and Eve. They were the reason God created everything else during those six days. He prepared a world that would support human life, animal life, and plant life. The God who made the giant stars and the tiny atoms and living cells also created an ecology that was in perfect balance so that it could support life.

God created human beings because He wanted additional intelligent beings whom He could love. He created us as physical beings with physical brains that are conscious and can experience emotion, and with intellects that can take in information, process it, and draw rational conclusions. The grand purpose of our consciousness, intellect, and emotions is that we can love God and experience His love in return.

There's more! God created these first humans with the ability to reproduce themselves. So each time a baby was born, God would have one more intelligent being whom He could love and who could love Him. This child would grow up, marry, and have children of his or her own—and God would have that many more intelligent humans whom He could love and who could love Him.

Now pause again to consider the implication of all this. Today planet Earth has seven and a half billion inhabitants,* and the numbers keep growing. And this is with every generation dying off. But there would have been no death in God's ideal world. So what would today's world population be if nobody ever died? By now, there would be standing room only! This would present God with a huge dilemma: what to do with all those extra human beings? As I see it, He would have had two options for solving the problem:[†]

1. After several hundred years, when the planet reached its ideal number

---

* That was the population of the world in 2017 when this book was published..

† God, being God, might have come up with other options.

49

of inhabitants, He could cause every human being to be sterile (or at least sterilize one gender).

2. He could create more planets like our world, which would be capable of supporting life and move some human beings from Earth to populate those new worlds.

I believe God intended to implement the second option. After all, He was looking for additional intelligent beings with whom He can have loving relationships, and He came up with this brilliant idea that instead of creating each new human individually, He would make two intelligent humans beings, a male and a female, who could do the creating for Him. Their offspring, in male and female pairs, would create more males and females to pair up and create more males and females ad infinitum. And now that we understand the vastness of the universe and the billions and trillions of other planets that exist out there, we can begin to understand what God was working toward. He had to begin by creating this vast universe of suns and planets so that He would have places to put the ever-growing multitude of humans. Then He created the first human pair to start the reproduction process rolling.

So now the question becomes, how long would it take the human race to create enough offspring to fill up all the planets in the universe? That's a problem I'll leave for God to solve.

The Sabbath

Several years ago the Idaho Transportation Department built a new bridge across Interstate 84, which runs through Nampa, Idaho, near where I live. When the construction was finished, the city and the state planned a grand ceremony to celebrate the opening of the new bridge, complete, as I recall (I wasn't there), with a ribbon-cutting ceremony. My family never could stop laughing about that one. A grand ceremony to celebrate the opening of a bridge? Come on! Nevertheless, the grand opening of the bridge illustrates an important fact of life on our planet: we humans celebrate the important events in our lives, whether graduations, weddings, or even the completion of a new building, such as a university science hall or student union center. We plan special programs for these events, and we invite interested parties to join us in celebrating the events.

God also celebrated His work of creating our world on that first Sabbath. Here's how Genesis describes it:

Thus the heavens and the earth were completed in all their vast array.

By the seventh day God had finished the work he had been doing; so on the seventh day he rested from all his work. And God blessed the seventh day and made it holy, because on it he rested from all the work of creating that he had done (Genesis 2:1–3).

Just as we have anniversaries such as birthdays, marriages, alumni reunions, and national independence days, so God made the Sabbath a weekly reminder of His creation of the world. We can draw several lessons from what Genesis 2:1–3 tells us about the origin of the Sabbath.

Creation or evolution? These verses strike the death knell to any notion of evolution.* Notice: "Thus the heavens and the earth were *completed*," and "by the seventh day God had *finished* the work he had been doing" (emphasis added).† The creation of our planet with all its living things took just six days, and no more. At the end of the sixth day, creation stopped. The popular theory of evolution has this "creation" taking place over a period of millions of years and still going on. Not so according to the Bible. The Bible says that creation was finished, done, and stopped.

Some Christians are so convinced that evolution is true that they try to wed it with the Genesis account. They call it theistic evolution. God is the Creator, they say, and evolution is how He created. In this scenario, the days of creation become eons of time that God used to create our world and its living things by the evolutionary process. However, theistic evolution doesn't solve the problem. Verses 1 and 2 of Genesis 2 say that on the seventh day God *finished* His work of creation. Both naturalistic evolution and theistic evolution fail to meet that biblical requirement. Thus, we have a choice: we can accept either the biblical account of origins or the modern scientific account, but we cannot embrace both. They are mutually exclusive.

An immaterial creation. Everything God made during the first six days was physical: light, air, land, and vegetation; sun, moon, and stars; birds and fish; and land animals and humans. But the Sabbath is made out of time, not matter. Animals are very aware of day and night; but for them, each day of the week is like every

---

* Microevolution does happen. It's the adaptation of plants and animals that have already been fully created to their environment. What creationists dispute is *macro*evolution—the idea that a single cell just happened to develop in some primordial soup and that all of today's plants and animals evolved their infinitely complex characteristic from that one single cell.

† While translated as "completed" and "finished" in the NIV, the Hebrew word is the same for both: *kalah.*

other day. They don't have minds that can understand the Sabbath concept. Thus, God made the Sabbath strictly for humans, who have the intelligence to distinguish between time that is sacred and time that is not sacred.

The purpose of the Sabbath. The question then becomes, why did God create the Sabbath for humans? Actually, He didn't create the Sabbath just for humans. God created the Sabbath as much for Himself as for us. Keep in mind that God is a God of relationships, and He created humans so that He could have loving relationships with intelligent beings who could also relate lovingly to Him. It goes without saying that God wants to relate with us on the other six days of the week, but He created the Sabbath as a special time for Him to have a more intimate relationship with us. That's an awesome thought: this Deity who created the vast universe with its galaxies and suns and planets longs for an intimate relationship with us. But that's why God created us, and it's why He set aside the Sabbath as a special day every week to deepen that relationship.

Sabbath as holy time. What is there about the Sabbath that makes it holy? The fact that God *pronounced* the day holy is part of the answer to the question. "God said it; I believe it; that settles it." True enough. But I propose that the primary reason the Sabbath is holy is that God's presence is in it. Anytime and anywhere God is present, that time and place are holy. That's why God told Moses that the ground around the burning bush was holy (Exodus 3:5). And this reinforces what I've already said about the Sabbath: it's a time when God meets with us in a special way, and it's a time for us to meet with Him in that special way. So it's God's presence in the day that makes the Sabbath holy. Because the Sabbath is holy *time*, there is no holy ground. The Sabbath is holy all around the world. God has left it to us to create holy spaces with churches, temples, and cathedrals. When we build these holy spaces, God commits Himself to meet with us in them. In fact, each individual can create his or her own holy place where he or she can meet with God in Bible study and prayer.

Relationships with each other. The Sabbath is also about relationships between Sabbath keepers. That first Sabbath there were just two people. But God made the Sabbath for the human race, not just for Adam and Eve. This is evident in Jesus' statement that "the Sabbath was made for *man*" (Mark 2:27; emphasis added). God's plan was for Adam and Eve to have children, who would have more children, who would have more children. Soon there would have been a world full of people meeting with each other and with God on the Sabbath.

Some people refuse to meet with others on the Sabbath because they say they can worship God at home. In our broken world, there are sometimes valid reasons why a person here and there can't meet with other Christians on the Sabbath. Illness and old age are two of those reasons, and there are others. But where we are physically able to do so, God's plan is for each Sabbath keeper to meet with fellow Sabbath keepers every Sabbath so that we can worship Him corporately.

I wonder what the Sabbath was like for Adam and Eve before they sinned. Genesis 3:8 suggests an answer. It says that Adam and Eve "heard the sound of the LORD God as he was walking in the garden in the cool of the day." I propose that this was a daily occurrence during the time of Adam and Eve's innocence. Every evening God came down to the earth He had just created and met for an hour or two with that first pair of humans because He longed for intelligent creatures with whom He could relate. I propose that God met personally with them the entire day on the Sabbath. And I'm sure many angels joined them.

Sometimes life gets so busy that we have a hard time setting aside the time to keep the Sabbath. That's because we have our priorities mixed up. I'll illustrate with a story of two lovers. Before they meet, their days are so full of all kinds of responsibilities that they have to turn down occasional requests for favors that would require more of their time. But after they meet, finding the time to spend together is no problem. They gladly give up all kinds of other obligations so they can be together. It happens all over the world every day: two people meet, fall in love, and carve out time to spend together.

That's what I believe the Sabbath means to God. He set it aside because of His longing desire to meet with humans and engage in that profound loving relationship. We too often think of what God wants *us* to do on the Sabbath, forgetting what *God* wants to do on the Sabbath. He wants to spend the day with us! *How disappointed He must feel when we refuse to meet with Him on that day!* How disappointed He must feel when we turn the day into mere rules and regulations about what we should and shouldn't do on the Sabbath. And how disappointed He must feel when we sit around on Sabbath afternoon and chat about our jobs and the things we plan to do during the coming week, and all that time He's longing for us to spend time with Him!

God's commitment. In the ideal world that God created, humans and God would both be fully committed to meeting together on the Sabbath. In that ideal world, we would *want* to meet with Him all day. We would *long* to meet with Him all day! The Sabbath couldn't roll around soon enough for us each week! That's pretty much gone with most seventh-day Sabbath keepers these days. We rush around trying to squeeze as much into Friday before sunset as possible, and I must confess that I'm as guilty of that as any other Sabbath keeper.

Then, of course, there are the people who don't even spend time with God on the seventh day at all. Sunday is their big day, and I believe most Sunday keepers would agree with an Episcopalian gentleman I met in Uvalde, Texas, when I was a pastor there. We were chatting in his office one day, and the conversation turned to the Sabbath. I explained our Adventist understanding of the Sabbath. When I was through, he thought for a moment, then said, "Well, I figure that once I get out of church the rest of the day is mine." I think the majority of Sunday keepers would agree. But that's not true of the Sabbath. The entire day is sacred—set apart as sacred time for us to meet with God and with each other.

Now let's look at the Sabbath from God's point of view. He longs for Sabbath keepers who will truly understand the purpose of the day and who will take the day seriously and spend quality time with Him. And He does get that with some Sabbath keepers. I try to be one of them, and I hope you do too.

I propose that God is absolutely committed to observing that weekly anniversary celebration, even if we aren't. And He welcomes every one of us to the celebration at any time. He will be there! I cannot emphasize strongly enough that God is present every seventh day, even if we ignore it. *Our absence cannot determine His presence.*

When we're just learning. I believe God rejoices even at our most feeble efforts to fellowship with Him on the Sabbath. He's cheering us on, encouraging us, and trying to help us understand the real purpose of the day. And He's relishing the new relationship with us.

Do you enjoy helping people in need? People who are out of work and need food to put on their tables. Older people who need their lawns mowed. Young people who need a friend. Depressed people who need someone to talk to. A single mother who has three children and needs someone to watch them now and then. God loves to be involved in that kind of thing too. He rejoices when people discover the Sabbath, and He loves to help them learn how to keep it. He's committed to entering into a love relationship with them on the Sabbath, feeble though their effort may be, and He helps them to grow in their understanding of the day and their appreciation of it.

Suppose there were no Sabbath-keeping people in the world. Zero. I propose that God would still keep the day. When He made the Sabbath in the beginning, He committed Himself to meeting with humans on that day whether they chose to or not. And once God makes a commitment, you can count on Him to keep it. God keeps every Sabbath!

I hope these reflections help you to understand the Sabbath a little better and find more meaning in keeping it. When you and I fully understand the Sabbath and fully keep it, we will discover that it's a powerful deterrent to the attacks on us by the Kingdom of Darkness.

Unfortunately, as I've said, the vast majority of the human race has forgotten about the Sabbath on the seventh day of the week, and many of those who are aware of it either ignore it or observe it on another day of the week. But the Sabbath is so important to God that He included it in His Ten Commandment law. During the final crisis at the end of Earth's history, the Kingdom of Darkness will make it the focal point of its attack on God and His people. Revelation 13 says that the beast that rises from the earth "forced everyone, small and great, rich and poor, free and slave, to receive a mark on his right hand or on his forehead, so that no one could buy or sell unless he had the mark, which is the name of the beast or the number of his name" (verses 16, 17). This will be Satan's final attack on God's law, His authority, and the freedom He intended His human friends to experience. This will be the opposite of the love on which His law and authority are based.

That's how important the Sabbath is to God!

CHAPTER 6

The Great Divorce

T rudy was thrilled when Jerry proposed. She felt so proud of him as she walked down the aisle toward him several months later. When she said, "I do," she meant every word—both of them—from the bottom of her heart. She couldn't imagine anything more rewarding than to spend the rest of her earthly life with the man she had come to love so dearly. Their first night together was passionate beyond anything she could ever have imagined. The only problem with their honeymoon in Hawaii was that it ended too soon.

The next few weeks were consumed with setting up their new home together. She felt troubled by some of the disagreements they had, but she brushed them off as a part of the adjustment that all couples have to go through once they start living together. However, as time went on, the disagreements became more and more intense. Jerry was demanding and controlling. He insisted that all their differences be resolved his way, and "No" was never an acceptable answer. Trudy decided that maybe he would change if they had children, and she was almost as thrilled when she became pregnant as she was when Jerry proposed. He seemed more gentle and patient with her as her pregnancy progressed, and the joy on his face when he held his first son in his arms assured her that their relationship would be better now. "Let's name him Donald, after my father," he said. Trudy agreed.

Unfortunately, the tension soon returned. Donald—or Donny, as they called him—was a restless baby and often woke up crying in the middle of the night. This upset Jerry. He would roll over in bed and tell Trudy to go take care of the problem. Jerry got upset anytime Donny fussed or cried during the day. Trudy tried to explain that Donny was only a baby, but this seemed to make Jerry even more moody. He accused Trudy of being an unfit mother because, as he put it, she failed to comfort Donny. Cindy's birth two years later only intensified the tension. By then, Jerry was drinking heavily, and he went from complaining to bitter accusations, not only against Trudy but against the children. At times, he threw temper tantrums like a two-year-old.

Trudy sensed that a parting of the ways was coming. On the day that Jerry slapped Donny on the face to get him to stop crying, she knew she had to do something. She told her parents what had happened, and they insisted that she bring the children and come live with them. They also recommended a good lawyer. Six months later the divorce was final. The marriage that began so happily was over.*

In one sense, divorce is unbiblical. Jesus said that Moses granted it only "because your hearts were hard. But it was not this way from the beginning" (Matthew 19:8). Unfortunately, the same hardness of heart that existed during Moses' time still exists with many people today, including Christians. Sometimes an intolerable situation *has* to end. Ask God. Ask Christ. Ask the angels. They'll agree. Why? Because that's what happened in heaven. In the chapters on the Kingdom of Darkness, we reviewed what the Bible and Ellen White had to say about Lucifer's jealousy of Christ and his ambition to take Christ's place. The time finally came when the disruption to the harmony of heaven was so severe and Satan's rebellion, which was causing it, became so intense that a parting of the ways was inevitable.

Revelation 12:7–9 is the only place in the Bible that speaks of a war in heaven between Christ and Satan and their angels. The context of that passage is Christ's victory over Satan at the cross, not the war in heaven prior to the creation of the world. Verse 10 says,

> "Now have come the salvation and the power and the kingdom of
> our God,
> and the authority of his Christ.
> For the accuser of our brothers,
> who accuses them before our God day and night,
> has been hurled down."

I agree that the primary application of these words is Christ's defeat of Satan at the cross. That's when the plan of salvation was secured.

However, many Christians, including Seventh-day Adventists, also apply Revelation's description of the war between Michael and Satan to the conflict in heaven at the time of Lucifer's original rebellion, and I agree with that conclusion as well. Every reference to Revelation 12:7–9 in Ellen White's writings applies these verses to the fall of Lucifer and his angels from heaven. Speaking of the interpretation of these verses, *The Seventh-day*

---

* This story is true to life. It has happened over and over again throughout the millennia of history.

Adventist Bible Commentary says, "Though the revelator is focusing primarily on the turning point of the controversy reached at the time of the cross, it is proper to understand the words, 'there was war in heaven,' as referring also to the time prior to the creation of the earth, when the hostility of the dragon began, and Lucifer aspired to be like God."[1]

The original war in heaven is the focus of this chapter.

Questions

I'm curious to know more about the details of that conflict. That's why I'm looking forward to getting acquainted with my guardian angel when I get to heaven. I have several questions I want to ask him about Lucifer. When did my angel first become aware that something was wrong? What did Lucifer say, or what did he do, that caused that first alarm to go off in my angel's mind? I also want to know more about how the conflict developed. Maybe my angel will show me a movie that tells the whole sad story of Lucifer's growing disaffection against Christ, how he gained the sympathy of more and more angels, and how my angel and his friends tried to reason with Lucifer and his followers and pleaded with them to abandon their rebellion. Did they succeed in redeeming some of these angels? Who knows, maybe my guardian angel was one of those who was influenced by Lucifer at first and then returned his loyalty to Christ. But all the effort of the loyal angels failed to persuade Lucifer and his most devoted followers to abandon their rebellion.

Another interesting question we can ask about the war in heaven is who initiated it. Who made the first move? Who was the first to attack—God or Lucifer? The Bible doesn't answer this question. The New International Version of the Bible, which is the primary version I'm using in this book, says that Satan and his angels "fought back," which suggests that Michael and His angels initiated the battle and Satan and his angels responded. However, the word *back* is not in the original. The Greek simply says that "Satan and his angels fought." But Inspiration doesn't leave us in the dark on this question. Ellen White gave us the answer in her book *The Great Controversy*. She wrote, "God in His wisdom permitted Satan to carry forward his work, *until the spirit of disaffection ripened into active revolt.* It was necessary for his plans to be fully developed, that their true nature and tendency might be seen by all."[2]

When enough of heaven's angels sided with Lucifer in his rebellion, he decided that he could win. At that point, he initiated the war, and God responded. That's how I understand the war in heaven to have started.

I also have a question for my angel about the nature of the war. Was it just a war of words, or was it in some sense physical? And if it was physical, what weapons did the two sides use? Christ and His loyal angels had to use some kind of force to cast Lucifer and his angels out of heaven? What was it?

In his book *Revelation of Jesus Christ*, Ranko Stefanovic says, "The battle they fought must be understood to be verbal rather than physical."[3] I will agree that during Christ's time on earth no pitched battle occurred with Him and His angels on one side and Satan and his angels on the other. However, battles of words often end up as physical battles, and there was a sense in which the battle between Christ and Satan turned physical even during Christ's time on earth. Satan saw to it that Jesus was slapped and flogged and that a crown of thorns was shoved down on His head, and finally He was crucified. All this is physical, not just verbal and spiritual. The war in heaven that began with words turned violent in some sense. And that's what I want my angel to explain to me. What was the nature of the war? I believe it was partly physical, if we can refer to a war between angels as physical when the Bible refers to angels as "ministering *spirits*" (Hebrews 1:14; emphasis added).

I was discussing these issues once with a group of friends, and I asked them how they thought Satan and his angels were cast out of heaven. The general opinion was that God used His supernatural power, and presto, the evil angels found themselves on planet Earth. However, I pointed out that Revelation 12:7 says that "Michael and his angels *fought* against the dragon, and the dragon and his angels *fought back*" (emphasis added). In other words, there was some kind of pitched battle in which Michael's angels were involved in casting Satan and his evil angels out of heaven. Speaking of the war in heaven, Ellen White wrote that "angels were engaged in the battle; Satan wished to conquer the Son of God and those who were submissive to His will. But the good and true angels prevailed, and Satan, with his followers, was driven from heaven."[4] Notice the words Ellen White used: "*Angels were engaged in the battle*"; "the good and true angels *prevailed*"; and "Satan, with his followers, was *driven* from heaven." Angels were involved in the conflict. I want to learn more about how that happened.

Satan's reaction to losing the war

Predictably—and fortunately—Satan lost and was cast out of heaven, and the next time the Bible has anything to say about him, he's tempting Eve at the tree of the knowledge of good and evil in Eden. However, in the book *The Story of Redemption*, Ellen White devotes an entire chapter to Satan's immediate reaction to losing the war. She tells an interesting story.

> Satan stood in amazement at his new condition. His happiness was gone. He looked upon the angels who, with him, were once so happy, but who had been expelled from heaven with him. Before their fall not a shade of discontent had marred their perfect bliss. Now all seemed changed. Countenances which had reflected the image of their Maker were gloomy and despairing. Strife, discord, and bitter recrimination were among them. . . . He [Satan] shuddered, and feared to face the future. . . .
> . . . Where is he? Is it not all a horrible dream? Is he shut out of heaven? Are the gates of heaven never more to open to admit him? . . .
> Could he be again as he was when he was pure, true, and loyal, gladly would he yield up the claims of his authority. But he was lost! beyond redemption, for his presumptuous rebellion![5]

Reality was finally beginning to dawn on Satan. Both Michael and the angels who were loyal to Him had warned Lucifer of what would happen if he persisted in his rebellion, but in his arrogant pride he had thought he could conquer Michael and take His place as the highest angelic authority in heaven. He took a chance on winning; he lost; and now he was feeling that loss. He wanted back. Ellen White went on to write, "And this was not all; he had led others to rebellion and to the same lost condition with himself—angels, who had never thought to question the will of Heaven or refuse obedience to the law of God till he had put it into their minds, presenting before them that they might enjoy a greater good, a higher and more glorious liberty. This had been the sophistry whereby he had deceived them. A responsibility now rests upon him from which he would fain be released."[6]

God created both angels and humans with a moral sense and a conscience, and Satan did not entirely lose that when he rebelled and was cast out of heaven. Now that moral sense was activated, and he was feeling guilty. It seems strange to think of Satan as having a conscience and feeling regret for the harm he's caused to others. We can safely assume that after six thousand years he's so compromised his conscience that little, if any, of it remains. But in the immediate aftermath of losing his place in heaven, much of it still remained in his mind. Ellen White continues her description:

> Satan trembled as he viewed his work. He was alone in meditation upon the past, the present, and his future plans. His mighty frame shook as

with a tempest. An angel from heaven was passing. He called him and entreated an interview with Christ. This was granted him. He then related to the Son of God that he repented of his rebellion and wished again the favor of God. He was willing to take the place that God had previously assigned him, and be under His wise command. Christ wept at Satan's woe but told him, as the mind of God, that he could never be received into heaven. Heaven must not be placed in jeopardy. All heaven would be marred should he be received back, for sin and rebellion originated with him. The seeds of rebellion were still within him.[7]

If I'm a lifelong smoker and come down with inoperable lung cancer at the age of seventy-two, God isn't going to heal me of something that was the result of the choices I made during most of my life. God presents us with evidence, which we are free to accept or reject, but we also have to live with the results of our choices.

It's the same in the area of morality and loyalty or disloyalty to God. Over a fairly long time in heaven, Lucifer and his angels made choices that molded their thinking and their brains to the point that the effect could not be reversed. Ellen White went on to explain why he couldn't change:

He repented not of his rebellion because he saw the goodness of God which he had abused. It was not possible that his love for God had so increased since his fall that it would lead to cheerful submission and happy obedience to His law which had been despised. The wretchedness he realized in losing the sweet light of heaven, and the sense of guilt which forced itself upon him, and the disappointment he experienced himself in not finding his expectation realized, were the cause of his grief. To be commander out of heaven was vastly different from being thus honored in heaven. The loss he had sustained of all the privileges of heaven seemed too much to be borne. He wished to regain these.[8]

Satan's repentance was not genuine. True repentance would have led him to recognize that his feelings toward Michael were wrong. He would have recognized his feelings of jealousy and hatred for what they really were, and he would have repented of them. As Ellen White put it, "This great change of position [in which Satan found himself] had not increased his love for God, nor for His wise and just law."[9] The best evidence of this is that "when Satan became fully convinced that there was no possibility of his being reinstated in the favor of God, he manifested his malice with increased hatred and fiery vehemence."[10] Had his repentance been genuine, his hatred would not have reignited.

This is a profound lesson for us. Terminal lung cancer that results from our choice to smoke all our adult lives cannot be reversed, and the spiritual cancer in our minds that is the result of a life of sinful choices also cannot be reversed. We have to live and *die* with the results of our choices—both physical and spiritual. There is one major difference, however. If we accept Jesus as our Savior today, at His second coming He will reverse the results of our physical choices; but beyond a certain point, our spiritual choices are fixed for eternity.

1. Francis D. Nichol, ed., *The Seventh-day Adventist Commentary*, vol. 7 (Washington, DC: Review and Herald® Pub. Assn., 1957), 809.

2. White, *The Great Controversy*, 497; emphasis added.

3. Ranko Stefanovic, *Revelation of Jesus Christ* (Berrien Springs, MI: Andrews University Press, 2009), 395.

4. White, *Early Writings*, 146.

5. White, *The Story of Redemption*, 24, 25.

6. Ibid., 25.

7. Ibid., 26.

8. Ibid., 26, 27.

9. Ibid., 27.

10. Ibid.

CHAPTER 7

The Kingdom of Darkness Comes to Earth

I have a friend whom I'll call David. David works at a natural foods store in Caldwell, Idaho, where I live, and I drop in there every month or so. He isn't a Christian, but he enjoys discussing religious questions. So whenever I have a bit of extra time on my hands and he isn't busy with other customers, we spend some time chatting. During a recent session, the big question was about the problem of God, evil, and suffering. This is without a doubt the most pressing question in all of Christian theology. Why did God create a devil? And why did He have to cast him to our planet? With all the other billions and perhaps trillions of planets that must exist in the universe, why did God have to choose ours to be Satan's prison house? Why didn't He stick Satan and his rebellious associates off on some uninhabited planet where they could waste away the years by themselves instead of plunging our world into six-thousand-plus years of agony? David and I chatted for twenty or thirty minutes, but I wasn't able to give him an answer that satisfied him.

Unfortunately, the Bible's writers didn't respond to this question; partly, I suspect, because it would never have occurred to them to ask it. They had no idea that the universe contains billions of galaxies and trillions of stars, solar systems, and planets. Today we know this, so it makes sense to us to ask why Satan and his angels weren't sent to some uninhabited planet. I believe there's a very good answer to that question.

I'll begin my response to this question with a quote from Ellen White's book *Early Writings*: "When God said to His Son, 'Let us make man in our image,' Satan was jealous of Jesus. He wished to be consulted concerning the formation of man, and because he was not, he was filled with envy, jealousy, and hatred."[1] We'll have to wait till the next life to be sure, but I suspect that one of the reasons God cast Satan and his angels into our world is that Satan *demanded* to be sent here, and God granted his request. He was angry at being left out of the planning for the creation of our planet, and he wanted to get even by coming down here and taking it over from God.

Of course, God could have refused to send Satan and his angels here. After all, why would He want to endanger His precious new creation of human beings? In our world, we protect our creative works. We have copyright laws that prevent others from appropriating our writings and works of art. In the case of very valuable works, we place them in museums, and sometimes we even put them in glass cases where people can see them but can't touch them. So why didn't God shield His new creation from Satan's attack?

In answer to that question, I will point out that God's creative art in making humans was much different from the inanimate objects we create. He couldn't shield them from the conflict between good and evil the way we protect our artworks without violating one of the most precious parts of His "artwork." God gave His newly minted human beings the same intelligence and freedom of choice that He gave the angels when He created them.

"God knew that . . . [Satan's] determined rebellion would not remain inactive. . . . He would seek to destroy the happiness of Adam and Eve. He would endeavor to incite them to rebellion, knowing that this would create grief in heaven."[2] Strange as that may seem, Satan had a hard time making that decision. We think of Satan as a totally depraved being who takes delight in inflicting as much pain and suffering on human beings as possible, and I have no doubt that is a correct assessment of him today. However, nobody becomes totally perverted in a split second. Those who choose to follow their rebellious feelings degenerate into perversion gradually. During the early stages of Satan's rebellion, he was not totally debased. Ellen White said that Satan still had enough of a conscience at the time he was cast out of heaven that "he shuddered at the thought of plunging the holy, happy pair [Adam and Eve] into the misery and remorse he was himself enduring. He seemed in a state of indecision: at one time firm and determined, then hesitating and wavering."[3] In the end, however, he decided to take out his hostility toward Christ on Adam and Eve. And he had a couple of interesting reasons for doing so.

Trying to manipulate God

Satan's original plan was to manipulate God into allowing him and his followers back into heaven. Having stood in God's presence for many years, he was very familiar with His loving nature, and he figured that "if he could in any way beguile them [Adam and Eve] to disobedience, God would make some provision whereby they might be pardoned, and then himself and all the fallen angels would be in a fair way to share with them of God's mercy."[4] *This was Satan's strategy for manipulating God into letting him and his evil companions back into heaven.* Deluded? Absolutely! But that's what happens when we allow our feelings to dominate our intellect. Our thinking gets screwed up.

Satan also knew that "if . . . [he] failed here, all prospect of *regaining* and *controlling* heaven, or any part of God's creation, was hopeless."[5] What distorted thinking! Satan was strategizing not only to *regain* an entrance back into heaven—he hoped when he got there to *control* heaven! That makes about as much sense as my trying to figure out a way to control the United States government, or even my local city government, for that matter. Satan didn't understand that he and his angels had totally unfitted themselves for the society of heaven. That's one of the consequences of allowing our feelings to control our thinking. It distorts our perception of reality. And after a time, our distorted, sinful thinking becomes so fixed in our minds that it can't be reversed. As Ellen White pointed out, God could not allow Satan back into heaven because "the seeds of rebellion were still within him."[6]

But back to Satan and his plan to manipulate God. His first objective was to tempt Adam and Eve to disobey God and then count on God to pardon them. If that happened, he assumed that in all fairness, God would be compelled to make the same pardon available to him and his evil followers. As I said, this was Satan's *first strategy* for manipulating God.

However, in case that didn't work, he had a plan B: "Once they [Adam and Eve] should transgress the law of God they would be subjects of God's wrath, like themselves [Satan and his followers]. Their [Adam and Eve's] transgression would place them, also, in a state of rebellion, and they [Satan and his angels] could unite with Adam and Eve, take possession of Eden, and hold it as their home. And if they could gain access to the tree of life in the midst of the garden, their strength would, they thought, be equal to that of the holy angels, and even God Himself could not expel them."[7]

This was Satan's plan B to manipulate God.

What Satan wanted was territory inhabited by intelligent beings whom he could rule over. His initial effort had been to conquer heaven and control its inhabitants. That plan having failed, he turned his attention to gaining control of planet Earth. As we know, he succeeded all too well. For the past six thousand years or so, he's been "the god of this world" (2 Corinthians 4:4, KJV). However, God outmaneuvered Satan. He granted him a period of time to rule over our world, but his rule will end someday with the battle of Armageddon. However, that's getting ahead of our story.

Satan gets his angels on board

Having come up with a strategy, Satan called a meeting of his followers and shared his plan with them. They listened, but "they did not all readily unite to engage in this hazardous and terrible work."[8] Having spent hundreds and perhaps thousands of years in heaven, they were very aware of God's great intelligence and power, and they were dubious of Satan's plan to get Adam and Eve on their side. So Satan told them that he wanted them to "consider the matter while he should leave them and seek retirement, to mature his plans. He sought to impress upon them that this was their last and only hope."[9]

Satan was very aware of the risk he was taking. "He had fears that his purposes might be defeated," and "even if he should be successful in leading Adam and Eve to disobey the commandment of God . . . no good [could] come to himself, his own case would not be improved; his guilt would only be increased." And, as I pointed out a moment ago, "he shuddered at the thought of plunging the holy, happy pair into the misery and remorse he was himself enduring. He seemed in a state of indecision: at one time firm and determined, then hesitating and wavering."[10] It's easy for us to think that when God cast Satan out of heaven, the very next thing Satan did was to boldly tempt Adam and Eve. Ellen White helps us to understand that he had a hard time reaching the decision to do that.

However, as Satan was pondering what to do, his angels returned "to acquaint him with their decision. They would unite with Satan in his plans, and with him bear the responsibility and share the consequences." With that, "Satan cast off his feelings of despair and weakness and, as their leader, fortified himself to brave out the matter and do all in his power to defy the authority of God and His Son."[11]

God gets His angels on board

God immediately "assembled the angelic host to take measures to avert the threatened evil."[12] By this time, I'm sure the Trinity had held Their own council meeting to decide how to respond to the decision by Satan and his evil angels to tempt Adam and Eve, and I find it very significant that one of the actions They took was to involve heaven's angels in the process of protecting Adam and Eve from Satan. God created intelligent beings, both angels and humans, who can think, reason, and take action on what they know. And the Godhead didn't just leave Their intelligent angels to sit around with nothing to do. In this particular instance, the Trinity involved the angels in two ways. First, the Trinity involved the angels in *devising* the plan to protect

Adam and Eve from Satan. Second, They gave the angels responsibilities to assist in *carrying out* the plan.

We know that, after creating Adam, "the LORD God commanded the man, 'You are free to eat from any tree in the garden; but you must not eat from the tree of the knowledge of good and evil, for when you eat of it you will surely die' " (Genesis 2:16, 17). The two Hebrew words for "LORD God" are *Yahweh Elohim*. The English translation of *Yahweh* is "Jehovah," who is God in the highest sense; the English translation of *Elohim* is "God," plural.

The Bible's statement that Jehovah commanded Adam not to eat of the fruit of the tree of the knowledge of good and evil brings up what at first glance seems to be an apparent contradiction of a comment by Ellen White. She said that one of the decisions of the heavenly council was for *angels* to "visit Eden and warn Adam that he was in danger from the foe. Two angels sped on their way to visit our first parents."[13] So was it God or the angels who warned Adam and Eve?

The simple solution to the problem is that it was Jehovah God who *commanded* Adam not to eat the fruit of the tree. However, the angels' conversation with the pair was a follow-up to God's order. They were told to share with Adam and Eve the "sad history of Satan's rebellion and fall." They were to inform Adam and Eve that "Satan purposed to do them harm, and it was necessary for them to be guarded, for they might come in contact with the fallen foe."[14] Thus, there's no contradiction between the statements of the Bible and Ellen White. God gave Adam the command. The angels followed up with the story of Satan's rebellion and a warning for Adam and Eve to be on their guard against him.

Adam and Eve join Satan

Once Satan decided to involve Adam and Eve and the human race in the same misery he was experiencing, he planned his strategy carefully. He knew that "if he should come boldly upon Adam and Eve and make complaints of God's own Son, they would not listen to him for a moment but would be prepared for such an attack. Should he seek to intimidate them because of his power, so recently an angel in high authority, he could accomplish nothing. He decided that cunning and deceit would do what might, or force, could not."[15]

Since the only place he could contact Adam and Eve was at the tree of the knowledge of good and evil, Satan probably had to wait some time for an opportunity to approach them. Occasionally, someone asks me how long

Adam and Eve were in Eden before they fell, and the simple answer is that we have no idea. The closest the Bible comes to answering that question is that Adam and Eve's son Seth was born when Adam was 130 years old (Genesis 5:3), and by then Cain and Abel and who knows how many other children had also been born. Adam and Eve may have been in Eden only a few weeks or months before their fall. However long it was, Satan no doubt spent a significant amount of his time watching the pair before finalizing his strategy. Probably, fairly early on he decided to approach one of them alone, and he had to spend some time observing them to decide which one to prey on. Then, once he decided that Eve would be his target, he may have had to sit around in the tree of the knowledge of good and evil for who knows how long, waiting for her to stroll up by herself.*

Then one day it happened! Eve approached the tree by herself. Here was Satan's chance! I can imagine his heart skipped a beat (assuming angels have hearts like humans do). He quickly found a snake (or maybe he had one waiting) and entered into it. He took a deep breath and let Eve stand around a bit, admiring the tree and wondering why God told them not to eat its fruit. Then he made his move.

I have to hand it to Satan. He was very subtle and very clever, and the way he approached Eve shows that he did indeed spend time in careful planning. He appeared in the guise of the snake that he had taken possession of. Speaking through the snake, Satan said, "Hello, Eve."† She probably turned around and looked this way and that, trying to figure out where the voice came from. Satan may have had to speak to her several times: "Up here, Eve, in the tree. It's me, the snake in the tree." That got her attention! *Hmm, a talking snake. How unusual!*

---

* Some people object to the idea that Eve was alone at the tree when the serpent tempted her, because Genesis 3:6 says that she ate the fruit and "she also gave some to her husband who was *with* her" (emphasis added). However, the Bible records only a conversation between the serpent and Eve. If Adam was present, why wasn't he also engaged in the conversation? He would almost certainly have recognized the temptation and warned his wife not to take the fruit. It seems more likely that Adam was "with her" in the same sense that a businessman who is accompanied by his wife on a work-related trip tells his business associates that his wife is *with* him, even though she isn't present during their actual meetings. Ellen White made it very clear that Eve wandered from her husband's side, which the angels had "cautioned her not to do," as noted on page 32 of *The Story of Redemption*.

† Neither the Bible nor Ellen White say that Satan's first words were, "Hello, Eve." However, on page 33 of *The Story of Redemption*, Ellen White did say that Satan flattered Eve with comments about her beauty before speaking to her about God's command. I'm guessing that Satan would most likely have begun his conversation with a simple greeting, such as, "Hello, Eve."

This should also have been a warning to Eve that something wasn't quite right. However, keep in mind that Adam and Eve were still discovering lots of things about their new world. So, while the idea of a talking snake would have struck Eve as unusual, she could have concluded that may have been how God had created snakes, and it aroused her curiosity. Satan specifically planned his strategy to avoid any warning bells going off in Eve's mind. Instead, he aroused her curiosity. And it worked. Instead of running away, Eve stayed and listened. Victory number one for Satan!

Then he worked the next part of his strategy. He asked a question: "Did God really say, 'You must not eat from *any* tree in the garden?' " (Genesis 3:1; emphasis added). Notice that Satan didn't begin by asking, "Did God say you must not eat from *this* tree?" He knew perfectly well that is what God had said. But his strategy at this point was simply to engage Eve in a conversation, so he asked her a question to which he knew the answer was No, because she would be more likely to correct his misunderstanding. He wanted to get her to talking, so he got *her* to tell *him* what God had actually said.

She fell for the trap. She replied, "We may eat fruit from the trees in the garden, but God did say, 'You must not eat fruit from the tree that is in the middle of the garden, and you must not touch it, or you will die' " (verse 2).

Satan got what he wanted. He got her to talk to him. Now was the time for the lie. He said, "You will not surely die" (verse 4). God had said you *will* die. Satan said you *won't* die. Satan then went on to tell a half-truth: "God knows that when you eat of it your eyes will be opened, and you will be like God, knowing good and evil" (verse 4). The truth is that if she ate the fruit she would indeed be like God insofar as knowing good and evil. What he did not tell her is that the knowledge of evil would bring her and her husband great anguish.

In saying that she would be like God, Satan also suggested that by eating the fruit she would enter upon a higher state of existence than God had given her. That's the same temptation that got Satan cast out of heaven. He coveted Christ's position and authority, which were higher than his.

Immediately after eating the fruit, Eve "imagined she felt the quickening power of a new and elevated existence as the result of the exhilarating influence of the forbidden fruit."[16] Then, "in a strange and unnatural excitement . . . she sought her husband with her hands filled with the forbidden fruit."[17] I can just imagine her enthusiasm. "Adam! Adam! Look what I have! This is fruit from the tree that God said we shouldn't eat from. But Adam, I ate it, and I feel *wonderful*! Here, try some. You'll like it!"

Let's say that Adam was trimming some vines that clung to a tree. When he heard his beloved wife's excited voice, he turned toward her expectantly, with a broad smile on his face. But then he heard her words, and his heart stopped. For the first time in his life, he felt fear—more than fear—panic. "Honey, you didn't! Oh, Eve, how could you? Honey, God said No!"

"But Adam, look at me. I'm still alive, and I feel *so good!*"

"Why, when God said we should *not* eat that fruit? Oh, darling, why did I let you stray from my side when the angels warned us to stay together?"

"Adam, listen to me. The snake ate the fruit, and it didn't hurt him. Besides, he said that if we eat the fruit we will become like God! Oh, Adam, try some! Here." She handed him a piece.

Adam took the fruit and looked at Eve, down at the fruit, and then back at Eve. "Oh, Eve, I can't! God said No."

Eve frowned. "So you don't believe me!"

A look of anguish crossed Adam's face, and his voice cracked. "Honey, I believe you when you say that a snake spoke to you and got you to eat the fruit. But you ate it when God said not to!" He looked at Eve with both a pained expression and the great love he felt for her. Then he looked down at the fruit, at Eve, and then down at the fruit again. "OK," he said, "if you die, I die with you!" He took a bite. "*Hmm!* Tastes good! And I feel great!"

"Honey, I told you so. That's how I felt when I ate the fruit. I wonder why God told us not to eat it when it makes us feel so good?"

Adam put an arm around Eve. "We'll tell God when He comes this evening and ask Him that question." Just then a slight breeze blew, and Adam held Eve a little closer. "Honey, I feel kind of chilly. Let's find a nice sunny spot where we can sit and warm up." They found a grassy knoll and sat down. Buried in their own thoughts, neither of them spoke for a while. Finally, Adam broke the silence. "I wonder what God will say."

Eve hesitated for a moment. "I'm wondering the same thing."

They sat in silence a few more minutes, then Eve started to cry. "Adam, I'm scared!"

Adam nodded. "Me too."

Suddenly, Adam jerked upright and stood to his feet. "Eve, look at yourself! You look the same way you did last night when we made love!"

Eve looked down at her body and then up at Adam with a startled look on her face. "But, but, but Adam, so do you!" Adam looked down at himself, and he cried out, "Oh, Eve, what have we done? We can't face God this evening looking naked like this. What are we going to do?"

Eve was silent for a moment. Her mind raced. "Let's think," she said. Adam put his arm around her and held her close. She pondered another moment and then said, "I know what we can do. Remember that fig tree in the meadow across the creek? Those leaves are huge. We can cover ourselves with them."

Adam frowned. "But how will we hold them together?"

"Oh, that's easy," Eve said. "We'll poke holes in them with the stem of a leaf. Then we'll cut some thin tendrils from the vine that's growing in the tree where we sleep, and we'll sew them together!" She looked up at Adam with a smile.

They proceeded to the fig tree, where they cut the leaves and sewed them together with tendrils from a vine. When they were through, they put on their new clothes and sat down on a grassy spot in front of the fig tree. The sun was about halfway down toward the horizon, so they waited. With each moment, the fear in their hearts grew.

Then they heard it—God's voice called them. "Adam, it's Me, God. I've come to see you again."

Adam felt his heart lurch, and he grabbed Eve's hand and leaped to his feet. "Honey, we can't let God see us like this. Let's hide."

"But where, Adam?"

Adam paused and then said, "Follow me!" He took off at a run. Minutes later, breathless, they burrowed deep into some bushes in the darkest part of the forest.

"Adam, Eve, where are you?" The voice was nearer now, and every second it drew closer. Moments later they heard the branches parting. Adam's heart raced.

"Adam, Eve, is that you?"

Adam crouched, pushing himself deeper in a bush. Then he looked up and saw God, and he gasped. "God, is that You? You look so different! Where's the glory?"*

God didn't say anything. He had a sad look on His face, and His voice was gentle when He spoke. "Why did you hide from Me, Adam?"

Adam took a deep breath, looked down at his and Eve's fig leaves, and then he said, "I was naked, and I was ashamed. That's why I ran and hid."

---

* Sinful human beings cannot look upon God in His glorious form and live. Even though neither the Bible nor Ellen White say so, I'm assuming that God visited Adam and Eve prior to their sin in His glorious form, but after they sinned He hid His glory, appearing to them more as a human.

"Adam," God asked softly, "did you eat the fruit from the tree I told you not to eat from?"

Adam gulped. Then he nodded toward Eve and said, "Well, uh, the woman You gave me, she brought some of the fruit to me. She said that she had eaten it, and obviously nothing bad had happened to her, so I ate some too."

God turned to Eve. His voice still gentle, He asked, "Eve, is that true? Did you eat the fruit?"

Just then a snake flew past one of the bushes. Eve glared and pointed to the snake. "He spoke to me from the tree, and he gave me some, and I ate it."

Suddenly, Adam and Eve gasped. A shadowy figure appeared in front of them. Satan stood beside the snake, with a look of triumphant glee on his face. Then he vanished.

A brief reflection

God instructed Adam very specifically that he was *not* to eat the fruit from the tree of the knowledge of good and evil. That was a law, a very simple law, but it was law nonetheless, and it carried with it a specific penalty for its violation: death. As we learned in the first chapter, the law is one of the important characteristics of God's government, the Kingdom of Light, and closely related to it is the authority to enforce the law. When Lucifer and his angels rebelled against God's law and His authority in heaven, God exercised His authority to cast them out of heaven to our planet. In the same way, Adam and Eve were cast out of Eden when they disregarded God's authority by violating His simple law that barred them from eating the forbidden fruit. At the same time, they lost the Holy Spirit's presence in their minds and hearts, which caused them to lose two other characteristics of God's Kingdom of Light—love and freedom. So the basic principles underlying the Kingdom of Light were very much at play in what happened in Eden. We will see these same principles involved in the conflict between good and evil from that time until the battle of Armageddon.

---

1. White, *Early Writings*, 145.

2. White, *The Story of Redemption*, 27.

3. Ibid., 28.

4. Ibid., 27.

5. Ibid., 28; emphasis added.

6. Ibid., 26.

7. Ibid., 28.

8. Ibid.

9. Ibid.

10. Ibid.

11. Ibid., 28, 29.

12. Ibid., 29.

13. Ibid.

14. Ibid., 30.

15. Ibid.

16. Ibid., 35.

17. Ibid.

CHAPTER 8

A Way of Escape for Humans

S atan's closest followers gathered around him. They slapped him on the back and cheered. Then the evil angels celebrated with a grand party. Satan's next in command raised his cup and said, "Hail to the chief!"* And they all raised their cups and cheered again.

"Friends," Satan said, "God gave dominion over the world to Adam and Eve, but we have wrested that dominion from them. The world is our kingdom now. As the human race multiplies, our kingdom will grow and expand over the earth, and we will have an opportunity to demonstrate the superiority of our plan of government. There are only two humans right now, so there may not be much for each of you to do for a while, but I assure you that as more and more of them are born you will increasingly be very, very busy. Michael and His crowd are most unhappy with us right now, which is exactly what I had hoped for. And we're going to keep them unhappy for a long, long time. Now let's wait and see what Michael does for Adam and Eve that we can cash in on."

The Kingdom of Darkness won that round.

The reaction in heaven

What was the reaction of God's loyal angels as Satan and his angels were cheering their victory over Adam and Eve? A cloud of gloom settled over heaven as the news spread that Adam and Eve had disobeyed God's command. "Every harp was hushed. The angels cast their crowns from their heads in sorrow. . . . The angels feared that they [Adam and Eve] would put forth the hand and eat of the tree of life, and thus perpetuate a life of sin."[1] At this point, it seemed to the angels that "man was lost and that world which God

---

* On page 45 of *The Story of Redemption*, Ellen White said that "Satan . . . rejoiced with his angels" over the fall of the human race. That they would celebrate their victory seems like a reasonable conclusion, even though there's no inspired source to tell us exactly how they did so. We don't know whether angels depend on food and water the way humans do, though I suspect that they don't. I've described their celebration in human terms.

had created was to be filled with mortals doomed to misery, sickness, and death, and *there was no way of escape for the offender.*"[2]

Then, wrote Ellen White, "I saw Him [Jesus] approach the exceeding bright light which enshrouded the Father. Said my accompanying angel, He is in close converse with His Father. . . . Three times He was shut in by the glorious light about the Father," and during this time "the anxiety of the angels seemed to be intense."[3]

When Jesus emerged from His conversation with the Father, "He . . . made known to the angelic host that a way of escape had been made for lost man."[4] I'm sure the angels rejoiced, breathed a sigh of relief, and then cheered—until they heard the nature of the escape plan. Jesus "told them that He had been pleading with His Father, and had offered to give His life a ransom, to take the sentence of death upon Himself, that through Him man might find pardon."[5]

The angels were horrified. They "prostrated themselves before Him . . . [and] offered their lives."[6] However, Jesus told them that "His life alone could be accepted of His Father as a ransom for man."[7] He explained that the sacrifice of their lives "would avail nothing. The transgression was so great that an angel's life would not pay the debt. Nothing but the death and intercessions of His [God's] Son would pay the debt and save lost man from hopeless sorrow and misery."[8] When the angels heard the entire plan explained to them, they poured forth "praise and adoration . . . for the self-denial and sacrifice of Jesus; that He would consent to leave the bosom of His Father and choose a life of suffering and anguish, and die an ignominious death to give life to others."[9]

Jesus also explained to the angels that they would have a part to play both in ministering to Jesus while He was on Earth and "to guard and keep the subjects of grace from the evil angels and the darkness constantly thrown around them by Satan"[10] (see Matthew 4:11; Hebrews 1:14).

Now here's a significant question: when in the order of events did this happen in heaven? Logic tells us that what I've described here—the angels' sorrow over the sin of Adam and Eve, Christ's meeting with His Father,* and then Jesus explaining the plan of salvation to the angels—must have taken

---

* I believe the Trinity had already agreed upon the plan of salvation at the time Adam and Eve sinned. Revelation 13:8 says that Jesus was "the Lamb that was slain from the creation of the world." This means that the Trinity had already agreed on the plan of salvation at the time They created the world, and I believe long before that. In Titus 1:2, Paul spoke of "the hope of eternal life, which God, who does not lie, promised before the beginning of time." Thus, the purpose of the meeting that Jesus had with His Father (and no doubt the Holy Spirit as well) at the time Adam and Eve sinned would have been to *confirm* the plan that They had already agreed on.

place between the time when the human pair sinned and the time when God met with them that evening.

Jesus informs Adam and Eve

I believe it was Jesus who communed with Adam and Eve each evening during the period of their innocence, and it was He who met with them that fateful evening and informed them of the consequence of their disobedience. Adam and Eve had hoped that God would forgive them and spare them the death penalty for their transgression. They "flattered themselves that God, who had given them everything to make them happy, might yet excuse their disobedience because of His great love to them and that their punishment would not be so dreadful after all."[11] Instead, He had to tell them that the death penalty still applied.* However, God was also able to give Adam and Eve hope because the Trinity had agreed upon the plan of salvation by this time. His words are found in Genesis 3:15:

> "I will put enmity
> > between you [Satan] and the woman [Eve, who is a symbol of
> > > God's people throughout the ages],
> > and between your offspring and hers;
> he [Christ] will crush your head,
> > and you will strike his [Christ's] heel."

I find it interesting that God's words of hope for Adam and Eve are found, not in what He said to them, but in what He said to Satan, the serpent. That's because the real culprit in this situation was Satan, not Adam and Eve. He was the perpetrator of all that had taken place. Adam and Eve were the victims. The most fundamental issue was the conflict between Christ and Satan, and God put Satan on notice that Christ would eventually defeat him. But the same words that pronounced Satan's doom also gave hope to Adam and Eve.

---

* A question I've asked myself now and then is why God could allow Lucifer to rebel in heaven over a period of time and offer to restore him to his position if he would submit to Michael's authority, yet He could not accept and forgive even one act of disobedience on the part of Adam and Eve without going through the plan of redemption. Why was He more tolerant of Lucifer's growing disaffection, which was clearly sinful, than He was of Adam and Eve's one sin? And the answer, at least in part, is that when Adam and Eve sinned, they sold out to Satan. He took over dominion of planet Earth that God had given to them, and they were now subjects of his kingdom, not God's. Part of the purpose of Christ's death was to buy (redeem) them back from Satan.

So what do God's cryptic words to Satan mean? They have two parts.[12] In the first part, God said, "I will put enmity between you and the woman, and between your offspring and hers." Because God was addressing the serpent, which is Satan, the word *you* refers to him. The woman is Eve, but more broadly she's a symbol for her descendants (her offspring); that is, God's people throughout the ages of human history.* *Enmity* is a condition of hostility or antagonism between two parties. So why did God say He would put enmity between the woman (God's people) and Satan? Adam and Eve were the total sum of God's people at that time. Didn't they already hate Satan for what he had done to them? To answer that question we need to explore what actually happened to Adam and Eve when they ate the forbidden fruit.

What happened when they sinned

Something of critical importance happened to Adam and Eve when they disobeyed God. We get a clue what this was from their mental and emotional reaction to their sin. They felt shame and fear. Adam admitted as much when he told God why they hid. He said, "I was afraid because I was naked" (Genesis 3:10). Compare this with their attitude toward their nakedness at the time God created them. Genesis 2:25 says that "the man and his wife were both naked, and they felt no shame."

So why were Adam and Eve afraid of God after they had eaten the forbidden fruit? Why did they flee from His presence and hide? It's because they felt differently about Him than they had before. I propose that more was going on than simply that they got caught with their hands in the cookie jar. The Bible doesn't say exactly what I will say next, but I believe it's a reasonable conclusion from other things the Bible does say.

We know that after the Fall, throughout human history, sinful humans are lost until they are born again. In His nighttime conversation with Nicodemus, Jesus said that "no one can enter the kingdom of God unless he is born [again] of water and the Spirit" (John 3:5; see also verse 3). In other words, if we want to be saved in God's kingdom, we must receive the Holy Spirit into

---

* Revelation 12 helps us to correctly interpret Genesis 3:15. In Revelation 12:1, 2, we see a woman who is pregnant and is about to give birth. Verse 3 shows us "an enormous red dragon," which verse 9 identifies as Satan. Throughout the rest of chapter 12, the dragon and the woman are in conflict. Verse 17 shows the dragon—"that ancient serpent called the devil, or Satan" (verse 9)—attacking the rest of the woman's offspring, who represent God's true people. This symbolism is clearly drawn from Genesis 3:15. We can also apply the symbolism the other way around from Revelation back to Genesis. And when we do that, it's evident that the woman in Genesis 3:15 represents God's people, and the serpent is a symbol of Satan.

77

our minds and hearts. The Holy Spirit is the One who writes God's laws on our hearts (see Hebrews 8:10; Jeremiah 31:33). It's reasonable to conclude, then, that because God created Adam and Eve with the ability to obey His laws, He must have placed the Holy Spirit in their minds and hearts at the time He created them. Ellen White affirmed as much when she said that "man, *as God created him, connected with the Father and the Son,** could obey every divine requirement."[13]

However, when Adam and Eve sinned, the Holy Spirit departed, and that's why they felt shame and fear. The logic is this: When Adam and Eve ate the fruit from the forbidden tree, they came into harmony, mentally and spiritually, with Satan. However, God was telling both Satan and Adam and Eve that this harmony between them would be broken. In other words, Adam and Eve and their descendants would have the opportunity to restore their harmony with God, which would put them once again at enmity with Satan. Even though He couldn't just arbitrarily do it, God devised a strategy by which He could place His Holy Spirit back into their minds and hearts so that they would once more resonate with His mind and heart. Human nature, which was depraved by sin, would be made whole again.

Let's look at what happened to Adam and Eve in light of the characteristics of the Kingdom of Light that I shared with you in chapter 1—love, law, authority, and freedom. God had given Adam and Eve a very simple law: don't eat the fruit from the tree of the knowledge of good and evil. He also placed them under His loving authority, but He gave them the freedom to disobey that law if they chose to do so. When they disobeyed this simple law, they placed themselves under Satan's law and his brutal authority, and they lost their freedom of choice. But by His death, Christ restored the opportunity for them, and us, to regain our freedom to choose God's law and His loving authority. All we have to do to regain what was lost is to choose to accept Jesus' death on our behalf. Then the Holy Spirit will come into our minds again and give us the power to overcome the debilitated spiritual faculties that we have under the Kingdom of Darkness.

Informing Adam and Eve

There were two steps in the process of informing Adam and Eve of the consequences of their sin and God's plan to deal with it. First, God told

---

* Ellen White said, "Connected with the Father and the Son," not "connected with the Holy Spirit." However, the meaning is the same regardless of which member of the Trinity is mentioned.

them the consequences of eating the forbidden fruit. Then the angels filled in more details, similar to the additional information they gave to Adam and Eve about Satan and his angels being cast to the earth.

God informs Adam and Eve. But how could God promise to create enmity between humans and Satan by placing His Spirit back into human minds and hearts when the removal of His Spirit was the penalty for their disobedience? Fortunately, the second half of verse 15 explains God's plan for resolving that apparent impasse. He said, "He will crush your head, and you will strike his heel."

There's something odd going on here. Keep in mind that the pronoun *you* in this verse refers to Satan, and the appropriate pronouns for the woman would be *she* and *her*. But in the second half of the verse God switched to *he* and *his*: "*He* [Christ] will crush your [Satan's] head, and you [Satan] will strike *his* [Christ's] heel." Shouldn't God have said that *she* (the woman) will crush your (Satan's) head? Shouldn't He have said that you (Satan) will strike *her* (the woman's) heel? Why the sudden switch to *he* and *his*?

The answer to this question is simple: The one who would crush Satan's head wouldn't be Eve or any of her female spiritual descendants. The One who would crush Satan's head would be Christ, a human male. In reality, God was saying that Christ would inflict a fatal wound on Satan (crushing his head), whereas Satan would inflict only a nonfatal wound on Christ (striking His heel). In other words, Christ would destroy Satan.

Genesis 3:15 brought a ray of hope to Adam and Eve that a way would be found to restore the Holy Spirit to their minds and hearts and break Satan's power over them. You and I know how it was all accomplished, because for us the story of Christ's life and death is history. But to Adam and Eve, the how and the when of Christ crushing Satan's head was a mystery. Nevertheless, they had the assurance that God had devised a plan for rescuing them from their death sentence, both physically and spiritually. He had devised a plan for restoring to them the Holy Spirit, whose presence in their lives they had lost when they sinned.

Ellen White wrote, "When Adam's sin plunged the race into hopeless misery, God might have cut Himself loose from fallen beings. He might have treated them as sinners deserve to be treated. He might have commanded the angels of heaven to pour out upon our world the vials of His wrath. He might have removed this dark blot from His universe. But He did not do this. Instead of banishing them from His presence, He came still nearer to the fallen race. He gave His Son to become bone of our bone and flesh of our flesh."[14]

Angels expand on God's explanation. God shared with Adam and Eve the fact that Satan would be defeated and that a way would be opened for them to restore their harmony with God, and then angels filled in the details of the plan. Ellen White wrote, "The angels of God were commissioned to visit the fallen pair and inform them that . . . the Son of God, who had conversed with them in Eden, had been moved with pity as He viewed their hopeless condition, and had volunteered to take upon Himself the punishment due to them, and die for them that man might yet live."[15] "To Adam were revealed future important events, from his expulsion from Eden to the Flood, and onward to the first advent of Christ upon the earth."[16]

The curse

God also told Adam and Eve that they would have to leave their garden home, and this caused them great anguish. "They entreated to be permitted to remain, although they acknowledged that they had forfeited all right to blissful Eden. They promised that they would in the future yield to God implicit obedience." However, God informed them that "in their fall from innocence to guilt they gained no strength but great weakness. . . . They were filled with keenest anguish and remorse. They now realized that the penalty of sin was death."[17]

There's a good reason why Adam and Eve had to leave their garden home: the tree of life was there, and people who eat of that tree don't die. God said, "The man has now become like one of us, knowing good and evil. He must not be allowed to reach out his hand and take also from the tree of life and eat, and live forever" (Genesis 3:22). Apparently, there's a nutrient in the tree of life that counteracts the aging process. Revelation 22:2 suggests something similar in its description of life on the new earth: "On each side of the river stood the tree of life, bearing twelve crops of fruit, yielding its fruit every month. And the leaves of the tree are for the healing of the nations."

Satan knew this, and, as I pointed out in the previous chapter, his hope was that

> once they [Adam and Eve] should transgress the law of God they would be subjects of God's wrath, like themselves [Satan and his followers]. Their [Adam and Eve's] transgression would place them, also, in a state of rebellion, and they [Satan and his angels] could unite with Adam and Eve, take possession of Eden, and hold it as their home. And *if they could gain access to the tree of life in the midst of the garden*, their strength, they thought, would be equal to that of the holy angels, and even God Himself could not expel them.[18]

God understood the danger of Adam and Eve remaining in the Garden and eating the fruit of the tree of life after they had sinned, so He "placed on the east side of the Garden of Eden cherubim and a flaming sword flashing back and forth to guard the way to the tree of life" (Genesis 3:24).

God also placed curses on Adam and Eve. To Eve, He said,

> "I will greatly increase your pains in childbearing;
>   with pain you will give birth to children.
> Your desire will be for your husband,
>   and he will rule over you" (verse 16).

And to Adam, God said,

> "Cursed is the ground because of you;
>   through painful toil you will eat of it
>   all the days of your life.
> It will produce thorns and thistles for you,
>   and you will eat the plants of the field.
> By the sweat of your brow
>   you will eat your food
> until you return to the ground,
>   since from it you were taken;
> for dust you are
>   and to dust you will return" (verses 17–19).

Other Bible writers acknowledge the presence of this curse on the world. Isaiah said that "the earth will wear out like a garment" (Isaiah 51:6), and the apostle Paul said that "the whole creation has been groaning as in the pains of childbirth right up to the present time" (Romans 8:22). We still see this curse today, especially in the way our modern culture is treating the environment. How long the earth can sustain this abuse is anyone's guess, but Revelation says that those who are causing this devastation will pay for it at Christ's second coming when He destroys those who destroy the earth (see Revelation 11:18). I suspect that the four winds that the angels of Revelation 7:1 are holding back have to do, at least to some extent, with postponing the consequences of our human environmental destruction.

Fortunately, God's cryptic promise to Adam and Eve that the woman's descendant would crush the serpent's head is also a promise that the curse will be lifted someday. Revelation tells us when that will happen. When God re-creates the earth at the end of the millennium, a voice will proclaim from God's throne that "the old order of things has passed away" (Revelation 21:4, NIV) and "there will no longer be any curse" (Revelation 22:3, NASB).

Summary of the Kingdom of Darkness in Eden

God gave one simple law to Adam in Eden: don't eat the fruit from the tree of the knowledge of good and evil. However, in eating that fruit Adam and Eve rejected God's authority and violated His law. Fear—a powerful negative emotion—immediately replaced love and peace. Because the Holy Spirit left them, they lost the freedom to again choose God and His Kingdom of Light. They became slaves of Satan. That's what the Kingdom of Darkness is like, and it has dominated world history ever since. Fortunately, the history of evil on our planet will come to an end with the battle of Armageddon.

---

1. White, *The Story of Redemption*, 39.

2. Ibid., 42; emphasis added.

3. Ibid., 42.

4. Ibid.

5. Ibid.

6. Ibid., 43.

7. Ibid., 43, 44.

8. Ibid., 45.

9. Ibid., 44, 45.

10. Ibid., 45.

11. Ibid., 38.

12. This paragraph and several that follow are adapted from chapter 5 of my book *The Close of Probation* (Nampa, ID: Pacific Press® Pub. Assn., 2014).

13. Ellen G. White, *Selected Messages*, bk. 1 (Washington, DC: Review and Herald® Pub. Assn., 1958), 253; Nichol, *The Seventh-day Adventist Bible Commentary*, 7:926; emphasis added.

14. Ellen G. White, *God's Amazing Grace* (Hagerstown, MD: Review and Herald® Pub. Assn., 2001), 176.

15. White, *The Story of Redemption*, 46, 47.

16. Ibid., 48.

17. Ibid., 41.

18. Ibid., 28; emphasis added.

CHAPTER 9

The World
Before the Flood

The Bible doesn't say very much about the world before the Flood, but what it does say is packed with meaning and makes it evident that the Kingdom of Darkness was alive and well and that it was rapidly gaining the upper hand over the Kingdom of Light. In 2 Peter 2:4–10, the apostle made an interesting and rather convoluted argument. He went through a series of three *if-but* lines of reasoning followed by a *then*. The chart below outlines his argument:

Verse	If	But
4	If God did not spare the angels when they sinned,	but sent them to hell . . . ;
5	if he did not spare the ancient world when he brought the flood . . . ,	but protected Noah . . . ;
6, 7	if he condemned the cities of Sodom and Gomorrah by burning them to ashes, . . .	[but] he rescued Lot . . .
9	then the Lord knows how to rescue godly men from trials and to hold the unrighteous for the day of judgment, while continuing their punishment.	

What Peter said next is of critical importance to our study. Commenting on the unrighteous whom the Lord held for the day of judgment, he said that they "follow the corrupt desire of the sinful nature* and despise authority" (verse 10). Lucifer fell from heaven because he despised Michael's authority, and he allowed his corrupt desire for self-exaltation to control his actions instead of what he knew to be right. That's exactly what happened to the

---

* Literally, "the flesh."

descendants of Cain who lived before the Flood. They despised authority, especially God's authority, which they knew, or should have known, was the right course to pursue, and instead followed the corrupt desires of their sinful natures. This trend continued to develop until, by the time the work on the ark was completed, *the Kingdom of Darkness had gained total control of the world with the exception of Noah and his family.*

Marriage

Genesis 6:1–13 describes two characteristics of the antediluvian world that help us to understand why God brought on the Flood. The first one is marriage. Jesus said that the world before the Flood was characterized by people "marrying and giving in marriage" (Matthew 24:38). The first two verses of Genesis 6 confirm His words: "When men began to increase in number on the earth and daughters were born to them, the sons of God saw that the daughters of men were beautiful, and they married any of them they chose."

Let's take a minute or two to analyze these verses. First, who were these "sons of God," and who were the "daughters of men"? It seems evident that the "sons of God" were the descendants of Seth—men such as Enoch, Methuselah, and Noah; and the "daughters of men" were the descendants of Cain—daughters of men such as Mehujael, Methushael, and Lamech.* A moment's reflection will lead to the obvious conclusion that both the sons of God and the daughters of men were mostly young people, because that's the age when we humans generally get married. And these marriages would have been the kind that God forbids, because they were uniting believers with unbelievers. This leads to a very significant conclusion: The pre-Flood young people were abandoning the faith of their fathers. They were "leaving the church" in droves.

Does this sound familiar? We, too, in the first few years of the twenty-first century, are seeing our young people leave the church in droves. It's a trend that fulfills Jesus' words: "As it was in the days of Noah, *so it will be at the coming of the Son of Man*" (Matthew 24:37; emphasis added).

I don't know what the pre-Flood patriarchs may have failed to do to keep their children loyal to God, but today we must not just shrug our shoulders and say, "Oh, well; Jesus predicted the apostasy of our young people, so

---

* The descendants of Seth are listed in Genesis 5, while the descendants of Cain are listed in Genesis 4:17–24. It's interesting to note that Cain named his son Enoch (Genesis 4:17), which was also the name of one of Seth's descendants (Genesis 5:18), and Noah's father was Lamech (verses 28, 29), which was also the name of one of Cain's descendants (Genesis 4:18).

there's nothing we can do about it." We absolutely *must* put forth every possible effort to lead our young people into a saving relationship with Jesus. We must make and implement well-thought-through plans to ground them in the faith. That's part of Christ's great commission. How tragic it is to put forth massive efforts at winning others to the faith while we're losing our young people at the same time!

Having said this, we also should not allow this departure of our youth to discourage us. Today's youth are being influenced by secularism and the scientific worldview, which increasingly denies the supernatural and the significant role of religion in society. They're also being profoundly influenced by movies, TV, the Internet, and video games. So once we've done our best to help them to have a saving relationship with Jesus, and once we've made every effort to instruct them in the teachings of the Bible and the church, we must give them the freedom to make their own choices. We must nurture them and then leave the results to God and to them.

Jesus asked a very significant question toward the end of His earthly life. He said, "When the Son of Man comes, will he find faith on the earth?" (Luke 18:8). The Bible indicates that the answer is clearly Yes. There will be faithful people living to greet Jesus when He comes. Paul said that at Christ's second coming "the dead in Christ will rise first. After that, *we who are still alive and are left* will be caught up together with them in the clouds to meet the Lord in the air" (1 Thessalonians 4:16, 17; emphasis added). However, with the exception of Noah and his family, pre-Flood society was characterized by universal apostasy.

Violence

A second characteristic of the pre-Flood world was violence. Genesis 6:11, 13 says, "Now the earth was corrupt in God's sight and was full of *violence*. . . . So God said to Noah, 'I am going to put an end to all people, for the earth is filled with *violence* because of them' " (emphasis added). Notice the description: the earth was "*full* of violence" and "*filled* with violence." The Bible doesn't tell us the nature of that violence, but Ellen White made several comments about the condition of society before the Flood.

> God had given men His commandments as a rule of life, but His law was transgressed, and every conceivable sin was the result. The wickedness of men was open and daring, justice was trampled in the dust, and the cries of the oppressed reached into heaven. . . .

. . . After the Fall, men chose to follow their own sinful desires; and as the result, crime and wretchedness rapidly increased. Neither the marriage relation nor the rights of property were respected. Whoever coveted the wives or the possessions of his neighbor, took them by force, and men exulted in their deeds of violence. They delighted in destroying the life of animals; and the use of flesh for food rendered them still more cruel and bloodthirsty, until they came to regard human life with astonishing indifference.[1]

That's the violence. Did you notice the cause? "After the Fall, men chose to follow their own sinful desires." That's the pattern we've seen both earlier in this chapter and in previous chapters of this book: people being controlled by their emotions instead of by what they know to be right according to God's law. Earlier in this chapter I pointed out that Peter called attention to the moral degeneracy of the ancient world's population. He described them as following the corrupt desires of their sinful natures and despising authority (2 Peter 2:10).

Notice also that our own world is becoming increasingly violent. Almost daily we read about people entering schools, stores, cafés, and other public venues and opening fire. Then there are the brutal acts of violence committed by ISIS, Boko Haram, and other radical groups.

Withdrawal of the Holy Spirit

Genesis 6:3 makes a very significant statement about God's relationship to the pre-Flood world: "Then the LORD said, 'My Spirit will not contend with man forever.' " The New King James Version says, "My Spirit shall not *strive* with man forever" (the King James Version also uses the word *strive*). The Hebrew word translated "contend with" or "strive" is *doon*, and footnotes in both the New International Version and New King James Version list alternate meanings to *doon* that I find to be very significant. Instead of "contend with," the footnote in the New International Version says "remain in"; and instead of "strive," the footnote in the New King James Version says "abide."

Let's look at Genesis 6:3 using these two meanings, with the emphasis added in each one: "My Spirit will not [*remain in*] man forever" (NIV) and "My Spirit shall not [*abide*] with man forever" (NKJV). Anytime the Holy Spirit ceases to remain in or abide with a person, that person's probation has closed. So, in effect, God was saying that a day was coming when He would bring human probation to a close.

The Seventh-day Adventist Bible Commentary states, "These words ['My Spirit shall not always strive"] indicate that the Holy Spirit could continue working but a little longer, and would then be withdrawn from the unregenerate and unrepentant of the human race."[2]

Satan managed to deceive the first humans, Adam and Eve, and get them to switch their allegiance from the Kingdom of Light to his Kingdom of Darkness. And he exulted in his victory, because he felt certain that with the dominion of the world in his hands he could lead the entire race of humans into joining with him. He had tried to get the entire host of angels to join with him, but two-thirds of them saw through his deception and refused his invitation. With human beings before the Flood, Satan was much more successful. He got the young people to abandon the faith of their fathers and intermarry with the descendants of Cain; and as the Spirit of God departed from people, they became increasingly incapable of controlling their anger, which resulted in a great increase of violence.

Among those of that generation who were totally loyal to God were Noah, his father Lamech, his grandfather Methuselah, and his great-grandfather Enoch (Genesis 5:21–29). However, by the time of the Flood, Enoch had been translated, and Lamech and Methuselah had both died. Of the entire human population, Noah and his family were the only ones left who were still loyal to God. One has to wonder how loyal Noah's wife, his three sons, and their wives really were. Did they remain faithful to God simply because Noah was their husband, father, or father-in-law? If that were the case—and I suspect it was—then God really had only one person in the entire world who was loyal to Him. And the Bible backs that up. Genesis 6:8 says that "*Noah* found favor in the eyes of the LORD" (emphasis added).

God's problem

Now stop and reflect a moment: God created humans because He wanted intelligent beings whom He could love and who would love Him in return. He must have been bitterly disappointed when Adam and Eve disobeyed Him and took the side of the Kingdom of Darkness,* but He didn't destroy them the way you and I often do when our creative projects don't turn out the way we want them to. He still loved them. So when sin first entered into

---

* Being omniscient (all-knowing), God surely was aware before Adam and Eve sinned that they would disobey His command not to eat of the fruit of the tree of life. Yet the idea that He was bitterly disappointed has a basis in Scripture. Genesis 6:5, 6 says that "the LORD saw how great man's wickedness on the earth had become, and that every inclination of the thoughts of his heart was only evil all the time. The LORD was grieved that he had made man on the earth, and his heart was filled with pain."

our human experience, He put in motion a plan to save us from our disobedience and restore us to His Kingdom of Light.

But hundreds of years later,* God had just one man in the whole world who was truly loyal to His Kingdom of Light. The prospect was that once Noah died the world's entire population would be loyal to Satan's Kingdom of Darkness!

Now think of the dilemma God faced. One of the fundamental principles of His Kingdom of Light is that its citizens must *choose* to be loyal to Him. He will not *force* their loyalty. Thus, once the entire population of the world had joined the Kingdom of Darkness there would be no way for God to restore even one of them to His side. He would have lost the battle, and Satan would have won. The situation wasn't as bad 120 years before the Flood, when God commanded Noah to build the ark, but it was that bad when the ark was completed. Noah and his family were the only human beings left on the earth who truly feared and served God. Satan had almost achieved his objective of taking control of the entire human race. I can imagine Satan and his demons celebrating their victory again with a banquet and with toasts to their leader and to their success.

But this time God did choose to destroy His creation. "So the LORD said, 'I will wipe mankind, whom I have created, from the face of earth—men and animals, and creatures that move along the ground, and birds of the air—for I am grieved that I have made them.' But Noah found favor in the eyes of the LORD" (verses 7, 8). When the Flood was over, Noah and his family became the new Adams and Eves of that blemished earth. God started over with them.

Summary of the Kingdom of Darkness before the Flood

While information about the time before the Flood is minimal, it's very evident that the four characteristics of God's Kingdom of Light were horribly disregarded during this period. Those who should have been God's people, especially the younger generation, were abandoning the moral principles that had undergirded the lives of their parents and grandparents. God's law and His authority were disregarded. As Ellen White put it,

---

* Depending on which ancient Hebrew tradition one chooses to follow, the world at the time of the Flood was anywhere from 1,948 years old (Masoretic text), 2,249 years old (Samaritan Pentateuch), 3,334 years old (LXX Alexandrinus), or 3,414 years old (LXX Vaticanus) according to figures given by Richard W. Coffen. "Am I Not Actually a Seventh-day Adventist?" *Adventist Today*, Spring 2015, 13.

His law was transgressed, and every conceivable sin was the result. The wickedness of men was open and daring, justice was trampled in the dust, and the cries of the oppressed reached unto heaven. . . .

. . . Neither the marriage relation nor the rights of property were respected.[3]

Clearly, love and freedom were sacrificed to the unbridled emotions of sinful human beings. This is because, as human beings abandoned God, His Spirit was slowly withdrawn from their hearts, and love can't exist in hearts that aren't controlled by the Holy Spirit.

Noah and his family lived relatively near the time when God created the world. The time when Adam and Eve had joined with the Kingdom of Darkness was not that far in the past. Today we live near the end of the conflict between the Kingdom of Light and the Kingdom of Darkness. Again, God is going to intervene globally to destroy the Kingdom of Darkness, and this time He will destroy it completely. Armageddon will bring it to a permanent end on our planet.

---

1. White, *Patriarchs and Prophets*, 91, 92.

2. Francis D. Nichol, ed., *The Seventh-day Adventist Bible Commentary*, vol. 1 (Washington, DC: Review and Herald® Pub. Assn., 1976), 250.

3. White, *Patriarchs and Prophets*, 91, 92.

CHAPTER 10

The Exodus

I magine for a moment that you are Moses at the burning bush. God tells you that He's heard the cries of the Israelites as they suffer under the heavy hand of their Egyptian taskmasters, and He says, "Now, go. I am sending you to Pharaoh to bring my people the Israelites out of Egypt" (Exodus 3:10).*

"What! Lord, I fled that place forty years ago for fear of Pharaoh, and now You want me to go back and confront him?"

"And God said, 'I will be with you' " (verse 12).

God also gave Moses a couple of miraculous signs to use in Pharaoh's presence: a rod that turned into a snake and then back into a rod; and a hand that turned leprous and then was healed. With these signs, and with God's promise to be with him, Moses returned to Egypt.

It's important to note, however, that Moses had no idea what lay ahead. All he had to go on were God's words: "I will be with you." The ten plagues and the parting of the Red Sea were the furthest things from his imagination. He simply did what God told him to do, trusting that God would see him through whatever difficulties he encountered along the way.

Partway to Egypt, Moses' brother, Aaron, met him in the wilderness and accompanied him back to Egypt. The first thing they did after they arrived was to call the elders of Israel together to hear Moses' story. "Aaron told them everything the LORD had said to Moses.† He [Moses] also performed the signs [God had given him] before the people, and they believed. And when they heard that the LORD was concerned about them and had seen

---

* The people of Israel were God's chosen people for about fifteen hundred years, from Abraham to the time of Christ. With the exception of the first twelve chapters, the entire Old Testament is entirely devoted to that story. And the whole account is a jostling back and forth between the Kingdom of Light and the Kingdom of Darkness. A full review of that conflict would go far beyond what we can consider in this book. Therefore, I have chosen to illustrate the conflict with an account of the rebellion at Kadesh and the apostasy that resulted in the Babylonian captivity.

† Apparently, after being away from Egypt for forty years, Moses had forgotten much of his Egyptian, so God arranged for Aaron to be his translator.

their misery, they bowed down and worshiped" (Exodus 4:29–31). This initial meeting went very well. I'm sure that when the elders shared the good news with the rest of the Israelites, they, too, praised the Lord. Everyone was excited about leaving Egypt for the Promised Land. What they didn't know was *how* God was going to deliver them.

Moses went to Pharaoh and asked that the people be allowed to take a three-day journey into the wilderness to worship their God. This made Pharaoh furious. He ordered the Egyptian slave drivers and their Israelite foremen to require the people to make the same number of bricks as before—and also to gather their own straw, which heretofore had been provided by the Egyptians.

Now, instead of welcoming Moses and Aaron, the foremen and many of the Israelite people turned against the two leaders. The foremen said to Moses and Aaron, "May the LORD look upon you and judge you! You have made us a stench to Pharaoh and his officials and have put a sword in their hand to kill us" (Exodus 5:21). They were *very angry*! Doubts began to arise among the Israelites over whether they should trust Moses and follow his directions, which he claimed had been given to him by God. Was he, in fact, a shyster trying to take advantage of a gullible people? Given the additional suffering they were experiencing, wouldn't it be better for them to follow their own judgment? After all, Moses was the man who had fled Egypt forty years earlier.

Moses knew that he had indeed been commissioned by God to lead His people out of Egypt and settle them in the Promised Land, yet even he had significant questions about the turn of events. Following the anger of the Israelite foremen, who blamed him for the additional burden the Egyptians had placed on them, he prayed, "O LORD, why have you brought trouble upon this people? Is this why you sent me? Ever since I went to Pharaoh to speak in your name, he has brought trouble upon this people, and you have not rescued your people at all" (verses 22, 23). Moses had expected an easy deliverance, and the sudden turn of events brought questions to his mind.

God replied, "Now you will see what I will do to Pharaoh: Because of my mighty hand he will . . . drive them [the Israelites] out of his country" (Exodus 6:1).

As the plagues followed one after the other, especially the last seven that fell only on the Egyptians, no doubt many of the Israelite dissenters changed their minds. And sure enough, after the tenth plague, Pharaoh *ordered* the people to leave Egypt. They were actually on their way to the Promised Land!

In fact, many of the Egyptian people were so impressed by what the God of the Israelites had done that they joined them and left the country with them.

The Red Sea

However, that joyful liberation was soon to change. The people had barely left Egypt when Pharaoh's army came charging after them, and with the Red Sea in front of them, there was no apparent way of escape. The people were terrified. "They said to Moses, 'Was it because there were no graves in Egypt that you brought us to the desert to die? What have you done to us by bringing us out of Egypt? Didn't we say to you in Egypt, "Leave us alone; let us serve the Egyptians"? It would have been better for us to serve the Egyptians than to die in the desert!' " (Exodus 14:11, 12).

This is an extremely important statement, because it leads to two significant conclusions. First, it provides an insight into what went on back in Egypt when Pharaoh increased the people's workload. The people and their leaders told Moses they didn't want to leave Egypt after all. They would rather stay, try to appease Pharaoh, and keep on working for him. We're going to see this sentiment repeated as we continue through the story of the Exodus.

The second conclusion is that while God had indeed commissioned Moses to be the people's civil leader, many of the people rejected him. They blamed him, not God, for their troubles. We'll also see this sentiment repeated throughout the story.

Fortunately, Moses was a man of courage and deep faith, and he wasn't swayed by the people's reminder of what they had said to him back in Egypt. He knew that God had called him at the burning bush. When he returned to Egypt, he had demanded ten times that Pharaoh let the Israelites go, and each time he saw God bring down plagues on the Egyptians because of Pharaoh's refusal. Now, at the Red Sea, he said to the Israelites, "Do not be afraid. Stand firm and you will see the deliverance the LORD will bring you today. The Egyptians you see today you will never see again. The LORD will fight for you; you need only be still" (verses 13, 14).

And sure enough, when Moses raised his staff over the Red Sea, it parted, and the people walked over on dry land! The Egyptians followed, but when they were halfway across, God brought the walls of water back down, and the entire Egyptian army drowned.

Food and water

Food is essential for survival, and there was very little available in the wilderness—certainly not enough to feed thousands of people. So, in due time, the Israelites ran out of the food they had brought with them from Egypt. While they didn't like being slaves back in Egypt, they at least had plenty of food, and the prospect of having *nothing* to eat in the desert shot their fears through the roof. They "grumbled against Moses and Aaron. The Israelites said to them, 'If only we had died by the LORD's hand in Egypt! There we sat around pots of meat and ate all the food we wanted, but you have brought us out into this desert to starve this entire assembly to death' " (Exodus 16:2, 3). Notice what the people said: *You*—Moses, not God—have brought us into the desert to starve us to death. Really? Did they think that *Moses* had brought the ten plagues that forced Pharaoh to let them leave Egypt? Did they think it was *Moses'* power that had separated the Red Sea so they could cross? Did they think that *Moses* brought the water down on the Egyptian army so that the army drowned?

The people were right about one thing: Moses could not have provided them with food. But God gave them manna to eat, demonstrating once again that He, not Moses, was the one ultimately responsible for the Israelites' well-being.

The same thing happened when they ran out of water. They blamed Moses. They said, "Why did *you* bring us up out of Egypt to make us and our children and livestock die of thirst?" (Exodus 17:3; emphasis added). The people said, in effect, "Moses, our lack of food and water is all *your* fault!" Moses did what any of us should do when we're faced with a trial: he "cried out to the LORD, 'What am I to do with these people?' " His next words reveal how serious the situation had become. He said, the people "are almost ready to stone me" (verse 4)! But again, God showed the people that *He*, not Moses, was the one responsible for providing for their needs. He instructed Moses to take his staff and go to "the rock at Horeb. Strike the rock, and water will come out of it for the people to drink" (verse 6). Moses did what God told him, and water gushed from the rock.

It's important to note that up to this point God had not rebuked the Israelites for their questions and lack of faith. When Pharaoh increased their workload and they questioned and complained, God didn't rebuke them. He didn't rebuke them for their panic at the Red Sea nor for their fear of death from starvation and thirst in the wilderness. And He didn't rebuke them for questioning Moses' leadership. God gave them time to see His mighty hand at work and develop their trust in Him and His servant Moses based on the supernatural ways God delivered them from these crises.

Sinai

The people finally arrived at Sinai, which was to be their place of residence for many months. Here God came down on the mountain. He spoke first with Moses, who went up on the mountain to visit with Him. God told him to say to the people, "You yourselves have seen what I did to Egypt, and how I carried you on eagles' wings and brought you to myself. Now if you obey me fully and keep my covenant, then out of all nations you will be my treasured possession" (Exodus 19:4, 5). Moses went back down the mountain and told the people what God had said, and they replied, "We will do everything the LORD has said" (verse 8). Moses returned to God and reported the people's response, and God told him to have the people wash their clothes and prepare for Him to appear on the mountain three days later (verses 10, 11).

"On the morning of the third day there was thunder and lightning, with a thick cloud over the mountain, and a very loud trumpet blast. Everyone in the camp trembled" (verse 16). The Bible says that the mountain "was covered with smoke, because the LORD descended on it in fire. The smoke billowed up from it like smoke from a furnace, the whole mountain trembled violently, and the sound of the trumpet grew louder and louder" (verses 18, 19).

Then God spoke the Ten Commandments to the people. His words were so loud and awesome that the people "trembled with fear. They stayed at a distance and said to Moses, 'Speak to us yourself and we will listen. But do not have God speak to us or we will die' " (Exodus 20:18, 19).

Prior to God's appearance on Mount Sinai, many of the Israelites had questioned whether God had really appeared to Moses at the burning bush as he claimed. But now God had appeared to the entire nation, and that was something they could not deny! Still, only a few weeks later, they built a golden calf, bowed down to it, and said, "These are your gods, O Israel, who brought you up out of Egypt" (Exodus 32:4). Did they really believe that a dumb idol had brought the ten plagues on Egypt? Did they really think that the idol had opened the Red Sea before them and provided them with food and water in the wilderness? This was blasphemy of the highest order!

The Israelites become a nation

It's important to understand God's purpose in bringing the Israelites out of

Egypt: He wanted to form this bunch of newly freed slaves into a nation. Every nation has to have laws, and God provided them with laws when He appeared on Sinai. First, He gave them the Ten Commandments, which are the moral basis for all human behavior for all time. He also gave them a variety of other laws—civil, religious, and health laws—that were especially applicable to them as a nation. Yet the principles behind these laws have a universal application, even though some of the details related particularly to the Israelites.

We can say, then, that it was at Sinai that the nation of Israel was formed. Not only did the Israelites receive the laws that were to be the foundation of the government, but God personally revealed Himself in awful grandeur to the entire nation at the very beginning of its national existence. He personally gave the Israelites their constitution—the Ten Commandments—and He personally gave them the other laws by which they were to be governed. He also appointed Moses as their first civil leader and Aaron as their first religious leader. The fact that God had commissioned these two men was beyond dispute. Yet it *would* be disputed, as we shall see in the next chapter.

CHAPTER 11

The Rebellion at Kadesh

The Israelites were excited! They were camped at a place called Kadesh, and when they crossed the southern border, they would be in the Promised Land (Numbers 13:26)!* Centuries earlier God had told Abraham that his descendants would possess this land forever (Genesis 13:14–17; 17:8), and here they were, the fortunate ones, about to see the fulfillment of that promise!

Today we can identify with their feelings. Christians have been looking forward to Christ's return for two thousand years, and Adventists have been expecting His immediate return for more than 170 years. What will it be like for the generation that actually *does* live to see Him come? That's how it was for the Israelites as they camped at Kadesh!

Spying out the land

But before they crossed the border, God instructed Moses to send twelve men, one from each tribe, to spy out the land.† The spies traveled north, south, east, and west; at the end of forty days, they returned, bringing back with them some of the fruit of the land, including a huge cluster of grapes that was so large it took two men to carry it on a pole between them!

Then came their report. In my imagination, I can picture the entire Israelite community gathered around the spies, eagerly anticipating their report and grasping at every word. All the spies agreed that the land did indeed "flow with milk and honey" (Numbers 13:27). They also gave a realistic account of the difficulties they would face when they attempted to take possession of the land. Its inhabitants were fearsome. "The people who live there are

---

* The Hebrew word *Kadesh* (sometimes spelled *kodesh*) means "holy place." Other places in Palestine are called Kadesh, so the place where the Israelites were camped is sometimes called Kadesh-Barnea (meaning "of Barnea") to distinguish it from these other places. Siegfried H. Horn, *Seventh-day Adventist Bible Dictionary* (Washington, DC: Review and Herald® Pub. Assn., 1960), s.vv. "Kadesh," "Kadesh-Barnea."

† See Numbers 13:1, 2. Ellen White said that "*it was proposed by the people* that spies be sent to survey the country. The matter was presented to the Lord by Moses, and permission was granted." *Patriarch and Prophets*, 387; emphasis added.

powerful," they said, "and the cities are fortified and very large" (verse 28). They went on to name some of the heathen tribes they had encountered— Amalekites, Hittites, Jebusites, Amorites, and Canaanites—and some of these people were giants.* That was the reality the Israelites faced. Anytime we face a difficult situation today it's vital that we get a realistic assessment of the problem before we attempt to deal with it. The key question was how the people would *respond* to the frightening report. The circumstances were challenging enough to throw any normal person into a horrible panic.

Caleb took the lead. "We should go up and take possession of the land, for we can certainly do it" (verse 30). Caleb had faith that God would go before the Israelite armies and help them drive out the inhabitants. He had seen God's powerful hand at work in the ten plagues and at the Red Sea. He had witnessed God's provision of food and water in the wilderness. He had heard God's voice at Sinai, and he trusted that a God who could deliver them from the Egyptians, open the Red Sea, and provide them with food and water in the wilderness could surely give them the victory over the Canaanites—no matter how powerful they might appear to be. Faith in God's leading in our lives is what we all need when we face challenging situations.

But ten of the twelve spies interrupted Caleb. "We can't attack those people," they said. "They are stronger than we are. . . . All the people we saw there are of great size. . . . We seemed like grasshoppers in our own eyes, and we looked the same to them" (verses 31–33).

The crowd suddenly went into a massive panic. They wept and grumbled against Moses and Aaron. "If only we had died in Egypt! Or in this desert!" they cried. "Why is the LORD bringing us to this land only to let us fall by the sword?" (Numbers 14:2, 3). They even proposed choosing a new leader and returning to Egypt (verses 3, 4)!

Again Caleb and Joshua tried to reason with the people. "Do not rebel against the LORD," they said. "And do not be afraid of the people of the land, because we will swallow them up. Their protection is gone, but the LORD is with us. Do not be afraid of them" (verse 9). But their effort to calm the crowd only angered the people to the point that "the whole assembly talked about stoning them" (verse 10).

At that point, God intervened. His glory appeared over the sanctuary, and He declared to Moses His intention to destroy the entire congregation and

---

* Numbers 13:28 says that the spies saw "the descendants of Anak" there. The Anakites were a tribe of giants in southern Palestine. Horn, *Seventh-day Adventist Bible Dictionary*, s.v. "Anak."

make Moses' descendants into a great nation.* Moses pleaded with God to forgive the people, which He did. But there was also to be a consequence for their rebellion, and it was based on the desire that the people themselves had expressed. They had said, "If only we had died In Egypt! Or in this desert!" (verse 2). So God said, "I will do to you the very things I heard you say: In this desert your bodies will fall—every one of you twenty years old or more. . . . Not one of you will enter the land I swore with uplifted hand to make your home, except Caleb son of Jephunneh and Joshua son of Nun" (verses 28–30). Next God declared that the people would wander in the desert for forty years—"one year for each of the forty days you explored the land" (verse 34). And He struck the ten faithless spies with a plague so that they died (verses 36, 37).

The people wept bitterly when Moses reported to them the Lord's declaration that they would wander in the wilderness for forty more years and that everyone who was twenty years old and older would die there. Mourning over their disobedience was appropriate, provided the mourning was genuine repentance. Unfortunately, that was not the case in this situation. The people were on an emotional roller coaster. They weren't thinking straight. They were bitterly disappointed at being denied an immediate entrance into the Promised Land. During the next night, they had time to remember their initial excitement at being the ones who would fulfill the long-cherished promise made to Abraham more than four hundred years earlier—and they changed their minds. The next morning they said, "We have sinned. . . . We will go up to the place the LORD promised" (verse 40). And so saying, they surged up to the top of a high hill where they could see across the border into the land that had just been denied them for the next forty years. The day before they had been weeping and wailing over the impossibility of conquering the Promised Land, wishing they were back in Egypt or that they had died in the desert. But now, a mere twenty-four hours later, they were excited about taking possession of the land!

Moses begged them not to cross the border and try to fight the enemy in defiance of God's explicit direction that they were to return to the wilderness and die there. "Why are you disobeying the LORD's command?" he said. "This will not succeed! Do not go up, because the LORD is not with you. You will be defeated by your enemies. . . . Because you have turned away from the LORD, he will not be with you and you will fall by the sword" (verses 41–43).

---

* God had made the same declaration to Moses at Sinai following the people's disobedience in making and worshiping the golden calf (Exodus 32:1–10, esp. verse 10).

Unfortunately, the crowd mentality prevailed. Disappointed at the prospect of postponing their entrance into Canaan for another forty years, they sent an army across the border to defeat their enemies and take over the land. However, just as Moses had said, God was not with them. They fought their enemies in their own weak power, and sure enough, "the Amalekites and Canaanites who lived in that hill country came down and attacked them and beat them down all the way to Hormah" (verse 45).* The Israelites retreated with their tails between their legs.

Korah, Dathan, and Abiram

You would think that with their defeat at Hormah the Israelites would have resigned themselves to following God's command that they return to the wilderness for forty more years. But the worst was yet to come, and this time it wasn't just a spontaneous rebellion incited by a fickle mob. This time it was a sinister plot that was hatched by a man named Korah.

Korah was a Levite and a prominent leader among the Israelites. As a Levite, he was given an important role in the care of the sanctuary. But that wasn't enough. He wanted to be the high priest, and he resented the fact that Aaron had been appointed to that position instead of himself (Numbers 16:8–10).[1] This resentment had probably been festering in Korah's mind for some time prior to the Israelites' arrival at Kadesh, and at some point, he began sharing his resentment among some of his close friends. At first, like Lucifer in heaven, he whispered his resentment secretly—and his friends listened and agreed.[†]

There was more. The covetousness and resentment didn't end with Korah's aspiration to be the high priest. Two of Korah's friends, Dathan and Abiram, thought that one of them should have been given Moses' authority as the civil leader of the nation, and they had a reason for that desire.[2]

Dathan and Abiram were from the tribe of Reuben, who was Jacob's oldest son (Genesis 35:23). Being the oldest, Reuben normally would have received the birthright, which would have given him authority over his brothers as the leader in the family. As the descendants of the twelve brothers formed into tribes, Reuben's tribe would have had civil authority over the other tribes. However, Reuben had sinned against his father by having

---

* Hormah is a city in the southernmost part of Judah near its border with Edom. Horn, *Seventh-day Adventist Dictionary*, s.v. "Hormah."

† The Bible doesn't say that Korah shared his feelings secretly, but Ellen White wrote, "For some time Korah had been secretly opposing the authority of Moses and Aaron, though he had not ventured upon any open act of rebellion." *Patriarchs and Prophets*, 395.

sex with one of his father's concubines (verse 22), and thus the rights of the firstborn were taken from him and given to Joseph (1 Chronicles 5:1, 2). Nevertheless, Dathan and Abiram felt resentful toward Moses as the nation's civil leader, because they didn't think Moses, a Levite, deserved that role. They felt that *their* tribe should have been the leader among the tribes, and because they were the current leaders of their tribe, they felt that one of *them* should have been given Moses' position. The truth was that both Moses and Aaron had been given their leadership roles by God, but this didn't seem to matter to Korah, Dathan, and Abiram. Like Lucifer, they allowed their feelings of covetousness to override what they knew—or should have known—to be right.

Getting the council on board

The conspiracy didn't stop with these three. Moses had apparently set up a council made up of several hundred respected leaders in the congregation whom he could call on to assist him in deciding important issues regarding the nation. Korah, Dathan, and Abiram were almost certainly members of this group. In due time, they began to share their resentment against Moses and Aaron with certain members of this council.

It isn't surprising that they found ready listeners. Challenges to Moses' leadership had begun even before the Israelites left Egypt, and they had continued unabated ever since. God's command for the people to turn back to the wilderness for forty years had only added fuel to the opposition against Moses. In fact, this situation provided an ideal opportunity for Korah, Dathan, and Abiram to assert themselves publicly.* Numbers 16:2 says that these three "rose up against Moses and Aaron."

This was a well-organized revolution!

This is especially evident in what the rebels said to Moses and Aaron: "You have gone too far! The whole community is holy, every one of them, and the LORD is with them. Why then do you set yourselves above the LORD's assembly?" (verse 3). These men no doubt agreed that God had appointed Moses and Aaron to lead the nation, but by accusing Moses and Aaron of going "too far" and setting themselves "above the LORD's assembly" they meant that Moses and Aaron had assumed more authority than

---

* Numbers 16:1 mentions a fourth person, named On, who initially joined Korah, Dathan, and Abiram in their rebellion, but he is never mentioned again in the story, which suggests that he changed his mind, followed Moses' advice, and maintained his loyalty to him and Aaron.

God had given them. Numbers 16:2 says that when Korah, Dathan, and Abiram challenged Moses and Aaron, they brought with them "250 Israelite men, well-known community leaders who had been appointed members of the council." This would be the equivalent of half the members of the United States (U.S.) House of Representatives and half of the U.S. senators challenging the authority of the U.S. president, seeking to take him down by their personal initiative rather than going through the legal impeachment process. This truly was a revolution!

Moses' response

So how did Moses respond to this challenge to his and Aaron's authority? The Bible says that "he fell facedown" (verse 4), and then he turned the problem over to God. "He said to Korah and all his followers: 'In the morning the LORD will show who belongs to him and who is holy, and he will have that person come near to him' " (verse 5).

Then Moses gave the following instruction: "You, Korah, and all your followers are to do this: Take censers and tomorrow put fire and incense in them before the LORD. The man the LORD chooses will be the one who is holy" (verses 6, 7). Then he challenged the entire group by throwing their own charge back in their faces. He said, "You *Levites* have gone too far!" (verse 7; emphasis added).

Next Moses defended Aaron's right to be the high priest. "Now listen, you Levites!" he said. "Isn't it enough for you that the God of Israel has separated you from the rest of the Israelite community and brought you near himself to do the work at the LORD's tabernacle? . . . It is against the LORD that you and all your followers have banded together" (verses 8, 11).

"Then Moses summoned Dathan and Abiram" (verse 12), but they remained defiant. They didn't yield an inch to Moses' authority. They said, "We will not come! Isn't it enough that you have brought us up out of a land flowing with milk and honey to kill us in this desert? And now you also want to lord it over us? . . . Will you gouge out the eyes of these men [the 250 council members who had joined them in their rebellion]? No, we will not come!" (verses 12–14). Notice that once again they blamed Moses for bringing them out of Egypt.

Verse 15 says that "Moses became very angry and said to the LORD, 'Do not accept their offering. I have not taken so much as a donkey from them, nor have I wronged any of them.' "

Then Moses turned to Korah and repeated the order for the rebels to appear the next morning before God with their censers, and he ordered Aaron to join them with his censer. He said, "You and all your followers are to appear before the LORD tomorrow—you and they and Aaron. Each man is to take his censer and put incense in it—250 censers in all—and present it before the LORD. You [Korah] and Aaron are to present your censers also" (verses 16, 17).

This time the rebels decided to follow Moses' demand. The next morning Korah, Dathan, and Abiram and their 250 followers appeared—each man with his censer filled with fire and incense. Moses and Aaron were also there, and Aaron had his censer. "When Korah had gathered all his followers in opposition to them [Moses and Aaron] at the entrance to the Tent of Meeting, the glory of the LORD appeared to the entire assembly. The LORD said to Moses and Aaron, 'Separate yourselves from this assembly so I can put an end to them at once' " (verses 19–21).

Please pay careful attention to what God said and what He *didn't* say. He did not order Moses and Aaron to separate from Korah, Dathan, Abiram, and the 250 men who had sided with them. He ordered Moses and Aaron to separate themselves from the entire *assembly*. Why? "So that I can put an end to *them* [the assembly] at once" (verse 21; emphasis added). Again God was threatening to destroy the entire Israelite community!

But once more "Moses and Aaron fell facedown and cried out, 'O God, God of the spirits of all mankind, will you be angry with the entire assembly when only one man sins?' " (verse 22).

God responded by telling Moses to "say to the assembly, 'Move away from the tents of Korah, Dathan, and Abiram' " (verse 24). So Moses "got up and went to Dathan and Abiram, and the elders of Israel followed him. He warned the assembly, 'Move back from the tents of these wicked men. Do not touch anything belonging to them or you will be swept away because of all their sins' " (verses 25, 26).

Notice that Moses gave this instruction to the entire assembly. Apparently, the entire camp of Israel was watching the dispute between God's appointed leaders and the rebels. My guess is that a significant majority of the people were sympathetic to the rebels. After all, it had been only a day or two since the entire congregation had been told they were being turned back to wander in the wilderness for forty years and that none of them who were twenty years old or older would enter the Promised Land. That was a bitter pill for them to swallow! Thus, Korah's challenge to Moses' leadership, which was joined by 250 other prominent leaders, gave the entire nation some hope.

They must have thought, *What if Korah was right when he said to Moses and Aaron, "You have gone too far"? What if he was correct when he said, "The whole community is holy, every one of them, and the Lord is with them. Why then do you set yourselves above the* LORD's *assembly?"*

God intervenes

I can imagine all the members of the community trying to jostle their way to the front of the crowd to get a better look at the action. But Moses had ordered the crowd to "move back from the tents of these wicked men." I can just see Moses waving his arms and shouting to the people, "Get back! Get back!"

No doubt grudgingly, the crowd began to move away from the tents of Korah, Dathan, and Abiram. As they were moving, Moses said, "This is how you will know that the LORD has sent me to do all these things and that it was not my idea: If these men die a natural death and experience only what usually happens to men, then the LORD has not sent me. But if the LORD brings about something totally new, and the earth opens its mouth and swallows them, with everything that belongs to them, and they go down alive into the grave, then you will know that these men have treated the LORD with contempt" (verses 28–30).

The words were scarcely out of Moses' mouth when the ground "under them split apart and the earth opened its mouth and swallowed them [Korah, Dathan, and Abiram], with their households and all Korah's men and all their possessions. They went down alive into the grave, with everything they owned; the earth closed over them, and they perished and were gone from the community. At their cries, all the Israelites around them fled, shouting, 'The earth is going to swallow us too!' " (verses 32–34).

It wasn't just Korah, Dathan, and Abiram and their families who perished that day. After these three leaders and their families died, "fire came out from the LORD and consumed the 250 men who were offering the incense" (verse 35).

You would think, wouldn't you, that the supernatural event that brought about the deaths of Korah, Dathan, and Abiram and their families would have been lesson enough to convince the Israelite community that Moses was carrying out his leadership on orders from God and not at his own initiative. You would think that the deaths of Korah, Dathan, and Abiram's 250 supporters would also have been enough to convince the people of this reality. But no! "The next day the whole Israelite community grumbled against Moses and Aaron. 'You have killed the LORD's people,' they said" (verse 41; emphasis added).

Really? These people were absolutely blind to what they had seen the day before! How could they say to Moses and Aaron, "You have killed the LORD's people"? Did they really believe that Moses was the one who caused the earthquake that opened the trench that swallowed up Korah, Dathan, Abiram, and their families? Did they really think that Moses and Aaron caused the fire that killed the 250 co-conspirators? All I can conclude is that they weren't listening to reason. They were acting totally out of their bitter, frightened, and disappointed emotions.

So how did God handle this crisis? He began by moving the cloud that accompanied the Israelites at every step of their journey and causing it to hover over the sanctuary, and He showed the people His bright, shining glory. Moses and Aaron then walked to the front of the sanctuary. But God said to them, "Get away from this assembly so I can put an end to them at once" (verse 45). God was again threatening to destroy the entire nation! Moses and Aaron again responded by falling facedown on the ground. When they got up, Moses said to Aaron, "Take your censer and put incense in it, along with fire from the altar, and hurry to the assembly to make atonement for them. Wrath has come out from the LORD; the plague has started" (verse 46). God had begun to carry out His threat to destroy the entire congregation. So Aaron grabbed his censer and ran among the people as Moses had instructed. He "offered the incense and made atonement for them. He stood between the living and the dead, and the plague stopped. But 14,700 people died from the plague in addition to those who had died because of Korah" (verses 47–49).

Aaron's rod that budded

Then God instructed Moses to do one more thing. "Get twelve staffs," He said, "one from the leader of each of their ancestral tribes. Write the name of each man on his staff. . . . Place them in the Tent of Meeting in front of the Testimony [the ark], where I meet with you. The staff belonging to the man I choose will sprout, *and I will rid myself of this constant grumbling against you by the Israelites*" (Numbers 17:2, 4, 5; emphasis added). God was getting very, *very* weary of the people's disbelief and negative behavior!

The leaders of each tribe brought their staffs, and God specifically instructed that Aaron provide the staff for tribe of Levi. That evening Moses placed them in front of the ark of the covenant. When Moses returned to the sanctuary the next morning, Aaron's rod had not only sprouted, it had also blossomed and produced almonds! The people came to Moses and said, "We will die! We are lost, we are all lost! Anyone who even comes near the tabernacle of the LORD will die" (verses 12, 13).

The rebellion was finally over!

Summary of the Kingdom of Darkness during the Exodus

The Bible's account of the Exodus says nothing whatsoever about Satan and the Kingdom of Darkness working behind the scenes to inspire the people's disaffection and the rebellion during the Exodus, especially at Kadesh. However, the story is a classic example of Satan's method of working. It begins with God meeting Moses at the burning bush, where He appointed Moses as the leader of the Israelites with the specific order to cooperate with Him in leading the children of Israel out of Egypt and into the Promised Land. Anytime God appoints a leader He gives that leader the authority to lead, and He expects the people to respect and obey that person and his authority. That's the way it was in heaven. Once God, in the grand meeting with all the angels, declared that Michael was their Leader, the angels were expected to obey Him. Those who didn't were eventually cast out of heaven.

The Israelites began questioning Moses' God-given authority even while they were still in Egypt. When Pharaoh ordered the Israelites to provide their own straw for making bricks, the Israelites who supervised the slaves became angry and questioned whether God had really appointed Moses to lead them out of Egypt. This disbelief in Moses' leadership persisted throughout the Exodus. In spite of the ten plagues that provided them with a miraculous deliverance from Egypt, the people panicked at the Red Sea. So God delivered them by parting the sea and giving them a dry path to safety on the other side. Then He destroyed their enemies by drowning them in the Red Sea.

When the people ran out of food and water, their fear again drove them to make complaints against God's appointed leader, even threatening to kill him and return to Egypt. Although they didn't carry out that plan, this was clear defiance of Moses' God-given authority. Nevertheless, God provided the people with the needed food and water.

Finally, at Sinai, God Himself met with the Israelites and made it absolutely clear over a period of at least forty days that He had appointed Moses to lead them. The people could no longer argue that Moses invented his claim to have received his commission to lead Israel at the burning bush.

But there was still sedition in the camp. In the rebellion at Kadesh, we see another classic example of how the Kingdom of Darkness works. In heaven, Lucifer kept his resentment against Michael to himself for a while; but in due time, he began to share it with those angels whom he could trust. And the very same thing happened at Kadesh. Ellen White said that Korah, the leader of the rebellion, at first kept his reservations about Moses' leadership to himself; but in due time, he shared them with Dathan and Abiram and eventually with all of the top 250 leaders of the nation.

Just as God dealt with the rebellion in heaven by casting Satan and his followers to this earth, so He dealt with the rebellion against Moses by eliminating the rebels from the camp of Israel. The ground split open and swallowed the top leaders in the rebellion and their families. Then God destroyed the 250 co-conspirators with fire, and He brought a plague upon the rest of the rebels in the congregation. In all, the number of those who died was nearly fifteen thousand people.

The Exodus contains these clear examples of defiance against God's laws and His authority. These rebellions also illustrate how people who turn away from God become selfish, which is the opposite of love and eventually results in a loss of freedom.

However, even after the crisis at Kadesh was over, Satan was still alive and well, and the story of the conflict between the Kingdom of Light and the Kingdom of Darkness continued throughout the history of Israel. Armageddon was still a long way off!

---

1. See also White, *Patriarchs and Prophets*, 395.
2. Ibid.

CHAPTER 12

From Canaan to Christ

After forty years, the Israelites camped on the east side of the Jordan River; they were ready to enter the land of Canaan and conquer it. But before they crossed over, God spoke to Joshua, Moses' successor. He told Joshua that the Israelites were to conquer the land "from the desert to Lebanon, and from the great river, the Euphrates . . . to the Great Sea on the west" (Joshua 1:4). He commanded Joshua to "be careful to obey all the law" (verse 7). And God said two other things. In verse 6, He said, "Be strong and courageous," and in verse 7, He said, "Be strong and *very* courageous" (emphasis added). He followed this up with "do not be terrified . . . for the LORD your God will be with you wherever you go" (verse 9). That was good advice, because fear of the giants in the land was one of the primary reasons God had had to keep the Israelites from entering Canaan forty years earlier.

The words *do not be afraid* occur thirty-five times in the New King James Version, and the words *fear not* occur eleven times, for a total of forty-six. So what's the significance of this? God almost never appears personally to us humans. He works through people to accomplish His will on the earth; some people have to labor under very difficult and threatening situations. And we humans are easily traumatized by events that appear frightening to us, which interferes with our doing what God wants us to do. That's why Jonah ran the other way when God told him to go preach in Nineveh. The Assyrians were among the most ruthless people of the ancient nations. I can just hear Jonah's reply, "God, are You serious? Do You *really* want me to go preach to those vicious people?" Fear is the reason God had to send the Israelites back into the desert to wander for forty years. That's why, on this second attempt to enter Canaan, God assured Joshua that "the LORD your God will be with you wherever you go." Jesus made the same promise to His disciples just before He returned to heaven: "Surely I am with you always, to the very end of the age" (Matthew 28:20). This promise is also for us today as we prepare to face the traumatic events of the world's final crisis.

After Joshua

The Bible says that "Israel served the LORD throughout the lifetime of Joshua and of the elders who outlived him and who had experienced everything the LORD had done for Israel" (Joshua 24:31). Then began a series of ups and downs that lasted for several hundred years. The people would start worshiping idols, and the Lord would send their enemies to oppress them. After enough of the oppression, they would cry to the Lord, and He would send judges, such as Gideon and Jephthah, to deliver them. The Israelites would serve God for several more decades, and then they would be back to their idols, followed by their enemies oppressing them, succeeded by a judge who would deliver them. God and Satan were keeping themselves very busy in their tug-of-war for the people's minds and hearts!

Things finally began to settle down when God raised up the prophet Samuel, who held the people reasonably steadfast in their loyalty to God. And the years of the first three kings of Israel were far more prosperous, especially the reign of David and the early years of his son Solomon. But then Satan got Solomon to marry heathen wives and set up idols in Jerusalem for them to worship, and Solomon also worshiped these pagan gods (1 Kings 11). He repented during his later years, but by then the damage had been done. For the next several centuries, the Israelites struggled between loyalty to God and their strong attachment to their idols.

I have to ask myself, What on earth was there about these dumb idols that made them such a fascinating temptation? The last thing in the world that I'm interested in is making a god out of a block of wood or stone and bowing down and worshiping it!

But an important reason why I'm not attracted to dumb idols is that I live in the twenty-first century. I know what causes earthquakes and storms and droughts. I know what causes illness, and my modern age has provided treatments to cure all kinds of diseases. But three thousand years ago the people hadn't a clue what caused illnesses and bad weather. So they concluded that there must be gods who controlled these devastating disasters. This was the perception of reality held by all the nations around Israel, and the Israelites absorbed that perception into their worldview.

Today we face the very same problem. Evolution is the prevailing worldview of our culture, and anyone who believes otherwise is considered to be naïve at best and more likely stupid. There's a huge temptation today for creationists to yield to the prevailing worldview in our culture in the matter of the origin of life on our planet. And it was the same with the Israelites.

They faced the huge temptation to succumb to the worldview of the nations around them, and this led them to ignore God's Word and worship idols. We today need to trust God's worldview as it's taught in the Bible instead of yielding to the popular worldview of the culture around us.

After Solomon's death, the northern kingdom of Israel split off from the tribes of Judah and Benjamin, making two kingdoms instead of one (1 Kings 12). Descent into idolatry was immediate, for Jeroboam set up idols in the cities of Dan in the north and Beersheba in the south. From there on, the trend in the northern kingdom was mostly away from God, in spite of the efforts of two of the most famous prophets in the Old Testament—Elijah and Elisha—to turn the people back to God.

The northern kingdom of Judah fared better, but even its people eventually succumbed to idolatry. Several kings of Judah were very loyal to God and led the people back to serving Him, most notably Asa, Hezekiah, and Josiah. But some of the kings of Judah, such as Manasseh during the early part of his reign, were evil to the core, and they led the people into profound idolatry.

Jeremiah

God sent the prophet Jeremiah to lead the people back to Him. Jeremiah labored for God during the final years of Judah's existence as a nation, and he experienced the Babylonians' destruction of Jerusalem and Solomon's temple. But prior to that calamity, Jeremiah begged and pleaded with the people of Judah, especially their rulers and the prominent people, to give up their idols and other wicked ways. Jeremiah spoke the words of God:

> "Return, faithless Israel," declares the LORD,
>   "I will frown on you no longer,
> for I am merciful," declares the LORD,
>   "I will not be angry forever.
> Only acknowledge your guilt—
>   you have rebelled against the LORD your God,
> you have scattered your favors to foreign gods,
>   under every spreading tree,
>   and have not obeyed me,"
>   declares the LORD (Jeremiah 3:12, 13).

God called Jeremiah to his prophetic ministry in the thirteenth year of good King Josiah, and he continued through the remaining eighteen years of Josiah's reign and up to the destruction of Jerusalem by the Babylonians. After Josiah's death, his son Jehoahaz was installed as the next king of Judah, even though he wasn't Josiah's oldest son, because the people of Judah favored him.[1] Jeremiah hoped that he could influence the nation's leaders to continue Josiah's reforms. Unfortunately, Jehoahaz "did evil in the sight of the LORD, just as his fathers had done" (2 Kings 23:32) and as did the three kings who followed him.

It's important to understand that a shift was taking place in the balance of power in the Middle East at this time.[2] Egypt had been the dominant nation for almost 140 years, but Babylon was now in the ascendancy. Nevertheless, Egypt still dominated Palestine, including the kingdom of Judah. Jehoahaz had probably favored Babylon over Egypt because three months after he came to the throne Pharaoh Necho deposed him and exiled him to Egypt, where he lived out the rest of his life.[3]

Necho installed Jehoahaz's brother Jehoiakim as king of Judah—a position he held for the next eleven years. Jehoiakim was also a wicked king who "did evil in the eyes of the LORD, just as his fathers had done" (verse 37). It didn't take him long to reverse all the religious reforms that his father Josiah had instituted. Ellen White wrote, "From the beginning of Jehoiakim's reign, Jeremiah had little hope of saving his beloved land from destruction and the people from captivity."[4] Nevertheless, he did his best to avert the threatened doom.

Jeremiah was very direct in pointing out the sins of the Israelites:

> "From the least to the greatest,
>   all are greedy for gain;
> prophets and priests alike,
>   all practice deceit" (Jeremiah 6:13).

"If you really change your ways and your actions and deal with each other justly, if you do not oppress the alien, the fatherless or the widow and do not shed innocent blood in this place, and if you do not follow other gods to your own harm, then I [God] will let you live in this place, in the land I gave your forefathers for ever and ever" (Jeremiah 7:5–7). Jeremiah warned that if the people didn't turn from their evil ways, God would "make this house [the temple] like Shiloh" (Jeremiah 26:6; see also verses 4, 5). Shiloh was the location of the wilderness tabernacle for three hundred years after the Israelites entered Canaan until the Philistines captured the ark.[5]

Back in the late 1920s, a group of archaeologists excavated the remains of Shiloh and found that the city had been destroyed by fire just about the time the Philistines captured the ark. So even though the Bible doesn't mention that event, it forms the background to Jeremiah's warning that God would "make this house like Shiloh." That is, the temple in Jerusalem would be destroyed.

During his first three years as king, Jehoiakim was loyal to Egypt, but in 605 B.C. Nebuchadnezzar defeated Egypt, subdued Judah, and took some of its prominent citizens as captives to Babylon, among them were Daniel and his three friends. Nebuchadnezzar also took some of the vessels from the temple and carried them to Babylon.

Jeremiah warned the Israelites of the danger they faced from the rising power of Babylon, and he repeatedly advised the leaders and the people to submit to Nebuchadnezzar's authority. At one point, God instructed Jeremiah to "take a scroll and write on it all the words I have spoken to you . . . from the time I began speaking to you in the reign of Josiah till now" (Jeremiah 36:2). He then instructed Jeremiah to read those words before the people, for "perhaps when the people of Judah hear about every disaster I plan to inflict on them, each of them will turn from his wicked way; then I will forgive their wickedness and their sin" (verse 3).

Jeremiah dictated his message to his secretary, Baruch, who was a scribe. Baruch wrote Jeremiah's words on a scroll. Then, because Jeremiah was not permitted to enter the temple at that time (verse 5), he instructed Baruch to go to the temple and read the scroll in the presence of all the people. God chose for His message to be read in the temple at this time because a great many people from Judah were gathered in Jerusalem to fast because of the crisis the nation faced from the Babylonians. In the message that Baruch read, Jeremiah warned the citizens of Judah and their king that they should submit to the Babylonians.

A man by the name of Micaiah, who was a leading Jew during Jehoiakim's reign,[6] heard Jeremiah's warning message and immediately reported it to some of the officials in the king's government. They sent for Baruch, and he read the writings on the scroll to them. When he was finished, they were filled with fear and said, "We must report all of these words to the king" (verse 16).* When they told King Jehoiakim about the scroll, he demanded that it be brought and read to him. But instead of heeding Jeremiah's warning, the king

---

* The entire story of Jeremiah dictating the scroll to Baruch and his report to the officials and the king is found in Jeremiah 36.

cut the scroll in pieces, burned it, and maintained his loyalty to Egypt.

Nebuchadnezzar allowed some of his troops, together with those of several neighboring nations, to invade Judah. They captured Jehoiakim, and he died shortly after that, probably as a result of the rough treatment he experienced from the Babylonians.[7]

Following Jehoiakim's captivity, his son Jehoiachin, who was only eighteen years old at the time, succeeded him on the throne. However, it wasn't long until Nebuchadnezzar again laid siege to Jerusalem. Jehoiachin surrendered to the Babylonian king, who took him captive to Babylon along with his closest family members and about ten thousand others, including the prophet Ezekiel. This was the second of three invasions by Nebuchadnezzar into Judah.

Nebuchadnezzar put Jehoiachin's uncle Zedekiah on the throne, apparently believing that he would be loyal to Babylon. Jeremiah urged the new king to remain loyal to Nebuchadnezzar. "Serve the king of Babylon, and you will live," he said. "Why should this city become a ruin?" (Jeremiah 27:17). Zedekiah was inclined to follow Jeremiah's advice. Unfortunately, unlike Jehoiakim's officials, who were alarmed when they heard Baruch's warning, Zedekiah's officials were incensed by Jeremiah's advice to yield to Babylonian domination, and they urged the king to pay no attention to the warning.

Jeremiah also wrote a letter to the Jewish captives in Babylon advising them to accept their captivity and to settle down there, but this only aroused their anger. Their leaders wrote back to Jerusalem, demanding that the prophet be imprisoned. As a result, Jeremiah "was confined in the courtyard of the guard in the royal palace of Judah" (Jeremiah 32:2). Later he was accused of trying to defect to the Babylonians. The king's officials beat him and put him in prison. Zedekiah had Jeremiah brought from the prison and asked the prophet for his advice. Jeremiah said, "Whoever stays in this city will die by the sword, famine or plague, but whoever goes over to the Babylonians will live. . . . This city will certainly be handed over to the army of the king of Babylon, who will capture it" (Jeremiah 38:2, 3).

When the king's officials heard of Jeremiah's advice, they said, "This man should be put to death. He . . . is not seeking the good of these people but their ruin." Instead of courageously rejecting the demand of his officials, Zedekiah said to them, "He is in your hands. . . . The king can do nothing to oppose you" (verses 4, 5). However, Jeremiah managed to stay alive.

The people of Judah were also strongly opposed to yielding to Babylon, and Zedekiah, who had a weak and indecisive personality, yielded to their opposition and rebelled against the Babylonians. The result was Nebuchadnezzar's third invasion of Judah, and this time he destroyed Jerusalem and its temple and carried off to Babylon most of the rest of the citizens of Judah. Zedekiah tried to escape, but the Babylonians captured him and took him to Nebuchadnezzar. The Babylonian king killed Zedekiah's sons in his presence, had his eyes put out, and took him to Babylon in chains.[8] Jeremiah was right! The king and his officials should have listened to him!

Thus ended the kingdom of Judah.

After the Babylonian captivity

Jeremiah had foretold that in seventy years the Jews would be restored to their homeland (see Jeremiah 29:10), and it happened as he predicted. Three Persian kings—Cyrus, Darius, and Artaxerxes—issued decrees authorizing the Jews to rebuild the temple. The seventy years of captivity foretold by Jeremiah ended with Cyrus's decree, which probably occurred in 536 B.C.— seventy years after the first Jewish deportation to Babylon in 605.[9] The third decree, by Artaxerxes, authorized the Jews to establish their own government (under dominion of the Persian Empire), and it also authorized the rebuilding of the city of Jerusalem. This decree was issued in 457 B.C., which is also the date for the beginning of the 2,300-day prophecy of Daniel 8:14.

The destruction of Jerusalem and the exile to Babylon finally cured the Jews of their fascination with idol worship. This experience taught them as a nation that God was serious about obedience to His law, and they determined to keep it at all costs. This was good; unfortunately Satan used their determination to keep the law as a means of leading them into a severe form of legalism. Their experts in the law scrutinized the law and interpreted it and reinterpreted it, which resulted in a pile of traditions that had nothing to do with the law itself. But they treated the traditions as the law. Several centuries later Jesus arrived on the scene, and He challenged these false interpretations, including the more than six hundred traditions about keeping the Sabbath. And that's one of the reasons the Jewish leaders crucified Him.*

Summary of the Kingdom of Darkness from Canaan to Christ

I've said little in this chapter about the history of Israel from Canaan to

---

* Another reason the Jewish leaders crucified Jesus is that He challenged their authority with the people.

Jeremiah, choosing to let Jeremiah's story be an example of that entire period. God called Jeremiah to his prophetic office during the reign of good King Josiah, and he continued to carry out that ministry all the way up to the Babylonian captivity. Josiah respected Jeremiah's authority as a spokesperson for God; but the last three kings of Judah rejected him, and by rejecting his authority, they rejected God's authority. In continuing to worship their false gods, they also rejected God's law. Their unjust treatment of foreigners, widows, and the fatherless showed their lack of love, and finally they lost their freedom both as a nation and as individuals when they were taken over by Babylon. The influence of the Kingdom of Darkness was clearly evident in the lives of the people of Judah during the prophetic ministry of Jeremiah.

By this time, about thirty-five hundred years had elapsed since Creation. However, Armageddon was still some twenty-five hundred years in the future.

---

1. Horn, *Seventh-day Adventist Bible Dictionary*, s.v. "Jehoahaz."

2. Ibid., 313.

3. Ibid., s.v. "Jehoahaz."

4. Ellen G. White, *Prophets and Kings* (Mountain View, CA: Pacific Press® Pub. Assn., 1943), 412.

5. See Nichol, *The Seventh-day Adventist Bible Commentary*, 4:387, 388.

6. Horn, *Seventh-day Adventist Bible Dictionary*, s.v. "Micaiah."

7. Ibid., s.v. "Jehoiakim."

8. Ibid., s.v. "Zedekiah."

9. Ibid., 558.

CHAPTER 13

Jesus' Birth

L et's take a moment to review where we've been in this story of the long road to Armageddon. We've learned that Satan rebelled against God in heaven, especially against Christ. But why would he do that? The answer is *jealousy*. Lucifer had held a very high position in heaven. He had stood next to God's throne as the covering cherub, and he was adorned with all kinds of jewelry (Ezekiel 28:13, 14).

Christ, who was fully divine and a member of the Trinity, nevertheless appeared to the other angels as one of them.* Lucifer became jealous of Christ because he could see no difference between himself and Christ, yet Christ was permitted into the counsels of the Godhead and he, Lucifer, was not. So he rebelled, secured the loyalty of a third of the angels, and went to war against Christ.

You know the story. Lucifer and his angels were cast to our planet. Satan got Adam and Eve to yield to his temptation, and with that, he took over dominion of the world from them. Adam and Eve themselves became sinful in the very core of their humanity. Satan rejoiced, because a group of intelligent beings whom God had created were now under his control. He figured that since God couldn't forgive him, neither could He forgive Adam and Eve. But God was one jump ahead of Satan. He devised a plan by which He *could* pardon Adam and Eve and any other human being who would accept Jesus. But Satan and his angels were left out of the plan. God announced this plan to Adam and Eve:

> "I will put enmity
>   between you [Satan] and the woman [God's people],
>   and between your offspring and hers;
> he [Christ] will crush your head,
>   and you [Satan] will strike his heel" (Genesis 3:15).

In other words, when Christ came, Satan would inflict severe pain on Him

---

* For an explanation of why Jesus appeared as an angel in heaven, see chapter 2.

and inspire the religious leaders to crucify Him. But Christ would be resurrected from the dead, which is why God told Adam and Eve that Satan would inflict a nonfatal blow upon Christ (strike His heel), but that Christ would defeat Satan and ultimately destroy him (crush his head).

Satan infused the human race with his attributes, and evil proliferated to the point that God had to destroy that first world with a global flood. This stemmed the tide of terrible evil that had developed up to that point, but immediately after the Flood Satan resumed inculcating his principles into human minds and hearts. Evil began to proliferate again.

God established the Jewish nation to be His representative in the world, but the Jews succumbed to idolatry to the point that God had to destroy the northern kingdom entirely. About a hundred years later, He allowed Nebuchadnezzar to destroy Jerusalem and take the majority of its citizens captive to Babylon. Satan was extremely successful!

In their Babylonian captivity, the Jews learned their lesson; they never succumbed to idolatry again. Instead, they made sure to keep every single precept of the law *to the letter*; over a period of about four hundred years, the spiritual leaders among them piled on a huge number of traditional interpretations of the law that became a horrible burden to the people. Ellen White wrote, "The people whom God had called to be the pillar and ground of the truth had become representatives of Satan."[1] During this same four hundred years, the Gentile world sank deeper and deeper into sin. Speaking of the entire human race—Gentiles as well as Jews—Ellen White noted,

> The bodies of human beings, made for the dwelling place of God, had become the habitation of demons. The senses, the nerves, the passions, the organs of men, were worked by supernatural agencies in the indulgence of the vilest lust. . . .
>
> . . . Rebellion had struck its roots deep into the heart, and the hostility of man was most violent against heaven.[2]

This was the condition of the world at the beginning of the first century A.D. How would God respond? Ellen White pointed to one option that God had: "With intense interest the unfallen worlds had watched to see Jehovah arise, and sweep away the inhabitants of the earth."[3] That's the option Satan hoped God would choose. Had God chosen that option, "Satan was ready to carry out his plan for securing to himself the allegiance of heavenly beings. He had declared that the principles of God's government make forgiveness impossible. Had the world been destroyed, he would have claimed that his accusations were proved true. He was ready to cast blame upon God, and to spread his rebellion to the worlds above."[4]

But God chose another option. It's summarized in that best-loved text in all the Bible: "God so loved the world that he gave his one and only Son, that whoever believes in him shall not perish but have eternal life" (John 3:16). But Satan wasn't about to give up! Revelation tells the story in dramatic language:

A great and wondrous sign appeared in heaven: a woman clothed with the sun, with the moon under her feet and a crown of twelve stars on her head. She was pregnant and cried out in pain as she was about to give birth. Then another sign appeared in heaven: an enormous red dragon with seven heads and ten horns and seven crowns on his heads. His tail swept a third of the stars out of the sky and flung them to the earth. The dragon stood in front of the woman who was about to give birth, so that he might devour her child the moment it was born. She gave birth to a son, a male child, who will rule all the nations with an iron scepter. And her child was snatched up to God and to his throne (Revelation 12:1–5).

This passage of Scripture is a mini description of the conflict between Christ and Satan at the point of Christ's birth. How was it fulfilled?* Joseph and Mary traveled to Bethlehem to register with the Roman government. They had barely arrived when Mary went into labor and gave birth to Jesus. That's the meaning of John's statement that the woman who was clothed with the sun "gave birth to a son, a male child" (verse 5).

A woman in biblical prophecy typically represents God's people. For example, in Hosea 2:16, the prophet quoted God as saying, "In that day . . . you will call me 'my husband.' " In verse 19, He said, "I will betroth you to me forever." God was referring here to the Israelite people. In the New Testament, Paul wrote to the church in Corinth, "I promised you to one husband, to Christ, so that I might present you as a pure virgin to him" (2 Corinthians 11:2). John expressed the same idea in Revelation 19:7, 8, when, speaking of Christ's second coming, he said,

"Let us rejoice and be glad

---

* John wrote Revelation about a hundred years *after* Christ was born, so we can't say that his description of Satan trying to destroy Christ when He was born was fulfilled in the same sense as Daniel's prophecies, which Daniel wrote several hundred years *before* the events he predicted actually happened.

and give him [God] glory!
For the wedding of the Lamb has come,
and his bride has made herself ready" (verse 7).

In each of these texts, God, or Christ, is the husband or the groom, and His people are the bride. That's why we should understand the woman in Revelation 12:1 to represent the Christian church, not just Mary.

But how can we say that the *church* gave birth to Jesus? This idea goes all the way back to Genesis 3:15, where God said that He would put enmity between the woman's *descendants* and Satan's *descendants*.* So the woman there has to be more than Eve. It's the entire group of descendants on both sides—Satan's side and the woman's side. God went on to say that Jesus, the descendant of Eve, would crush Satan's head, while Satan would injure only Jesus' heel. The fulfillment of that prediction began when Jesus died on the cross. That was the injury to Jesus' heel, from which He fully recovered three days later when He rose from the dead. However, God said that Jesus would crush Satan's head—that is, Jesus would destroy Satan. That will be fulfilled at the end of the millennium, when Satan and all his evil followers, both angels and humans, are cast into the lake of fire. So Jesus is the offspring of the entire body of believers throughout world history, not just Eve or Mary, which is why we can say that the woman in Revelation 12:1 represents God's people—the nation of Israel in the Old Testament and the Christian church in the New Testament.

Now let's continue with Revelation 12. Verse 4 says that "the dragon stood in front of the woman who was about to give birth, so that he might devour her child the moment it was born." This was fulfilled some time after Jesus' birth, probably no more than two years, when King Herod tried to kill Jesus by slaying all the baby boys in Bethlehem who were two years old and under (Matthew 2:16). However, God was one step ahead of Satan. He sent an angel to warn Joseph, and he and his family left Bethlehem for Egypt before the massacre. The reason for going to Egypt was because Satan might lead Herod to try to kill Jesus again, so the family waited in Egypt until an angel told them Herod had died and it was safe to return to Nazareth.

Satan was perfectly aware of who Jesus was even before He was born into our world. He knew that this was the One whom he had been so bitterly jealous of back in heaven thousands of years before. He knew Jesus was the one who, with His angels, had cast him and his angels out of heaven. Satan had

---

* Instead of "descendants," the KJV and the NKJV say "seed," and the NIV says "offspring."

conquered God and Christ in Eden by tempting Adam and Eve to sin. Now he was determined to conquer Christ Himself, for this was his last stand. If he won this conflict, he would defeat Christ and claim the earth as his rightful kingdom forever. In fact, Ellen White indicated that had Jesus failed in His mission, Satan believed he could "spread his rebellion to the worlds above."[5]

Of course, that was part of Satan's delusion. I'm sure that God would not have permitted Satan to spread his sinister plans to the rest of the universe had Christ failed. Fortunately, Christ did *not* fail, so we don't need to worry about Satan's deluded intentions.

Jesus as a human being

Jesus came to this world as a fully human person, while at the same time He was fully divine. John stated it in simple language. First, the divine part: "In the beginning was the Word, and the Word was with God, and the Word *was* God" (John 1:1; emphasis added). Next, the human part: "*The Word became flesh* and made his dwelling among us" (verse 14; emphasis added). So why did Jesus have to become a human being? I'm sure we'll learn more about that throughout the ceaseless ages of eternity, but I'll share with you five reasons why Jesus became one of us.

1. *To respond to Satan's charge.* Satan had claimed that it was impossible for human beings to keep God's law, and he pointed to Adam and Eve's sin as evidence that he was right. But Jesus proved him wrong by coming to earth and living a sinless life as a human. Peter said that Jesus "committed no sin" (1 Peter 2:22), and Ellen White commented, "In thought, word, and deed Jesus was sinless."[6]

2. *To give us His righteousness.* Paul said that "God made him [Christ] who had no sin to be sin for us, so that in him we might become the righteousness of God" (2 Corinthians 5:21). Think of that. We can become righteous like God! However, it's critically important to understand how that happens. We can't accomplish this through our own efforts, even in our converted state. Christ attributes His righteousness to us when we accept Him as our Savior. Ellen White explained the concept well when she wrote, "Christ's character stands in place of your character, and you are accepted before God just as if you had not sinned."[7] And in order for Him to have a righteous, sinless character to give us, Jesus had to develop that sinless character during the thirty-three years He lived among us. Had He sinned even once, He would not have had that sinless character to give us.

3. *To teach us the truth about God.* By the time Jesus came to earth as a

human, "the world was dark through misapprehension of God."[8] Thus, His character had to be manifested in contrast to the character of Satan, and "this work only one Being in all the universe could do. Only He who knew the height and depth of the love of God could make it known."[9] That's why, when Philip said to Jesus,

> "Lord, show us the Father and that will be enough for us."
>
> Jesus answered, "Don't you know me, Philip, even after I have been with you such a long time? Anyone who has seen me has seen the Father" (John 14:8, 9).

Jesus' life was a revelation of what God is like.

4. *To restore the lost dominion.* When Adam and Eve sinned, they became slaves of Satan, and the dominion over the earth that God had given them passed to their adversary. Paul said that Satan is "the god of this world" (2 Corinthians 4:4, KJV). One of the important reasons Jesus came to this planet was to restore that lost dominion—not to Adam and Eve or to any of their descendants, but to Himself. Daniel made this very clear. In Daniel 7, he told about a pre-Advent judgment that would take place in heaven prior to Christ's second coming. This judgment, which is going on right now, is a legal process that involves all the angels in heaven. Daniel said that at the conclusion of this judgment a "son of man," who is clearly Christ, came before God's throne, and "he was given authority, glory and sovereign power. . . . His dominion is an everlasting dominion that will not pass away, and his kingdom is one that will never be destroyed" (verses 13, 14). This "son of man" is obviously a reference to Christ, who will take over dominion of the world from Satan at His second coming.

5. *To pay the death penalty for our human sins.* God told Adam in Eden that he and Eve must not eat the fruit of the tree of the knowledge of good and evil or they would die. You know the story: Adam and Eve *did* eat the fruit, and God had to impose that death penalty on them and the entire human race after them. But nothing is more clearly stated in the New Testament than that Jesus died to pay that death penalty for us. Paul said that "Christ died for our sins" (1 Corinthians 15:3); Peter said that Jesus "bore our sins in his body on the tree" (1 Peter 2:24); and John said that Jesus "is the atoning sacrifice for our sins" (1 John 2:2). Ellen White said that "in this speck of a world the whole heavenly universe manifests the greatest interest, for Christ has paid an infinite price for the souls of its inhabitants."[10]

But why did Christ have to die for our sins? Because humans disobeyed, a Human had to pay the penalty. And the only way God could save us from that penalty was for His divine Son, who was a member of the Godhead, to become a human being and pay the death penalty for us. Paul affirmed this truth when he wrote, "For as in Adam all die, so in Christ all will be made alive" (1 Corinthians 15:22).

That's why Jesus is called our Redeemer. The word *redeemer* comes from an Old Testament custom. If a man had a debt he could not pay, a relative could pay it for him, and this relative was called a redeemer. In the same way, Christ redeemed us from the penalty of death by paying it for us.

Whose nature did Christ take?

There's another issue we need to discuss before leaving this chapter. It's a question that has created a significant debate among Seventh-day Adventist students of the Bible and Ellen White's writings. The question is, when Christ came to earth, did He take on the human nature Adam had *before* the Fall or *after* the Fall? Vigorous arguments have been made by both sides, often so strongly that it has been a war of words at times. The problem is that each side has staked out its position without realizing that there's truth on both sides. One of the major evidences put forth by the post-Fall side is this quote by Ellen White:

> It would have been an almost infinite humiliation for the Son of God to take man's nature, even when Adam stood in his innocence in Eden. But Jesus accepted humanity when the race had been weakened by four thousand years of sin. Like every child of Adam He accepted the results of the working of the great law of heredity. What these results were is shown in the history of His earthly ancestors. He came with such a heredity to share our sorrows and temptations, and to give us the example of a sinless life.[11]

Notice the first sentence in that quote: "It would have been an almost infinite humiliation for the Son of God to take man's *nature,* even when Adam stood in his innocence in Eden." In other words, Christ did *not* take our human nature in the condition it was before the Fall. *Thus,* the proponents of the post-Fall position are correct. The rest of the paragraph clarifies the part of our human nature that Christ did take: "But Jesus accepted humanity when the race had been weakened by four thousand years of sin. Like every child of Adam He accepted the results of the working of the great law of

heredity. What these results were is shown in the history of His earthly an-
cestors. He came with such a heredity to share our sorrows and temptations,
and to give us the example of a sinless life."

It really had to be that way, because if Christ had taken the human nature
Adam had before the Fall, Satan could have argued, "Of course Jesus lived
a sinless life, because He didn't come in the human nature Adam and Eve
had after they sinned and after four thousand years of sin and degeneracy."
So the post-Fall proponents are absolutely correct.

However, the pre-Fall proponents also make a very valid point. The
question is this: what enabled Christ to live that sinless life? I will answer
that question by asking another one: what is it that enables any of Christ's
true followers to live godly life today? The answer is simple: conversion, the
new birth, the active presence of the Holy Spirit in our minds and hearts,
by which He changes our thoughts and motives. Paul said it well: "The
man without the Spirit does not accept the things that come from the Spirit
of God, for they are foolishness to him, and he cannot understand them,
because they are spiritually discerned" (1 Corinthians 2:14). To turn Paul's
statement around, we can say that those who *do* have the Spirit of God—that
is, the new birth—*can* discern "the things that come from the Spirit of God."

Think of it like this: Would it have been possible for Jesus in His humanity to live a perfect life without the presence of the Holy Spirit in His life?
Of course not! This means that Christ experienced the working of the Holy
Spirit in His life from the moment of His birth until shortly before His crucifixion. His anguished cry on the cross, "My God, my God, why have you
forsaken me?" (Mark 15:34) is clear evidence that by then the Holy Spirit had
left Him. I will have more to say about this in the chapters on Gethsemane,
Jesus' trial, and His crucifixion. God created Adam and Eve with the Holy
Spirit's presence built in. They didn't have to be converted like we do, because they were filled with the Holy Spirit from the moment they took their
first breaths.*

It's in this sense that Christ was made like Adam before the Fall. Consider
this: if Christ had been born without the presence of the Holy Spirit in His
mind and heart, the Savior would have *needed* a Savior before He could *be* a
Savior. That just doesn't make sense!

---

* I'm not aware of any statement in the Bible or Ellen White's writings that says this. It's
a logical conclusion that I draw from the fact that they were sinless until they made the fatal
choice to eat the forbidden fruit. The only way they could be sinless is they had to have the
Holy Spirit implanted in their minds and hearts from the moment they were created.

Ellen White confirms this conclusion in one sentence: "Christ came to the earth, taking humanity and standing as man's representative, to show in the controversy with Satan that *man, as God created him, connected with the Father and the Son,* could obey every divine requirement."[12] This is the pre-Fall part of Christ's nature. Man had to be "connected with the Father and the Son." What we call conversion, which we must experience by accepting Jesus as our Savior after we're born, He experienced from the moment of His birth. He had to experience what we call conversion from the moment of His birth* (or, probably more correctly, from His conception) so He could demonstrate that "in the controversy with Satan" the rest of us humans could also "obey every divine requirement." Satan had claimed all along that it was impossible for created beings to obey God's laws, but Jesus proved him wrong. By having the power of the Holy Spirit in *our* human lives, obedience to every one of God's requirements is possible for us too.

This is the Jesus who was born of a virgin in Bethlehem. This is the Jesus that God sent to earth because He loved us. This is the Jesus who loved us so much that He came as one of us and by His death redeemed us from our slavery to sin and Satan.

Praise the Lord for Jesus' birth!

1. Ellen G. White, *The Desire of Ages* (Mountain View, CA: Pacific Press® Pub. Assn., 1940), 36.

2. Ibid., 36, 37.

3. Ibid., 37.

4. Ibid.

5. Ibid.

6. Ellen G. White, *The Faith I Live By* (Washington, DC: Review and Herald® Pub. Assn., 1973), 219.

7. Ellen G. White, *Steps to Christ* (Nampa, ID: Pacific Press® Pub. Assn., 2000), 62.

8. White, *The Desire of Ages,* 22.

9. Ibid.

10. Ellen G. White, *Christ's Object Lessons* (Washington, DC: Review and Herald® Pub. Assn., 1969), 176.

11. White, *The Desire of Ages,* 49.

12. White, *Selected Messages,* bk. 1, 253. See also White, *The Desire of Ages,* 123.

* Luke says that John the Baptist was "filled with the Holy Spirit even from birth" (Luke 1:15). There may be others throughout human history who experienced the same thing.

CHAPTER 14

Jesus' Temptation

From the very beginning, the primary issue in the conflict between Christ and Satan has been dominion, and it's important to understand how that dominion works. You will recall that one-third of the millions of angels in heaven joined Lucifer in his rebellion against Michael (Revelation 12:4). I pointed out in chapter 3 that Lucifer didn't just twist the arms of these angels and say, "OK, you're on my side now whether you like it or not!" He had to persuade them of the "legitimacy" of his cause. And he achieved this through deception—misrepresenting God's character and His laws of love.

God, Christ, and the Holy Spirit also work to persuade human beings to pledge their allegiance to Them. Thus, the conflict between Christ and Satan for dominion is a conflict over the minds and hearts of intelligent beings. Through deception, Satan was able to gain the loyalty of Adam and Eve; and through them, he gained control of the entire human race. With this method, Satan achieved in a smaller way the goal he had aspired to in heaven: to have dominion over an entire race of intelligent beings. At first, he thought that they were all his forever. However, God interposed with a plan to win back the loyalty of those humans who would choose Jesus as their supreme Leader. The plan was for Jesus to become a human being and pay the death penalty for humanity. Then those who chose to accept His sacrifice on their behalf and who pledged their loyalty to Him could be restored to fellowship with the Trinity. As a result, there are now two dominions on the earth that seek to win the minds and hearts of human beings to their sides.

Of course, this plan was a direct challenge to Lucifer's dominion over the human race, and he resisted it mightily. Ellen White commented,

Christ entered upon His mission of mercy, and from the manger to the cross was beset by the enemy. Satan contested every inch of ground, exerting his utmost power to overcome Him. Like a tempest temptation after temptation beat upon Him. But the more mercilessly they fell, the more firmly did the Son of God cling to the hand of His Father, and press on in the bloodstained path.

The severity of the conflict through which Christ passed was proportionate to the vastness of the interests involved in His success or failure. . . . Satan sought to overthrow Christ, in order that he himself might continue to reign in this world as supreme.[1]

Unfortunately, throughout human history, Satan has managed to win the minds and hearts of the large majority of humanity to himself—but not all! Some people in every age have pledged their allegiance to God and remained faithful to their commitment.

Satan knew, both from God's promise to Adam and Eve of a Redeemer and from his study of the Old Testament prophecies, that a coming Messiah would challenge his dominion. He also knew that if this Messiah succeeded it would spell the end of his (Satan's) dominion over the world, and he would eventually perish. Thus, Satan realized that it was crucial for him to recognize this Messiah when He appeared on the earth and to do everything in his power to defeat Him. That's why he inspired Herod to destroy all the baby boys in Bethlehem who were two years old or younger. And it's why he approached Jesus in the wilderness with three temptations. However, before getting into a discussion of Satan's three temptations, we need to understand how Jesus prepared Himself to meet those temptations.

Preparing for His temptations

Four factors were involved in Jesus' preparation for Satan's temptations:

1. A close, intimate relationship with His Father
2. A strong character that could endure the conflicts that lay ahead of Him
3. A clear understanding of His mission to rescue sinful human beings by paying the death penalty for their sins
4. A clear understanding of His conflict with Satan over the dominion of the world*

Without each of these factors being fully developed in His mind and His life, Jesus would have failed in His mission to save humanity from the death penalty first pronounced upon Adam and Eve. So let's examine each of these factors.

Intimacy with His Father. We know that during His three and a half years

---

* A fifth reason Christ came to Earth was to reveal God's character of love to a world that perceived Him as a cruel, angry tyrant. However, that issue isn't relevant to Satan's temptation of Jesus, which is the theme of this chapter.

of active ministry Jesus was often in prayer, sometimes all night long (Luke 6:12). We also know that He was a diligent student of the Scriptures—a fact that is evident in the other three kinds of preparations Jesus had to make in order to be ready to meet Satan in the wilderness. Jesus' awareness of the life that lay before Him, especially the final hours, drove Him to seek a profound trust in His Father. We can never approach the depth of Jesus' trust in God, but we should seek to come as close to it as possible.

His character development. It may come as a surprise to you that Jesus had to develop a character that could successfully resist Satan's temptations, both in the wilderness and for every day of His life. However, keep in mind that at the time He was born as a human being, Jesus' mind and emotions were as undeveloped as those of any other human child. Ellen White said that "Jesus was placed where His *character* would be tested."[2] Thus, He had to learn the lessons of self-control the same way the rest of us do. I'm sure that during the early years of His life God intervened to protect Him from Satan's temptations that would have been beyond His ability to deal with. After all, if God won't allow us to be tempted beyond our ability to resist (1 Corinthians 10:13), He would surely have protected His Son in the same way. Ellen White said that "from His earliest years, Jesus was guarded by heavenly angels." But these angels didn't shield Him completely from Satan's temptations, for she continues in the second half of this same sentence as follows: "yet His life was one long struggle against the powers of darkness."[3] Thus, as the young Child "grew and became strong in spirit" (Luke 1:80), God would have allowed Satan increasing access to tempt Him.

There are two ways to develop character. One is to just relax, go with the flow, and take the easy way out of every difficult situation. That's a sure path to developing a character that's unfitted for heaven. I will describe the hard way to develop character in the next few paragraphs.

The first requirement is to cultivate an intimate relationship with God, building trust in Him in every difficult situation. This relationship requires self-discipline to commune with God through the study of His Word and prayer, to serve others, and to worship and fellowship with other believers. And Jesus did all of this. Ellen White said that "His intimate acquaintance with the Scriptures shows how diligently His early years were given to the study of God's word. . . . From His earliest years He was possessed of one purpose; He lived to bless others."[4] In Luke 4:16, we learn that it was His custom to fellowship with others on the Sabbath—a habit that would surely have begun when He was a child.

It's evident that Jesus was very deliberate in developing His character. Ellen White said that "at a very early age, Jesus had begun to act for Himself in the formation of His character."[5]

One of the most important ways we develop character in this life is through dealing with conflict. If we're willing, trials and conflicts can teach us to depend upon God and to trust Him. Did Jesus have to endure conflict during His childhood? Ellen White devoted an entire chapter to this issue in her book *The Desire of Ages*; it's titled "Days of Conflict." She said that Jesus had to endure the efforts of the religious leaders of His time who tried to teach Him to conform to their standards; He had to deal with the misunderstanding of His brothers, because He wasn't like them; and He had friends who criticized Him for refusing to join in their frivolous amusements.[6]

As is true of every other son or daughter of Adam who has developed a holy character, Jesus had to take a personal initiative to study the Old Testament writings. I already pointed out that "His intimate acquaintance with the Scriptures shows how diligently His early years were given to the study of God's word."[7] This was a critical part of His character development. Jesus spent the first thirty years of His life developing a character that could successfully meet Satan's temptations.

His efforts in character development were also part of His gaining an intimate relationship with His heavenly Father.

His mission to die for human sin. The Bible doesn't tell us how Jesus learned that He was the long-awaited Messiah. I'm sure that at some point Mary and Joseph told him about Gabriel's visit to Mary and about Joseph's dream in which Gabriel told Joseph that he should marry Mary. It's also possible that an angel visited Jesus and gave Him some basic instruction about His mission. However, as we've already noted, Jesus was a diligent student of the Old Testament Scriptures, and I believe that most of what He learned of His mission came from that source. In any case, however He learned about His mission, it's evident that by the age of twelve He had a basic understanding of who He was and the nature of His life's work.

I say this because of something Mary said to Him and His response during the time of the family's Passover visit to the temple in Jerusalem. You will recall that it wasn't until the evening of the day Mary and Joseph left to return to Nazareth that they realized Jesus wasn't with them. Thus began a frantic search for Him, and they eventually found Him in the temple, visiting with the scribes and teachers of the law. Mary said, "Son, why have You done this to us? Look, Your father and I have sought You anxiously." Jesus replied, "Why did you seek Me? Did you not know that I must be about My Father's business?" (Luke 2:48, 49, NKJV). Notice that Mary referred to *Joseph* as Jesus' father, but in His reply Jesus clearly understood that His real Father was God. So some time prior to that incident Jesus had gained a basic understanding of who He was and the nature of His life's mission.

Another evidence that Jesus had obtained some understanding of His mission by the time of the Passover visit comes from a comment by Ellen White, again in *The Desire of Ages*. She said that as Jesus watched the Passover rituals in the temple each day, especially the offering of the lambs on the altar of sacrifice, He gained a clearer understanding of their meaning. "Every act seemed to be bound up with His own life. New impulses were awakening within Him. Silent and absorbed, He seemed to be studying out a great problem. The mystery of His mission was opening to the Saviour."[8]

I said earlier that Joseph and Mary would almost certainly have told Jesus about Gabriel's visit to inform Mary that she, a virgin, would give birth to a Son conceived by the Holy Spirit. Remember what the angel said about this Son: "He will be great and will be called the Son of the Most High. The Lord God will give him the throne of his father David, and he will reign over the house of Jacob forever; his kingdom will never end" (Luke 1:31–33). It's very obvious that Gabriel was telling Mary that she would give birth to the long-promised Messiah. But notice that he told her only about the Messiah's *royal* role. There wasn't a word in Gabriel's message to suggest the Messiah's *suffering* role. However, in His visit to the temple Jesus saw the meaning of its services more clearly. The sacrificial rituals "seemed to be bound up with His own life," and "the mystery of His mission was opening to the Saviour."

My point is that, since Mary and Joseph could not have told Jesus about the suffering aspect of His mission, He had to have learned it from some other source. I've suggested that perhaps God sent Gabriel or some other angel to give Jesus an idea of the purpose of His life. Neither the Bible nor Ellen White say anything about this. But even if that did happen, the angel left a lot for Jesus to figure out for Himself. I believe He learned it from a careful study of the Old Testament writings. After Mary and Joseph told Jesus about Gabriel's words, He would have intensified His study of the prophets concerning the Messiah, and when He visited the temple at the age of twelve, He began putting together everything He had learned up to that point. Then, after returning to Nazareth, He would have pursued His study of the prophets even more intently to understand His role in paying the death penalty for human sin.

His conflict with Satan over dominion. How would Jesus have obtained an understanding of His mission to wrest dominion of the world from Satan? We can assume that if God sent an angel to reveal His mission to Him, this angel would have given Him some understanding of that aspect of His life's work. However, since the Bible is totally silent on that point, we can't rely upon it for an explanation. We have to turn to Jesus' study of the Old Testament. So where in the Old Testament would He have gained an understanding of the dominion aspect of His mission?

First, He would have read the prophecies of Ezekiel and Isaiah that we examined in chapter 3 of this book. From Ezekiel 28:11–19 Jesus would have learned of a highly decorated being in heaven who was the covering cherub before God's throne. He would have learned that God created this angel blameless in every way until God *found* evil in him. Ezekiel would also have explained how this angelic being became evil: he became proud of his beauty and splendor. Ezekiel would have told Jesus of God's response to the evil in this angel's heart. God said,

> "I threw you to the earth. . . .
> . . . I made a fire come out from you,
>   and it consumed you,
> and I reduced you to ashes. . . .
> You have come to a horrible end
>   and will be no more" (verses 17–19).

Isaiah 14:12–15 would especially have informed Jesus about Lucifer's ambition for dominion. He would have learned that this supreme angelic being aspired to raise his throne "above the stars [angels] of God" and make himself "like the Most High" (verses 13, 14). In other words, Satan wanted to put himself in charge of the government of the universe! But this angel did not succeed. He fell from heaven, was "cast down to the earth," and was "brought down to the grave, to the depths of the pit" (verses 12, 15).* Jesus would have learned from both Ezekiel and Isaiah that Satan's ultimate fate would be annihilation.

But where would Jesus have obtained the idea that *He* was destined to wrest dominion over the world from Satan? The answer is simple: from the first three chapters of Genesis. In Genesis 1:26, Jesus would have learned that God gave dominion over the world to Adam and Eve, and from

---

* In the Hebrew language during Old Testament times, the word *pit* was often used to mean "the grave."

Genesis 2:16, 17, He would have learned of God's warning to Adam that they should not eat fruit from the tree of the knowledge of good and evil, because the penalty for transgression was death. From Genesis 3, He would have learned that they yielded to Satan's temptation. Then from Genesis 3:15, He would have discovered that one of Eve's descendants would crush Satan's head—that is, destroy him. From there, it wouldn't have been a huge leap to put all these ideas together and conclude that He would be the one to defeat Satan and reclaim the lost dominion over the world.

I said at the beginning of this section that Jesus would have needed to prepare for Satan's temptations in the wilderness in four ways. First, He would have had to develop a very intimate trust relationship with His Father. Second, He would have had to develop a character that could recognize and withstand Satan's temptations. Third, He would have had to gain a clear understanding of His mission to pay the penalty for human sin. And fourth, He would have had to learn that another aspect of His mission was to reclaim the lost dominion over the world that Satan had stolen from Adam and Eve through deception.

We are now ready to investigate Satan's three temptations in the wilderness.

In direct conflict with Satan

From the moment Jesus was born, Satan knew that "he must either conquer or be conquered. The issues of the conflict involved too much to be entrusted to his confederate angels. He must personally conduct the warfare."[9] Immediately following His baptism, "Jesus was led by the Spirit into the desert to be tempted by the devil" (Matthew 4:1). He spent the next forty days and nights fasting and praying. By the end of those forty days, He was weak and famished—and Satan chose this as the time to strike. Ellen White wrote, "Satan knew that the Saviour had gone into the wilderness, and he thought this the best time to approach Him."[10] However, God also had a hand in the temptation of His Son, for Matthew 4:1 says that "Jesus was *led by the Spirit* into the desert to be tempted by the devil" (emphasis added). That sounds strange to our ears, especially since Jesus taught us to pray as part of the Lord's Prayer, "Lead us not into temptation" (Matthew 6:13).

However, we aren't Jesus, whom God sent to save the world from its sins. Jesus came to regain the dominion that Adam and Eve had forfeited when they yielded to Satan's temptation, so He had to deal with Satan directly and in person in order to recover what had been lost. Satan claimed that it was impossible for created intelligences to keep God's law. Jesus had to prove him wrong, and the only way to do that was to allow Himself to be tempted by Satan in person the way Adam and Eve were. Not all temptations are inspired directly by Satan. Some arise from the random circumstances of our lives, and I'm sure Jesus faced some of these temptations too. But in order to wrest back the lost dominion, He also had to face Satan directly, and that's what His temptations in the wilderness were about. That's why Matthew, Mark, and Luke all say that the *Holy Spirit led* Jesus into the desert to be tempted by Satan (Matthew 4:1; Mark 1:12; Luke 4:1). While neither the Bible nor Ellen White say so, I'm sure that Satan planned carefully before he tempted both Eve in Eden and Jesus in the desert but with one significant difference. With Eve, he could approach her only at the forbidden tree, so all he had to do was figure out a strategy for catching her off guard at that one place and then wait for her to wander by alone. With Jesus, he had no idea ahead of time when or where would be the best time to catch Him off guard, so he had to constantly watch Jesus' movements and His circumstances. I'm sure God didn't inform Satan ahead of time that Jesus would be spending forty days in the wilderness. But as the days turned into weeks, with Jesus spending a lot of time fasting and praying, Satan recognized an excellent opportunity. I can just hear him saying, "Aha! Now's the time!"

Satan's three temptations

God seldom warns us about Satan's temptations prior to our encountering them. So if Jesus was to be our example in overcoming temptation, then I'm reasonably certain that He had to recognize Satan's temptations in the desert the same way we recognize ours—by maintaining a close relationship with His Father and being on guard every moment.

The first temptation. Satan approached Jesus with the same strategy he used on Eve: disguising himself and appearing as something or someone other than who he really was. "There came to the Saviour, as if in answer to His prayers, one in the guise of an angel from heaven."[11] And as he did with Eve, Satan tried to get Jesus to doubt God's Word. To Eve, he said, *"Did God really say,* 'You must not eat from any tree in the garden?' " (Genesis 3:1; emphasis added). To Jesus, he said, *"If you are the Son of God,* tell these stones to become bread" (Matthew 4:3; emphasis added). Only a little more than forty days earlier Jesus had heard God say, "You are my Son, whom I love; with you I am well pleased" (Luke 3:22). Now Satan tried to get Jesus to doubt those reassuring words.

Notice that Jesus didn't enter into any conversation with Satan. That had

131

been Eve's first mistake. When Satan asked her, "Did God really say, 'You must not eat from any tree in the garden?' " she tried to explain what God had really said—that they *could* eat of any tree in the garden *except* for the one from which the serpent was speaking to her. The important point is that Jesus didn't try to reason with Satan or explain Himself. He simply quoted a verse from the Bible: "It is written, 'Man does not live on bread alone, but on every word that comes from the mouth of God' " (Matthew 4:4; see Deuteronomy 8:3).

Satan also took advantage of Jesus' circumstances at that moment: He hadn't had a bite to eat for forty days, and the Bible says that "he was hungry" (Matthew 4:2). To say that Jesus was hungry is to put it mildly. He was famished! Satan would never come after you and me with the temptation to work a miracle to satisfy our hunger because he knows—and we know—that we couldn't do it. That's precisely what made Satan's challenge to Jesus so powerful. Because Jesus was divine as well as human, He *could* work a miracle to provide Himself with food. But Jesus had two reasons for refusing Satan's temptation on this point. First, He had a very strict policy of never performing a miracle to benefit Himself. He used His divine power only to bless others. Second, Jesus became a human being with the specific purpose of meeting temptation the way we must, and you and I can't work miracles to provide food when we're hungry. To be like us, Jesus had to depend on God to provide His food. Had He used His divine power to satisfy His hunger by turning stones into bread, He would not have been an example to us in meeting Satan's temptations.

Satan's first temptation for Jesus has other important lessons for us today. Overindulgence of physical desires is rampant in our world today, including everything from the consumption of unhealthful foods and the overeating of good foods to sexual immorality and drunkenness and soaking our brains in street drugs. We violate the laws of health to satisfy our distorted emotions, and we pay a heavy price in various diseases and mental and emotional stress. Worst of all is the damage these wrong habits do to our spiritual nature.

Satan may not demand that we work a miracle to prove we are God's children, but he surely does tempt us to doubt God's love and care for us. The apostle John said, "Now are we the sons [and daughters] of God" (1 John 3:2, KJV). Yet we're afraid that we're too sinful for God to forgive us.

"Oh, but Jesus was sinless," you may say. True enough. He was sinless so that He could pay the death penalty for our sins and thereby gain the right to forgive us, because we aren't sinless. And His death on our behalf was precisely *because* we are *not* sinless. He died so that we can be absolutely certain that once we accept Him as our Savior, repent of our sins, and confess them, we *truly are* God's sons and daughters.

So don't let Satan trap you into the idea that you aren't good enough for God to accept you. For even if you haven't yet met the conditions, you still can.

The second temptation. The devil lost with his first temptation, but he had two backups. In his next temptation, he took Jesus "to the holy city and had him stand on the highest point of the temple."* Then he said, "*If you are the Son of God, . . .* throw yourself down. For it is written: 'He [God] will command his angels concerning you, and they will lift you up in their hands, so that you will not strike your foot against a stone' " (Matthew 4:5, 6; emphasis added; see also Psalm 91:11, 12).

It's easy to wonder what was so tempting about that. Trying to get Jesus to turn a stone into bread at a time when He was famished makes sense. But no normal person would be tempted to throw himself or herself off the side of a cliff! That would be plain stupid, and I'm sure Satan understood that as well as you and I do.

There were at least two issues going on in this temptation that help us to make sense of it. The first was the same as in Satan's temptation to turn stones into bread. Both temptations were prefaced with the words, "If you are the Son of God . . ." Satan was demanding that Jesus prove what he (Satan) already knew to be true: that Jesus truly was God's Son. The second issue was that Satan was trying to get Jesus to manipulate God. In the first temptation, Satan tried to get Jesus to doubt God and perform a miracle on His own behalf. In the second temptation, beside trying to get Jesus to doubt God, Satan also tried to get Jesus to create a situation that would demand that *God* perform a miracle on Jesus' behalf. And since Jesus had quoted the Bible in response to Satan's first temptation, this time Satan managed to find a Bible text he could twist in order to get Jesus to demand a miracle from God.

But Jesus wasn't persuaded. Again He didn't try to reason with Satan. He just quoted another verse back to him: "It is also written: 'Do not put the Lord your God to the test,' " or, as the New King James Version states it, "You shall not tempt the LORD your God" (Matthew 4:7; see Deuteronomy 6:16).

The third temptation. By this time, Satan realized that Jesus knew exactly who he was, and he ceased all efforts to conceal himself. He took Jesus

---

* Luke records this temptation as the third one, and Matthew's third temptation is Luke's second one (Luke 4:1–13).

to a very high mountain and made all the world's fairest kingdoms pass in front of Him. Ellen White described the scene that Jesus looked upon: "The sunlight lay on templed cities, marbled palaces, fertile fields, and fruit-laden vineyards. The traces of evil were hidden. The eyes of Jesus, so lately greeted by gloom and desolation, now gazed upon a scene of unsurpassed loveliness and prosperity."[12] Then Satan said, "All this I will give you . . . if you will bow down and worship me" (Matthew 4:9).

Satan understood all too well the nature of Christ's mission in the world. He had read the Old Testament prophets, and he knew that the Lord would lay "on him [Jesus] the iniquity of us all" (Isaiah 53:6). He knew that Jesus was to be "oppressed and afflicted" and "led like a lamb to the slaughter" (verse 7). That's the last thing Satan wanted. He was saying, in effect, "I have a better plan for You, Jesus. If You accept my offer, You won't have to suffer the agony of Gethsemane, the trial before the Sanhedrin and Pilate, and the torture of scourging and the cross."

However, as he had with Eve in Eden, Satan made statements in tempting Jesus that were misleading and only partly true. Satan told Eve that by eating the fruit she would know good and evil as God did. What he *didn't* tell her is that his statement that she would not die as a result was a bald-faced lie. Nor did he warn her that by eating the fruit she would bring untold suffering upon herself, her husband, and the world.

It was the same with Jesus. What Satan did not tell Him was that he, Satan, held dominion over the world only at God's discretion and that by bowing down to him Jesus would lose the very conflict He had come into the world to win! Ellen White commented, "When the tempter offered to Christ the kingdom and glory of the world, he was proposing that Christ should yield up the real kingship of the world, and hold dominion subject to Satan."[13]

Satan succeeded brilliantly with Eve. Fortunately, he utterly failed with Jesus. Jesus' response to Satan was curt and to the point: "Away from me, Satan!" Then He quoted another verse of Scripture: "It is written, 'Worship the Lord your God, and serve him only' " (Matthew 4:10; see Deuteronomy 6:13).

Satan approaches us today using the same strategies he used with Eve and Jesus. He tempts us to believe that it's OK to lose our temper, because we perceive that we've been treated unfairly, when the best solution to the problem is to reply calmly, stating the issues, taking personal responsibility where that's needed, and pointing out facts on the other side of the question that shed a different light on the problem. Satan tempts us to make money or position or power our highest priority. He tempts us to indulge in pleasure and entertainment while we neglect Bible study, prayer, and fellowship with other believers. Or he tempts us to eat food that tastes good but isn't good for us and drink that which makes us feel good but clouds our minds so that we fail to understand the spiritual lessons God wants us to learn. One of Satan's cleverest and most successful strategies is to get us worked up emotionally to the point that our feelings override our reason and common sense.

The aftermath of the three temptations

Luke informs us that "when the devil had finished all this tempting, he left him [Jesus] until an opportune time" (Luke 4:13). Ellen White said that "Satan had no power to resist . . . [Christ's] command. Writhing with humiliation and rage, he was forced to withdraw from the presence of the world's Redeemer."[14]

Jesus, on the other hand, "fell exhausted to the earth, with the pallor of death upon His face. The angels of heaven had watched the conflict, beholding their loved Commander as He passed through inexpressible suffering to make a way of escape for us. He had endured the test, greater than we shall ever be called to endure. The angels now ministered to the Son of God as He lay like one dying. He was strengthened with food, comforted with the message of His Father's love and the assurance that all heaven triumphed in His victory."[15]

What a victory for Jesus, for all heaven, and for you and me!

---

1. Ellen G. White, *Reflecting Christ* (Hagerstown, MD: Review and Herald® Pub. Assn., 1985), 58.

2. White, *The Desire of Ages*, 71; emphasis added.

3. Ibid.

4. Ibid., 70.

5. Ibid., 86.

6. Ibid., 85, 88, 89.

7. Ibid., 70.

8. Ibid., 78.

9. Ibid., 116.

10. Ibid., 114.

11. Ibid., 118.

12. Ibid., 129.

13. Ibid., 130.

14. Ibid.

15. Ibid., 131.

CHAPTER 15

Jesus in Gethsemane

After being tempted by Satan in the wilderness, Jesus spent three and a half years teaching and healing the Jewish people in Palestine. He walked their streets and ate their food. He lived the life of an itinerate preacher, but He was much more than that. He was God in the flesh, living out God's love for lost humanity. When Philip asked Him to "show us the Father," Jesus replied, "Anyone who has seen me has seen the Father" (John 14:8, 9).

Throughout these years of ministry, Jesus knew that at some point in the near future He would be killed. This was so strange to His disciples' ears that the first time He told them about it Peter rebuked Him. " 'Never, Lord,' he said. 'This shall never happen to you!' " (Matthew 16:22).

Peter meant well, but notice Jesus' reply: "Get behind me, Satan! You are a stumbling block to me; you do not have in mind the things of God, but the things of men" (verse 23). To use a modern expression, Jesus said, "Get out of My sight!" But why did Jesus respond so forcefully? Put yourself in His place. Suppose you knew that sometime in the next few months you would be violently persecuted and murdered, causing you excruciating mental and physical pain. How would you feel? Fear would be a mild word.

But why did Jesus address Peter as Satan? Because at that moment Satan was using Peter's concern for Jesus' well-being to tempt Him to give up going to the cross, and Jesus was not going to allow profound feelings of fear and pain to deter Himself from what He had *come* to do and what He knew He *had* to do. The fate of humanity lay in His choice, whether to go through with the pain or give up and return to heaven. Satan was determined to prevent Jesus from going to the cross, and Jesus was even more determined that He *would* go to the cross.

The Kingdom of Light and the Kingdom of Darkness were battling it out again. But the real battle would begin a few months later in Gethsemane.

The Kingdom of Light versus the Kingdom of Darkness

Sometimes in a war between two earthly powers there's a decisive battle that determines the outcome of the conflict, even though other battles remain to be fought. The Battle of Normandy during World War II is a good example. In spite of bad weather, the Allies crossed the English Channel and landed their troops on French soil, taking the Germans by surprise. Significant battles were yet to be fought, but Germany was doomed.

That's how it was in the conflict between the Kingdom of Light and the Kingdom of Darkness during Christ's time on Earth. The decisive battle was not fought at the cross. It was fought in Gethsemane. I don't say this to minimize the significance of the cross in any way, because that's where Jesus paid the price for human sin. That's why the cross is the central symbol of Christianity. That's why Paul could exclaim, "May I never boast except in the cross of our Lord Jesus Christ" (Galatians 6:14). It's why he could tell the believers in Corinth that he was determined "to know nothing while I was with you except Jesus Christ and him crucified" (1 Corinthians 2:2). It's also why the billions of angels surrounding God's throne can sing in a loud voice, "Worthy is the Lamb, who was slain, to receive power and wealth and wisdom and strength and honor and glory and praise" (Revelation 5:12).

Nevertheless, Gethsemane was a crucial lead-up to the cross. If Gethsemane hadn't happened, the cross would never have happened. So let's take a good hard look at Gethsemane.

At the conclusion of the Last Supper, Jesus and His disciples sang a hymn and left for Gethsemane, which was on the Mount of Olives (Mark 14:26). As they approached the garden, Jesus was gripped with a profound sadness. He said, "My soul is overwhelmed with sorrow to the point of death" (Matthew 26:38). Here's how Ellen White described the scene: "As He proceeded, this strange sadness deepened; yet they [His disciples] dared not question Him as to the cause. His form swayed as if He were about to fall. . . . Every step that He now took was with labored effort. He groaned aloud, as if suffering under the pressure of a terrible burden. Twice His companions supported Him, or He would have fallen to the earth."[1]

When they arrived at Gethsemane, Jesus asked nine of His disciples to stay near the entrance to the garden while He and Peter, James, and John went deeper into the olive grove (verses 36, 37). Then leaving the three disciples and going alone a little farther, "he fell with his face to the ground and prayed, 'My Father, if it is possible, may this cup be taken from me. Yet not as I will, but as you will' " (verse 39).

By this time, Jesus was experiencing such extreme stress and anxiety that "his sweat was like drops of blood falling to the ground" (Luke 22:44). Why was that? Based on his research into the physical and psychological effects of Jesus' experience in Gethsemane, His scourging, and His crucifixion, author Terry McDermott made the following comment about Jesus' sweating blood:

> There is a rare condition called hematidrosis that may occur in cases of extreme anxiety caused by fear. . . . It manifests as sweat that contains blood or blood pigments.
>
> Anxiety due to intense fear affects the autonomic nervous system. Fear triggers the amygdala, which is the brain's fear centre. We know the reaction as the fight-or-flight response. The response results in the following: profuse sweating (diaphoresis), accelerated heart rate, vasoconstriction of blood vessels, increased blood pressure, diversion of blood from non-essential areas in order to increase blood perfusion to the brain and muscles of the arms and legs, skin pallor, and decreased function of the digestive system, which may result in vomiting and abdominal cramps.
>
> Jesus' fight-or-flight response lasted several hours as He prayed alone while His apostles slept nearby. He would have been completely exhausted and dehydrated because of diaphoresis and vomiting.[2]

As Jesus prayed to His Father in Gethsemane, He was obviously experiencing extreme anxiety and fear because of the torture He knew He would experience during approximately the next eighteen hours. Terry McDermott explained the effects of the crown of thorns, the flogging, and the crucifixion as we will see in the next two chapters, and this will help you to understand the reason for Jesus' sweat mixed with blood in Gethsemane.

However, anticipation of the physical pain He would experience was only part of the cause of Jesus' profound fear. There were two other causes: separation from His Father and His struggle with Satan's Kingdom of Darkness.

Separation from His Father

Ellen White's description in *The Desire of Ages* of Jesus' struggle in Gethsemane is dramatic and detailed. For that reason, I will quote extensively from what she said and keep my comments to a minimum.

I pointed out in the chapter about Jesus' birth that He was born with the Holy Spirit already dwelling in His mind and heart. That was necessary, because otherwise the Savior would have needed a Savior. And Jesus kept that relationship with His Father through the Holy Spirit for the rest of His life—until Gethsemane. The reason He lost it there is simple: He had to die the death of every sinner. How will sinners who don't experience the new birth die? Without the Holy Spirit; without a relationship with God and Jesus.

Jesus Himself, on the cross, cried out, "My God, my God, why have you forsaken me?" (Matthew 27:46). God had removed His presence from His Son. Ellen White made it very clear that God actually began removing His presence from Jesus in Gethsemane:

- Jesus "seemed to be shut out from the light of God's sustaining presence."[3]
- "He felt that by sin He was being separated from His Father."[4]
- "Christ felt His unity with the Father broken up."[5]
- "Christ's soul was filled with dread of separation from God."[6]
- "Could mortals have viewed the amazement of the angelic host as in silent grief they watched the Father separating His beams of light, love, and glory from His beloved Son, they would better understand how offensive in His sight is sin."[7]

The withdrawal of God's presence from Jesus in Gethsemane is clear evidence that He was beginning even then to pay the penalty for humanity's sins. But there was one who bitterly opposed what was taking place in that grove of olive trees.

The decision to save humanity
Lucifer had hated Michael in heaven with a bitter passion. He hated Him even more when, after he was cast out and requested reinstatement, Christ told him that this was impossible. Satan's hatred was intensified again when God (probably Christ) informed Eve that one of her descendants would crush Satan's head (Genesis 3:15). Satan watched for the coming descendant, and Satan tried to have Him killed when He was born, but God outwitted Satan by removing Jesus to Egypt.

When Jesus resisted Satan's temptations in the wilderness, Satan's hatred rose to a fever pitch—and so did his anxiety, I'm sure. Satan's last chance to defeat his bitterest enemy began when Jesus stepped into Gethsemane, so Satan unleashed every weapon of hell against Him. He knew that he had fewer than twenty-four hours to accomplish the task. It wasn't a physical wrestling match. Satan couldn't use a sword to compel Jesus to yield to him. As has always been the case in the conflict between the Kingdoms of

Light and Darkness, Satan had to use persuasion. Ellen White describes the struggle: "Now [in Gethsemane] the tempter had come for the last fearful struggle. For this he had been preparing during the three years of Christ's ministry. Everything was at stake with him. If he failed here, his hope of mastery was lost; the kingdoms of the world would finally become Christ's; he himself would be overthrown and cast out. But if Christ could be overcome, the earth would become Satan's kingdom, and the human race would be forever in his power."[8]

Jesus had to deal with this struggle at the same time that the Father was withdrawing His power and presence from Him, for "Christ's soul was filled with dread of separation from God."[9]

> In its harshest features Satan pressed the situation upon the Redeemer: The people who claim to be above all others in temporal and spiritual advantages have rejected You. They are seeking to destroy You, the foundation, the center and seal of the promises made to them as a peculiar people. One of Your own disciples, who has listened to Your instruction, and has been among the foremost in church activities, will betray You. One of Your most zealous followers will deny You. All will forsake You. Christ's whole being abhorred the thought. That those whom He had undertaken to save, those whom He loved so much, should unite in the plots of Satan, this pierced His soul. The conflict was terrible. . . . The sins of men weighed heavily upon Christ, and the sense of God's wrath against sin was crushing out His life.[10]

> Jesus . . . fell prostrate, overcome by the horror of a great darkness. The humanity of the Son of God trembled in that trying hour. . . . The awful moment had come—that moment which was to decide the destiny of the world. The fate of humanity trembled in the balance. Christ might even now refuse to drink the cup apportioned to guilty man. It was not yet too late. He might wipe the bloody sweat from His brow, and leave man to perish in his iniquity. He might say, Let the transgressor receive the penalty of his sin, and I will go back to My Father. Will the Son of God drink the bitter cup of humiliation and agony? Will the innocent suffer the consequences of the curse of sin, to save the guilty? The words fall tremblingly from the pale lips of Jesus, "O My Father, if this cup may not pass away from Me, except I drink it, Thy will be done."

Three times has He uttered that prayer. Three times has humanity shrunk from the last, crowning sacrifice. But now the history of the human race comes up before the world's Redeemer. He sees that the transgressors of the law, if left to themselves, must perish. He sees the helplessness of man. He sees the power of sin. The woes and lamentations of a doomed world rise before Him. He beholds its impending fate, and *His decision is made*. He will save man at any cost to Himself. He accepts His baptism of blood, that through Him perishing millions may gain everlasting life. . . .

Having made the decision, He fell dying to the ground.[11]

This is why I said earlier that the decisive battle between Christ and Satan was not fought on the cross. It was fought in Gethsemane. While recovery of dominion over the physical planet was involved, the real issue wasn't territory. The real issue was a choice, a decision, and it was up to Jesus to make that decision. God didn't force it upon Him. Jesus really could have chosen to return to heaven. During those agonizing hours in Gethsemane, the destiny of the world truly did tremble in His hands. And Jesus made the decision.

He . . . [would] save man at any cost to Himself. . . .

Christ's agony did not cease [following His decision], but His depression and discouragement left Him. The storm had in nowise abated, but He who was its object was strengthened to meet its fury. He came forth calm and serene. A heavenly peace rested upon His bloodstained face. He had borne that which no human being could ever bear; for He had tasted the sufferings of death for every man.[12]

Jesus' disciples didn't observe His suffering, because they were asleep. But there were other observers.

Angels beheld the Saviour's agony. They saw their Lord enclosed by legions of satanic forces, His nature weighed down with a shuddering, mysterious dread. There was silence in heaven. No harp was touched. Could mortals have viewed the amazement of the angelic host as in silent grief they watched the Father separating His beams of light, love, and glory from His beloved Son, they would better understand how offensive in His sight is sin.

The worlds unfallen and the heavenly angels had watched with intense interest as the conflict drew to its close. Satan and his confederacy of evil, the legions of apostasy, watched intently this great crisis in the work of redemption.[13]

Conclusion

Try though we may, we can but dimly comprehend the depth of Jesus' feelings as He pleaded with His Father in Gethsemane. We will gain a much greater understanding in eternity; yet this won't even approach what He really endured that night in the garden. The fate of the world depended on His decision. No other human being in history has had that responsibility. The president of the United States may be the most influential person on the planet, but there's no way he can determine its destiny. Jesus could—and He did.

What would have happened to the world had Jesus chosen to abandon it and return to heaven? I believe God would have had no choice but to destroy it, if not immediately, eventually.

It wasn't just the fate of the world that was determined by Jesus' decision in the garden. The destiny of the entire universe depended upon the choice Jesus made that night in Gethsemane. Speaking on the condition of the world after four thousand years of sin, Ellen White stated the following:

> Sin had become a science, and vice was consecrated as a part of religion. Rebellion had struck its roots deep into the heart, and the hostility of man was most violent against heaven. . . .
>
> With intense interest the unfallen worlds had watched to see Jehovah arise, and sweep away the inhabitants of the earth. And if God should do this, Satan was ready to carry out his plan for securing to himself the allegiance of heavenly beings. He had declared that the principles of God's government make forgiveness impossible. Had the world been destroyed, he would have claimed that his accusations were proved true. He was ready to cast blame upon God, *and to spread his rebellion to the worlds above.*[14]

Now I don't think for a moment that had Jesus failed to complete the plan of redemption, God would have allowed Satan to claim sovereignty over the rest of the universe. As I see it, God would have had at least two options. One would have been to destroy Satan, his angels, and the world immediately or at some point in the future. The other would have been to allow Satan to continue his form of government on the earth until the human race became extinct from people killing each other or dying out from their physical, mental, and moral degeneration.

But if Jesus had returned to His Father with His mission unfulfilled, He would have broken a promise that He and the Father had made to Their loyal followers for four thousand years: that They would send a Redeemer. Had Jesus returned to heaven with His mission unfulfilled, He would have had to renege on that promise. What would this have done to His reputation among the loyal inhabitants of the universe? Could they truly have trusted any other promises He might make to them in the future? Was He really as powerful as He claimed to be? This doubt would eventually have led to further rebellion, and the whole sad history of sin would have been repeated. And where would it all have ended? Would God ultimately have had to destroy all His created intelligences and start over?

Fortunately, we don't have to waste our time wondering what would have happened had Jesus returned to His Father with His mission unfulfilled, because Jesus *did* make the choice to go through with the completion of the plan of salvation, and we *are* assured of eternal life in His kingdom—all because He made the right decision in Gethsemane!

"Worthy is the Lamb, who was slain!" (Revelation 5:12).

---

1. White, *The Desire of Ages*, 686.

2. Terry McDermott, "The Physical Effects of the Scourging and Crucifixion of Jesus," *Catholic Insight*, March 13, 2014, http://catholicinsight.com/the-physical-effects-of-the -scourging-and-crucifixion-of-Jesus/.

3. White, *The Desire of Ages*, 685.

4. Ibid., 686.

5. Ibid.

6. Ibid., 687.

7. Ibid., 693.

8. Ibid., 686, 687.

9. Ibid., 687.

10. Ibid.

11. Ibid., 690, 693; emphasis added.

12. Ibid., 693, 694.

13. Ibid., 693.

14. Ibid., 37; emphasis added.

CHAPTER 16

Jesus' Trial

I t will be helpful to consider two issues before we get into our discussion of Jesus' trial before the Sanhedrin, Pilate, and Herod.

First, the issue of Jewish perceptions about the Messiah. Expectation was running high among the Jews that the Messiah was about to appear. After all, they could read Daniel's seventy-week prophecy and do the math just as easily as we can. The problem was with their expectations of the Messiah's mission. They were suffering under the heavy hand of Rome, and they received hope from Daniel's prophecy about a great image that would "crush all those kingdoms and bring them to an end, but . . . will itself endure forever" (Daniel 2:44). This fed their anticipation of a Messiah who would destroy the Roman Empire, leaving Israel as the world's only superpower.

Now stop and think what would be going through the minds of these leaders in Israel. They would have been savoring the glory of the Messiah appointing them to high positions in the new empire. But then along comes this humble carpenter's Son who wanders all over Galilee and Judea teaching the people and supposedly performing all kinds of miracles—and who claims that, of all people, *He*, the illegitimate son of Mary, is the Messiah! It didn't make sense, given their expectation of a conquering Messiah who would defeat the Romans and lead Israel to worldly glory. To make matters worse, this so-called Messiah was gaining a *huge* following among the common people, who of course were totally unqualified to properly evaluate His claim.

Even Jesus' astonishing miracle of raising Lazarus from the dead failed to persuade these proud leaders of the Jewish nation that He was who He claimed to be. To the contrary, this only made them more firm in their decision that they had to get rid of Jesus. When the leadership learned that Jesus had raised Lazarus to life, they "called a meeting of the Sanhedrin." They asked,

"What are we accomplishing? . . . Here is this man performing many miraculous signs. If we let him go on like this, everyone will believe in him, and then the Romans will come and take away both our place and our nation."

Then one of them, named Caiaphas, who was high priest that year, spoke up, . . . "It is better for you that one man die for the people than that the whole nation perish" (John 11:47–50).

This is crystal-clear evidence of their selfish motives.

The second issue we need to discuss is one of Satan's key strategies in Jesus' trial. In chapter 4, I pointed out that our minds—our intellectual powers—are supposed to be in charge of our feelings; but it's possible for our feelings to override our reason, causing us to act on our feelings instead of what we know to be true. We humans have a variety of emotions, including the ability to experience joy, fear, anger, jealousy, and pain, to name a few. Joy is a positive emotion, and Satan wasn't interested in using that on the Sanhedrin. He used the negative emotions. The evidence of Jesus' messiahship was overwhelming, but the thinking of the Sanhedrin was so blinded by pride and selfish ambition that they *could not* see it. Satan had almost full control of the minds of these leaders, especially Annas and Caiaphas.

Jesus' trial before the Sanhedrin

The Roman soldiers arrested Jesus in Gethsemane and took Him to the place where the Sanhedrin was meeting. False witnesses were brought in to testify, but they couldn't get their stories to agree. Finally, two witnesses testified* that Jesus had said, "I am able to destroy the temple of God and rebuild it in three days" (Matthew 26:61). But when Caiaphas asked Jesus to respond to this testimony, He remained silent. So Caiaphas demanded that Jesus declare under oath whether He was "the Christ, the Son of God."† Jesus replied, "Yes, it is as you say. . . . But I say to all of you: In the future you will see the Son of Man sitting at the right hand of the Mighty One and coming on the clouds of heaven" (verses 63, 64).

Ellen White made the following significant comment about Caiaphas's reaction to Jesus' reply:

The words of Christ startled the high priest. The thought that there was to be a resurrection of the dead, when all would stand at the bar of God, to be rewarded according to their works, was a thought of terror to Caiaphas.

---

* Jewish law required that in a capital case two witnesses had to testify to the same evidence (Deuteronomy 17:6). The Jewish leaders obviously had a hard time meeting this legal requirement, but they finally made it with fabricated evidence.

† The Hebrew word *Messiah* means "anointed one," which is also the meaning of the Greek word *Christ*. So the high priest was asking Jesus whether He claimed to be the Messiah.

He did not wish to believe that in future he would receive sentence according to his works. There rushed before his mind as a panorama the scenes of the final judgment. . . . For a moment he felt as if [he were] standing before the eternal Judge. . . .

[But] the scene passed from the priest's vision, . . . [and] he was maddened by satanic fury.[1]

Caiaphas tore his robe and exclaimed, "He has spoken blasphemy! Why do we need any more witnesses?" (verse 65). The entire Sanhedrin agreed that Jesus deserved to die.

"Then they spit in his face and struck him with their fists. Others slapped him and said, 'Prophesy to us, Christ. Who hit you?' " (verses 67, 68).

Ellen White described the scene: "When the condemnation of Jesus was pronounced by the judges, a satanic fury took possession of the people. The roar of voices was like that of wild beasts. The crowd made a rush toward Jesus, crying, He is guilty, put Him to death! Had it not been for the Roman soldiers, Jesus would not have lived to be nailed to the cross of Calvary. He would have been torn in pieces before His judges, had not the Roman authorities interfered, and by force of arms restrained the violence of the mob."[2]

Something else was going on outside the vision of the angry rabble. Again in the words of Ellen White: "The angels of God faithfully recorded every insulting look, word, and act against their beloved Commander. One day the base men who scorned and spat upon the calm, pale face of Christ will look upon it in its glory, shining brighter than the sun."[3]

It's important to understand what was taking place in the Sanhedrin's judgment hall. In Gethsemane, Satan had used emotional pressure to try to get Jesus to give up the struggle to save humanity and return to His comfortable home in heaven. He pressed fear of the torture Jesus would experience in the following twenty-four hours and the ingratitude of the Jews— especially the lethargy and disinterest of His disciples. But Satan failed. Jesus decided to go through with His sacrifice to save humanity and secure the universe against evil ever arising again.

Now, in Jesus' trial, Satan used the intimidation of the mob and physical violence in an effort to get Jesus either to use His divinity to strike down His persecutors or to give in to His sense of the injustice at the way His persecutors were treating Him. Satan was trying to get Jesus to lash out in anger at His persecutors. Fortunately, in Jesus' trial before the Sanhedrin, Satan lost again. But he wasn't through yet. Other opportunities remained.

Jesus' trial before Pilate

The first thing you need to understand about Jesus' appearance before Pilate is that the Roman governor was afraid of the Jewish leaders over whom he was supposed to rule. This caused him to be hesitant and vacillating when what he knew to be his duty as a ruler clashed with their wishes. Satan used this character trait to his advantage.

The Jews completed their judgment of Jesus shortly after sunrise on Friday morning and immediately brought Him before Pilate. They understood the governor's weakness, and they hoped for a quick decision from him to have Jesus put to death. Pilate was at first irritated that the Jews had gotten him out of bed—or at least interrupted his early morning preparation for the day, and he was determined to give the quick decision the Jewish leaders wanted.[4] However, one look at Jesus brought him up short.

> He had had to deal with all kinds of criminals; but never before had a man bearing marks of such goodness and nobility been brought before him. . . .
>
> Christ's appearance made a favorable impression on Pilate. . . . He resolved to demand of the Jews their charges against the prisoner.[5]

Pilate asked the Jewish leaders what accusations they were bringing against Jesus. Knowing that they had a very weak case, they answered evasively: "If he were not a criminal, . . . we would not have handed him over to you." So Pilate told them, "Take him yourselves and judge him by your own law." They replied that they were bringing him to Pilate because under Roman law only the governor appointed by Rome could sign off on a criminal's execution (John 18:30, 31). Pilate wasn't impressed. By this time, the Jews had accused Jesus of claiming to be "the king of the Jews" (Matthew 27:11), so Pilate went back inside his palace and ordered that Jesus be brought to him. When the two were alone, Pilate asked Jesus, "Are you the king of the Jews?" (John 18:33). Jesus could tell that Pilate was under the conviction of the Holy Spirit,[6] so He replied with another question: "Is that your own idea, . . . or did others talk to you about me?" Pilate was irritated. " 'Am I a Jew?' . . . [he] replied. 'It was your people and your chief priests who handed you over to me. What is it you have done?' " (verses 33–35).

Jesus wanted to assure the governor that He wasn't trying to raise an army against the Roman government (which was the very thing the Jewish leaders were looking for their Messiah to do!), so He said,

> "My kingdom is not of this world. If it were, my servants would fight to prevent my arrest by the Jews. But now my kingdom is from another place." . . .
>
> . . . With this he [Pilate] went out again to the Jews and said, "I find no basis for a charge against him" (verses 36, 38).

"Pilate at this time had no thought of condemning Jesus,"[7] and this infuriated the Jewish leaders. "They insisted, 'He stirs up the people all over Judea by his teaching. He started in Galilee and has come all the way here' " (Luke 23:5). Pilate "knew that the Jews had accused Him [Jesus] through hatred and prejudice. He knew what his duty was. Justice demanded that Christ should be immediately released. *But Pilate dreaded the ill will of the people.*"[8] He saw a way out of his dilemma when he heard that Jesus was from Galilee. Herod was the governor of Galilee, where Jesus had lived for thirty years, and Herod happened to be in Jerusalem at the time. So passing Jesus off to Herod's jurisdiction, Pilate "delivered Jesus again to the soldiers, and amid the jeers and insults of the mob he was hurried to the judgment hall of Herod."[9]

In my imagination, I can picture Pilate smiling as he watched the Roman soldiers leading Jesus out of his presence, followed by those pesky Jewish leaders. I can hear him congratulating himself for getting rid of the problem so easily.

Jesus before Herod

Herod had heard about Jesus and was glad to see Him (verse 8). At first, when he received news of Jesus' miracles, he thought Jesus might be John the Baptist raised from the dead (Matthew 14:1, 2; Mark 6:16), and this filled him with terror. However, Herod knew that Jesus wasn't John by the time Pilate sent Jesus to him, and he was anxious to meet Him, because he hoped that Jesus would perform one of His miracles in his presence. Herod plied Jesus with many questions, but Jesus "maintained a profound silence."[10] During this entire time, "the chief priests and the teachers of the law were standing there, vehemently accusing him" (Luke 23:10). "Herod was irritated by . . . [Jesus'] silence. It seemed to indicate utter indifference to his authority. . . . He angrily threatened Jesus, who still remained unmoved and silent."[11] Hundreds of years before, Isaiah had predicted that the Messiah

> was oppressed and afflicted,
> yet he did not open his mouth;
> he was led like a lamb to the slaughter,
> and as a sheep before her shearers is silent,
> so he did not open his mouth (Isaiah 53:7).

Failing to get Jesus to speak to him, Herod tried a different strategy. Knowing that Jesus performed miracles of healing, he called for sick and deformed people to be brought in, and when they arrived, Herod ordered Jesus to work a miracle and heal them. He "promised that if Christ would perform some miracle in his presence, He should be released."[12] Satan was clearly the inspiration behind that promise, for if Jesus had worked a miracle to deliver Himself from the persecution He was enduring, the plan of salvation would have been broken, and Satan would have been the victor.

Herod's call for Jesus to save Himself by healing a few people in his presence filled the Jewish leaders with fear lest He should now work a miracle. "Of all things they most dreaded an exhibition of His power. Such a manifestation would prove a deathblow to their plans. . . . In great anxiety, [they] urged their accusations against Him. Raising their voices, they declared, He is a traitor, a blasphemer. He works His miracles through the power given Him by Beelzebub, the prince of the devils. The hall became a scene of confusion, some crying one thing and some another."[13]

But through it all, Jesus spoke not a word. Turning to the multitude, Herod angrily denounced Jesus as an impostor, and he and his soldiers ridiculed and mocked Jesus (Luke 23:11).

Instantly, the crowd made a rush for Jesus. "Like wild beasts, the crowd darted upon their prey. Jesus was dragged this way and that, Herod joining the mob in seeking to humiliate the Son of God. Had not the Roman soldiers interposed, and forced back the maddened throng, the Saviour would have been torn in pieces."[14] Satan controlled the minds and actions of the Jewish leaders and the crowd that was trying to break Jesus, but so far he had been unsuccessful. The war between the Kingdom of Light and the Kingdom of Darkness was approaching its end, and Satan was getting desperate. He realized that bringing Jesus to Herod hadn't achieved his desired objective. In spite of his anger at Jesus, Herod "dared not ratify the condemnation of Christ,"[15] so he dressed Him in a royal robe and sent Him back to Pilate (verse 11).

Back to Pilate

Pilate was *not* happy to see Jesus brought back to him for the final decision. He and Herod both realized that Jesus was innocent, but both feared the Jewish leaders and the rabble that accompanied them. "Pilate called together the chief priests, the rulers and the people, and said to them, 'You brought me this man as one who was inciting the people to rebellion. I have examined him in your presence and have found no basis for your charges against him. Neither has Herod, for he sent him back to us; as you can see, he has done nothing to deserve death. Therefore I will punish him and then release him' " (verses 13–17).

These events were all taking place at the time of the Passover feast, and "it was the governor's custom at the Feast to release a prisoner chosen by the crowd. At that time they had a notorious prisoner, called Barabbas. So when the crowd had gathered, Pilate asked them, 'Which one do you want me to release to you: Barabbas, or Jesus who is called Christ?' " (Matthew 27:15–17). The chief priests and the elders persuaded the crowd to ask for Barabbas and to have Jesus executed.

> "Which of the two do you want me to release to you?" asked the governor.
> "Barabbas," they answered.
> "What shall I do, then, with Jesus who is called Christ?" Pilate asked.
> They all answered, "Crucify him!"
> "Why? What crime has he committed?" asked Pilate.
> But they shouted all the louder, "Crucify him!" (verses 21–23).

Ellen White described the scene in vivid language:

> Like the bellowing of wild beasts came the answer of the mob, "Release unto us Barabbas!" Louder and louder swelled the cry, Barabbas! Barabbas! Thinking that the people had not understood his question, Pilate asked, "Will ye that I release unto you the King of the Jews?" But they cried out again, "Away with this Man, and release unto us Barabbas"! "What shall I do then with Jesus which is called Christ?" Pilate asked. Again the surging multitude roared like demons. *Demons themselves, in human form, were in the crowd*, and what could be expected but the answer, "Let Him be crucified"?[16]

Apparently, it hadn't occurred to Pilate that the mob would demand Christ's crucifixion, which was a horrible way to die, and he "was troubled.

150

He had not thought it would come to that. He shrank from delivering an innocent man to the most ignominious and cruel death that could be inflicted."[17] Three times Pilate tried to save Jesus from execution. Ellen White commented, "Wonder, O heavens! and be astonished, O earth! Behold the oppressor and the oppressed. A maddened throng enclose the Saviour of the world. Mocking and jeering are mingled with the coarse oaths of blasphemy. His lowly birth and humble life are commented upon by the unfeeling mob. His claim to be the Son of God is ridiculed, and the vulgar jest and insulting sneer are passed from lip to lip."[18]

Far more was going on than the human beasts demanding Jesus' death were aware of.

Satan led the cruel mob in its abuse of the Saviour. It was his purpose to provoke Him to retaliation if possible, or to drive Him to perform a miracle to release Himself, and thus break up the plan of salvation. One stain upon His human life, one failure of His humanity to endure the terrible test, and the Lamb of God would have been an imperfect offering, and the redemption of man a failure. But He who by a command could bring the heavenly host to His aid—He who could have driven that mob in terror from His sight by the flashing forth of His divine majesty—submitted with perfect calmness to the coarsest insult and outrage.[19]

Satan realized that he was losing the battle. His "rage was great as he saw that all the abuse inflicted upon the Saviour had not forced the least murmur from His lips. Although He had taken upon Him the nature of man, He was sustained by a godlike fortitude, and departed in no particular from the will of His Father."[20] Jesus had made His decision in Gethsemane to endure the trial that would be inflicted on His soul, and He adhered to it with absolute firmness.

Up to this point, the Kingdom of Darkness had lost, and the Kingdom of Light had won. No conflict between the nations of the earth could equal the one that was taking place in Pilate's judgment hall that day! But Satan wasn't about to give up. Pilate turned Jesus over to the Roman soldiers with instructions to flog Him. This was an utterly cruel punishment. Flogging was done with a whip of leather straps that had sharp metal pieces on the ends. People who were not under a death sentence received thirty-nine lashes across their backs, while prisoners who were condemned to die received forty.

Terry McDermott, whom I quoted in the previous chapter, has also explained the nature of this flogging and its effect on the victim.

Jesus would have been stripped naked and shackled by His wrists to a low column so that He would be in a bent-over position.

One or more soldiers would be assigned to deliver the blows from the flagrum [whip]. Standing beside the victim, he would strike in an arc-like fashion across the exposed back. . . . "The bits of metal would dig deep into the flesh, ripping small blood vessels, nerves, muscle, and skin." . . .

. . . Blows to the upper back and rib area caused rib fractures, severe bruising in the lungs, bleeding in the chest cavity and partial or complete pneumothorax (puncture wound to the lung causing it to collapse). As much as 125 millilitres of blood [a little more than four ounces] could be lost. The victim would periodically vomit, experience tremors and seizures, and have bouts of fainting. Each excruciating strike would elicit shrieks of pain. The victim would be diaphoretic (profusely sweating) and exhausted, his flesh mangled and ripped.[21]

Remember that Jesus was flogged twice! Pilate ordered the first flogging (John 19:1), hoping that the Jews would consider this enough punishment and give up their demand for crucifixion. This flogging would have been thirty-nine lashes. Satan was doing absolutely everything he could think of to break Jesus' spirit and make Him resist or give up! But through it all Jesus remained calm. The second flogging would come a bit later.

Pilate once again brought Jesus out before the Jews and said, "Look, I am bringing him out to you to let you know that I find no basis for a charge against him" (verse 4). But "as soon as the chief priests and their officials saw him, they shouted, 'Crucify! Crucify!' " (verse 6). Pilate kept trying to set Jesus free, "but the Jews kept shouting, 'If you let this man go, you are no friend of Caesar. Anyone who claims to be a king opposes Caesar' " (verse 12).

Finally, Pilate sat down on his judge's chair and said,

"Here is your king." . . .
But they shouted, "Take him away! Take him away! Crucify him!"
"Shall I crucify your king?" Pilate asked.
"We have no king but Caesar," the chief priests answered (verses 14, 15).

So Pilate finally yielded to their wishes. "When Pilate saw that he was getting nowhere, but that instead an uproar was starting, he took water and washed his hands in front of the crowd. 'I am innocent of this man's blood,' he said. 'It is your responsibility!' " (Matthew 27:24). At that point, Pilate turned Jesus over to them to be crucified, and this is when the second flogging occurred (verse 26). This time it would have been forty lashes. When the flogging was over, "the governor's soldiers took Jesus into the Praetorium and gathered the whole company of soldiers around him. They stripped him and put a scarlet robe on him, and then twisted together a crown of thorns and set it on his head. They put a staff in his right hand and knelt in front of him and mocked him. 'Hail, king of the Jews,' they said. They spit on him, and took the staff and struck him on the head again and again" (verses 27–30).

Jesus was wearing His crown of thorns, and the pain from being repeatedly struck on the head with the staff caused Him intense agony. Terry McDermott explained this at some length. I will share with you the most pertinent details.

[There is a nerve that] runs through the face, eyes, nose, mouth, and jaws. Irritation of this nerve . . . would have caused a condition called trigeminal neuralgia. . . . [It] causes severe facial pain. . . . Stabbing pain radiates around the eyes, over the forehead, the upper lip, nose, cheek, the side of the tongue and the lower lip. Spasmodic episodes of stabbing, lancinating, and explosive pain are often more agonizing during times of fatigue or tension. It is said to be the worst pain that anyone can experience. . . .

As the soldiers struck Jesus on His head with reeds, He would have felt excruciating pains across His face and deep into His ears, much like sensations from a hot poker or electric shock. . . . These pains would have been felt all the way to Calvary and while on the Cross. As He walked and fell, as He was pushed and shoved, as He moved any part of His face, and as the slightest breeze touched His face, new waves of intense pain would have been triggered. The pain would have intensified His state of traumatic shock.[22]

Matthew goes on to say that "after they had mocked him, they took off the robe and put his own clothes on him. Then they led him away to crucify him" (verse 31).*

The abuse, ridicule, and torture that Jesus received would have been

---

* I have used Matthew's account of the soldiers putting a robe over Jesus' shoulders and the crown of thorns on His head. Matthew's account has this happening just before Jesus was led out to be crucified. John, on the other hand, describes it as happening before Pilate made the decision that Jesus should be crucified (John 19:1–16).

enough to break any other man down. But the amazing thing is that Jesus maintained His composure through it all. He could have flashed His divinity before Pilate and the Jewish leaders and destroyed them—but He didn't. He could have called on a host of heaven's angels to deliver Him from the hands of His tormentors—but He didn't. He could have disappeared and gone back to heaven, leaving Pilate and the Jews with their mouths open, wondering where He had gone—but He didn't. Why? Because He loved you and me and wanted us to spend eternity with Him; because He knew He had to defeat Satan; and because He knew He had to secure the universe against sin *ever* raising its ugly head again.

But Satan wasn't about to give up! He still had one final strategy: the cross.

1. White, *The Desire of Ages*, 708.
2. Ibid., 715.
3. Ibid.
4. Ibid., 723, 724.
5. Ibid., 724.
6. Ibid., 726, 727.
7. Ibid., 728.
8. Ibid.; emphasis added.
9. Ibid., 728.
10. Ibid., 729.
11. Ibid., 730.
12. Ibid., 729.
13. Ibid., 729, 730.
14. Ibid., 731.
15. Ibid.
16. Ibid., 733; emphasis added.
17. Ibid., 733.
18. Ibid., 734.
19. Ibid.
20. Ibid., 735.
21. McDermott, "The Physical Effects of the Scourging and Crucifixion of Jesus." The excerpt includes quoted material from Frederick T. Zugibe, *The Cross and the Shroud* (New York: M. Evans & Co., 2005), 20.
22. McDermott, "The Physical Effects of the Scourging and Crucifixion of Jesus."

CHAPTER 17

Jesus' Crucifixion

Before getting into Jesus' crucifixion, let's briefly review the highlights of the ten or twelve hours prior to Calvary in order to get the setting. The last time Jesus had anything to eat was during the Passover meal that He celebrated with His disciples, perhaps around six o'clock on Thursday evening. Since then He had been through the emotionally draining experience in Gethsemane. He had endured a trial by the Sanhedrin in which He was condemned to die according to their law (or their perception of their law). Following this, the members of the Sanhedrin attacked Him verbally and physically with such force that they would have killed Him had the Roman soldiers appointed to guard Him not intervened. Then He was hauled off to Pilate, where He endured the screams of the maddened Jewish leaders and the mob surrounding them, who demanded His crucifixion. Pilate was convinced of Jesus' innocence and wanted to save Him from that cruel punishment. He thought he had found a way to avoid having to make that decision when he learned that Jesus was from Galilee, so Pilate sent Him to Herod.

The Galilean governor was actually glad to see Jesus at first, but his friendliness turned to rage when Jesus would neither speak to him nor work a miracle to save Himself. Jesus was attacked again by a ferocious mob similar to the one that attacked Him following His condemnation by the Sanhedrin. Roman soldiers once more protected Jesus from the maddened throng, and Herod sent Him back to Pilate. A frustrated Pilate had Jesus flogged with thirty-nine lashes—a punishment that was so brutal that some victims died before it was over. Pilate hoped this would satisfy the angry Jewish leaders, but they would accept nothing short of crucifixion. Pilate finally yielded to their wishes and condemned Jesus to forty more lashes and death by crucifixion.

At this point, Jesus was utterly exhausted. It's amazing that He was even alive! But then came another brutal experience. The Roman soldiers loaded the cross onto His horribly lacerated back, causing intense pain. And, mind you, the crosspiece didn't have a nice polished surface like your dining room table! Splinters would have pierced what was left of the skin and flesh across Jesus' back, causing excruciating pain. All this combined with His exhaustion, and it's no wonder He fell beneath the load!

The soldiers picked Jesus up off the street and loaded the cross on His back a second time, but again He collapsed. Realizing that Jesus really *could not* carry His own cross, the soldiers looked around for someone to carry it for Him. But no one in that angry mob volunteered for the job. Finally, they ordered a sympathetic Simon of Cyrene to carry the cross for Jesus (Matthew 27:32). Soon they arrived at the site for the crucifixion. Simon laid down the cross he had carried to the place of execution, and the two thieves unloaded the crosses from their backs, probably with the help of the soldiers.

Three large holes had been dug: the center one for Jesus' cross and the other two for the thieves, one on each side. The implication of this was that Jesus was the worst of sinners. In fact, He was, not because He had committed any sins—because He hadn't—but because He was bearing the guilt of all the sins ever committed by every human being from Adam and Eve to His second coming.

I pointed out in the previous chapter that throughout Jesus' time on Earth Satan used powerful emotions to try to get Jesus to yield to his temptations. At both Jesus' trial and His crucifixion, the Jewish leaders and the rabble taunted Him. They "hurled insults at him, shaking their heads and saying, 'You who are going to destroy the temple and build it in three days, save yourself! Come down from the cross, if you are the Son of God!' " (verses 39, 40). And the rulers "sneered at him," saying,

> "He saved others; let him save himself if he is the Christ of God, the Chosen One."
> The soldiers also came up and mocked Him. They offered him wine vinegar and said, "If you are the king of the Jews, save yourself" (Luke 23:35–37).

This was emotional pain. But physical pain was one of the most powerful methods Satan used in his effort to break Jesus down—both at the Savior's trial and on the cross.

The physical pain

Terry McDermott, whom I've quoted in the previous two chapters, again helps us to understand the physical pain Jesus experienced when He was crucified.

By the time He arrived at Calvary, Jesus was in exquisite pain, struggling to breathe and suffering from blood and fluid loss. One of the executioners threw Him to the ground and then made Him lie on His back. One other executioner pressed down on His chest, another held Him down by His legs, while a third soldier stretched His arms one at a time across the patibulum [the horizontal piece on the cross] and nailed down His hands.

The pain from the nails would have been like having hot pokers driven through His hands, causing bolts of radiating pain up His arm. He would have screamed out in agony.* "The process was repeated for the other hand, offering no relief from the agonizing pain. Then, two members of the execution squad likely manned the ends of the crosspiece while a third member grasped Jesus around the waist, getting Him to His feet. They backed Him up to the upright onto a platform device, and then two men lifted Him by the legs and inserted the crosspiece into a mortice on the top of the upright. . . . Again, Jesus would likely have screamed out in agony after each foot was nailed." . . .

The median nerve runs through the thenar furrow [just below the wrist] where the nail was hammered. A nail through this area would cause a burning, searing pain so severe that the slightest touch, movement, or gentle breeze felt here is agonizing. . . .

The Romans bent the legs of their victims at the knees and then placed their feet flush against the cross. Then they hammered one nail through the top of each foot, severing the plantar nerves. The pain would have been similar to . . . [the pain] caused by the palm injuries. In addition, the effect of bending the knees to align the feet against the stipes [the vertical part of the cross] would cause cramping and numbness in the calves and thighs. This would force Jesus to arch His back in an attempt to straighten His legs and alleviate the cramping.[1]

Jesus' cross was lifted up "and with great violence thrust into the place prepared for it. This caused the most intense agony to the Son of God."[2] Yet Jesus endured it all quietly, actually asking God to forgive His tormentors (verse 34)!

---

* This is how the average person would have reacted to having his or her hands nailed to the cross, and it's possible that Jesus reacted in the same way. While it's true that Isaiah said the Messiah would "not open his mouth" (Isaiah 53:7) and Ellen White, in *The Desire of Ages*, stated that "the Saviour made no murmur of complaint" (744), screaming at the instant the nails were driven through His hands and feet would have been a normal reaction to the intense pain Jesus was experiencing. It would not have been a complaint against the ones who were injuring Him.

Dr. C. Truman Davis was another medical doctor who spent a great deal of time examining the effects of crucifixion on Jesus' mind and body, and he provided a graphic description of what Jesus would have experienced during the six hours* He hung on the cross.

As Jesus slowly sagged down with more weight on the nails in the wrists, excruciating, fiery pain shot along the fingers and up the arms to explode in the brain. The nails in the wrists were putting pressure on the median nerves, large nerve trunks which traverse the mid-wrist and hand. As He pushed Himself upward to avoid this stretching torment, He placed His full weight on the nail through His feet.† Again there was searing agony as the nail tore through the nerves between the metatarsal bones of the feet.

At this point, another phenomenon occurred. As the arms fatigued, great waves of cramps swept over the muscles, knotting them in deep relentless, throbbing pain. With these cramps came the inability to push Himself upward. Hanging by the arms, the pectoral muscles, the large muscles of the chest, were paralyzed and the intercostal muscles, the small muscles between the ribs, were unable to act. Air could be drawn into the lungs, but could not be exhaled. Jesus fought to raise Himself in order to get even one short breath. Finally, the carbon dioxide level increased in the lungs and in the blood stream, and the cramps partially subsided. . . .

. . . [As the end approached,] the loss of tissue fluids had reached a critical level; the compressed heart was struggling to pump heavy, thick, sluggish blood to the tissues, and the tortured lungs were making a frantic effort to inhale small gulps of air. The markedly dehydrated tissues sent their flood of stimuli to the brain.[3]

Dr. Davis suggested that it was at this point that Jesus gasped, "I am thirsty" (John 19:28).

---

* The Jews divided the light part of the day into twelve hours, so depending on the season, the hours would be longer or shorter. Jesus was crucified at Passover, and at that time of the year, the twelve hours of the day would come close to equaling hours as we reckon them— sixty minutes. Mark said that Jesus was crucified at the third hour; assuming that the sun rose at six o'clock, the third hour, when Jesus was crucified, would be about nine o'clock. The sixth hour, when darkness covered the land, would be about noon, and the ninth hour, when He died, would be about three o'clock (see Mark 15:25, 33, 34).

† At the time Jesus was crucified, the feet of criminals were sometimes nailed with one nail driven through both feet or with two nails, each driven through one of the feet. The Bible doesn't inform us which way Jesus' feet were nailed to His cross.

The mental pain

However, the worst pain Jesus experienced was mental, not physical. Ellen White wrote that "the wrath of God against sin, the terrible manifestation of His displeasure because of iniquity, filled the soul of His Son with consternation. . . . So great was this agony that His physical pain was hardly felt."[4] It's hard for us to understand this, because physical pain of the kind Jesus endured was so utterly intense. Our imaginations recoil from the thought!

Jesus' mental pain actually began in Gethsemane, as we learned a couple of chapters previously. Ellen White wrote that in Gethsemane Jesus "seemed to be shut out from the light of God's sustaining presence," and His "soul was filled with dread of separation from God."[5] This feeling intensified on the cross, as evidenced by His cry, "My God, my God, why have you forsaken me?" (Matthew 27:46). Jesus "feared that sin was so offensive to God that Their separation was to be eternal."[6] You and I and all Christians know that this was not true. Jesus conquered gloriously, and He's now in heaven as our Mediator. But that isn't the point. The point is that on the cross Jesus *feared* that the separation between Himself and the Father was to be eternal. That's how He *felt*.

Ellen White states, "In the agony of Gethsemane, the death of Calvary, the heart of infinite Love paid the price of our redemption."[7] So the question is, what was that payment? What did it consist of? It consisted of two things: first, experiencing God's wrath against sin; and second, paying the death penalty for sin.

God's wrath. Revelation 6:16, 17 describes the wicked experiencing God's wrath against sin at the Second Coming: "They called to the mountains and the rocks, 'Fall on us and hide us from the face of him who sits on the throne and from the wrath of the Lamb! For the great day of their wrath has come, and who can stand?' " Now ponder for a moment how these wicked people will feel. They'll be utterly terrified. They'll be exposed to the full light of God and Christ at the Second Coming, and they'll long to die. It will be mass suicide! In order for Jesus to pay the price for our sins, He had to experience what sinners will experience at Christ's second coming and at the final judgment at the end of the millennium.

Three paragraphs earlier I mentioned Ellen White's comment that Jesus' mental agony was so great that He hardly felt His physical pain. I can begin to understand what she meant when I look at what sinners will experience at the end of time, because *that's* what Jesus felt on the cross.

Paying the death penalty. The wrath of God against sin was part of Jesus' payment for our sins. The other part was His actual death. God told Adam that he would die if he ate the fruit from the forbidden tree (Genesis 2:16, 17). Both Adam and Eve did eat the fruit, and they and every human being from that time to our day has died or will die, except the righteous who live to see Jesus come. Jesus, the Seed of the woman, came to earth to pay that penalty for Adam and Eve and us, and that's what was happening on Calvary. Both the Bible and Ellen White are very clear about this. Let's start with the Bible. Hundreds of years before Christ's time the prophet Isaiah declared that the Messiah

> was pierced for our transgressions,
>   he was crushed for our iniquities. . . .
> . . . He poured out his life unto death. . . .
> . . . He bore the sin of many (Isaiah 53:5, 12).

In the New Testament, Paul said, "God made him who had no sin to be sin for us" (2 Corinthians 5:21), and Peter, echoing Isaiah, said that Jesus "bore our sins in his body on the tree [the cross]" (1 Peter 2:24). This means that Jesus paid the death penalty for our sins. Ellen White wrote, "Jesus died to save His people from their sins."[8] "Jesus died, . . . not to save you in your sins, but from your sins."[9] "What is it to believe? It is to fully accept that Jesus Christ died as our sacrifice; that He became the curse for us, took our sins upon Himself, and imputed unto us His own righteousness."[10]

Kingdoms in conflict

During the entire time that Jesus agonized on the cross and was taunted by the priests and rulers and the mob, things were taking place outside the awareness of humans. The Kingdom of Darkness was desperately trying to defeat Jesus, and the Kingdom of Light was watching with bated breath to see how it would all turn out.

The Kingdom of Darkness. Ellen White tells us that Satan was so intent on defeating Jesus that he and his demons actually joined visibly and audibly in the conflict. "Satan with His angels, in human form, was present at the cross. The archfiend and his hosts were co-operating with the priests and rulers. . . . Priests, rulers, Pharisees, and the hardened rabble were confederated together in a satanic frenzy. Religious rulers united with Satan and his angels. They were doing his bidding."[11] Surely Satan was whispering in Jesus' ear (*shouting* would probably be a better word), "Why on earth are You putting up with all this pain and unjust condemnation? Just give up and go home, for goodness' sake!"

Jesus had at least three options at that point. First, He could have lashed out at His persecutors, in which case He would have sinned, joined Satan's side, and lost the conflict between good and evil. Second, He could have exercised His power to simply disappear from the cross and return to His Father. Third, He could have done what the priests and rulers were demanding—come down from the cross. Then He could have flashed His glory and stunned the entire crowd into submission. Emotionally, Jesus must have felt a profound temptation to take one of these escape routes, but He understood the issues involved, and He refused to use any of these means to spare Himself the torture of mind and body that He was going through. Ellen White wrote, "Had He in one particular yielded to Satan to escape the terrible torture, the enemy of God and man would have triumphed."[12] Why didn't He? Because Jesus "fully comprehended the results of the sacrifice made upon Calvary."[13]

Meanwhile God was intensifying Jesus' mental and emotional pain by removing His presence from His Son and pouring out His wrath against sin upon Him. It would almost seem that God was on Satan's side! This sounds strange to our human minds until we realize that God was simply implementing His part in the plan of salvation that had been laid "from the creation of the world" (Revelation 13:8). The Father had to impose on Jesus His full wrath against every sin committed by every human being from Adam to the Second Coming.

Even before coming to this planet, Jesus was fully aware that God would have to punish Him for human sin, and "in those dreadful hours He . . . relied upon the evidence of His Father's acceptance heretofore given Him. He was acquainted with the character of His Father; He understood His justice, His mercy, and His great love. By faith He rested in Him whom it had ever been His joy to obey. And as in submission He committed Himself to God, the sense of the loss of His Father's favor was withdrawn. By faith, Christ was victor."[14]

The Kingdom of Light. While Satan and his demons were fully engaged in the conflict, God's angels could only stand aside and watch. "With amazement angels witnessed the Saviour's despairing agony. The hosts of heaven veiled their faces from the fearful sight."[15] "With amazement, the angels beheld the infinite love of Jesus, who, suffering the most intense agony of mind and body, thought only of others."[16]

Jesus' death

Jesus was crucified at the third hour of Jewish time (Mark 15:25), which would be around nine o'clock in the morning as we count time. "At the sixth hour [noon] darkness came over the whole land" (verse 33). Ellen White described this darkness:

> Inanimate nature expressed sympathy with its insulted and dying Author. The sun refused to look upon the awful scene. Its full, bright rays were illuminating the earth at midday, when suddenly it seemed to be blotted out. Complete darkness, like a funeral pall, enveloped the cross. . . . There was no eclipse or other natural cause for this darkness, which was as deep as midnight without moon or stars. It was a miraculous testimony given by God that the faith of after generations might be confirmed.[17]

But in the midst of that darkness, "God and His holy angels were beside the cross. The Father was with His Son."[18] Even though He had withdrawn His presence from Jesus' mind and heart, and even though He was pouring out His wrath against sin upon Jesus, God was there with Him! Yet "in that dreadful hour Christ was not to be comforted with the Father's presence."[19] Apparently, God was there, but Jesus was not aware of it.

"At the ninth hour [about three o'clock in the afternoon] Jesus cried out in a loud voice, *'Eloi, Eloi, lama sabachthani?'*—which means, 'My God, my God, why have you forsaken me?' " (Mark 15:34; italics in the original). Someone again put a sponge soaked in wine vinegar on a stick and held it up to Jesus' mouth. "When he had received the drink, Jesus said, 'It is finished' " (John 19:30). Then He "called out with a loud voice, 'Father, into your hands I commit my spirit.' When he had said this, he breathed his last" (Luke 23:46).

Reflections

Jesus' words "It is finished" have a profound meaning. Jesus was the victor in the conflict between the Kingdom of Light and the Kingdom of Darkness. That war is still going on, as we all know; but the decisive battle has been fought—and Jesus won it! That's why Revelation 12:10 says,

> "Now have come the salvation and the power and the kingdom of
>   our God,
>   and the authority of His Christ.
> For the accuser of our brothers,

who accuses them before our God day and night,
has been hurled down."

Satan, who rebelled against Michael in heaven thousands of years earlier and who conquered Adam and Eve in Eden, was a defeated foe. Ellen White wrote, "All heaven triumphed in the Saviour's victory. Satan was defeated, and knew that his kingdom was lost."[20]

Jesus' victory was also a victory for us, because the promise God made to Adam and Eve in Eden that one of Eve's descendants would crush the serpent's head was now fulfilled. Throughout Old Testament history, God had promised His people that He would redeem them. Isaiah was especially emphatic on that point. In Isaiah 44:22, the prophet wrote, "I have blotted out, like a thick cloud, your transgressions, and like a cloud, your sins. Return to Me, for I have redeemed you" (NKJV). Over and over again—twenty-six times throughout his prophetic utterances—Isaiah spoke of God as Israel's Redeemer and of the people having been redeemed by Him (see, for example, Isaiah 41:14; 44:23; 52:3; 63:9, 16). And in chapter 53 of his prophecy, Isaiah foretold of a Messiah who would be stricken for the transgression of His people and bear their sins (verses 8, 12).

This was all very true—except that at the time Isaiah wrote these words the redeeming act had not yet happened, and there was a very real possibility that it might not be accomplished. You will recall the overwhelming difficulty Jesus had in Gethsemane while making the decision to go through with the plan of salvation. We can better understand His profound anxiety in light of the horrible, unrelenting pain that Satan and his human allies inflicted on Jesus during His trial and crucifixion. The possibility that He might choose to give up the struggle was very real. But we can praise God that Jesus made the decision to go through with this bitter trial of His soul, and with His final words, "It is finished," He sealed the Old Testament promises of a Messiah and a Redeemer. Salvation was now a reality, not just a promise.

That reality is for you and me as well. For the Old Testament saints, there was the possibility that Jesus *might* fail. We know that He *didn't* fail.

We can also understand something else now: there was a short time—no more than fifteen to eighteen hours, from the time Jesus entered Gethsemane until He cried out "It is finished"—when the fate of the world hung in the balance. This was *the* most critical bit of time in the history of the world and of the great conflict between good and evil.

Another question we can ask is, what made it possible for Jesus to endure those fifteen to eighteen hours? I'm sure there were several factors, but I will mention one: Jesus knew that the fate of the world hung in the balance. Nobody else understood that this was *the* most critical bit of time in the history of the great conflict between good and evil. No one else in the crowds of people around the cross during those hours had a clue that Jesus was settling the great controversy that began with Lucifer's rebellion in heaven and which will culminate in the lake of fire after the millennium. The furthest thing from their imaginations was that Jesus' act on the cross would have a profound effect on world history. All they saw was a Man who they thought had managed to get on the bad side of the Jewish religious leaders.

You and I can't *prove*, in a scientific way of proving things, that Jesus is the Savior of the world. For that, we have to turn to the Bible; Seventh-day Adventists also use the writings of Ellen White for additional insights. Without these two sources, we would have to agree with the perspective of the crowds that surrounded Jesus on the cross. Fortunately, we *do* have these sources, and because we trust them, we have the assurance of eternal life beyond the grave.

I hope that, after reading this chapter and the two before it, you can appreciate a little better what Jesus had to go through in order to obtain your salvation and mine. And I hope that it has drawn you closer to Him and increased your love for Him.

I will close this chapter with two quotes from Ellen White. You're probably familiar with the first one: "It would be well for us to spend a thoughtful hour each day in contemplation of the life of Christ. We should take it point by point, and let the imagination grasp each scene, especially the closing ones."[21]

The second quote presents us with a challenge:

Hanging upon the cross Christ was the gospel. Now we have a message, "Behold the Lamb of God, which taketh away the sins of the world." Will not our church members keep their eyes fixed on a crucified and risen Saviour, in whom their hopes of eternal life are centered? This is our message, our argument, our doctrine, our warning to the impenitent, our encouragement for the sorrowing, the hope for every believer. If we can awaken an interest in men's minds that will cause them to fix their eyes on Christ, we may step aside, and ask them only to continue to fix their eyes upon the Lamb of God. They thus receive their lesson. Whosoever will come after Me, let him deny himself, and take up his cross, and follow Me. He whose eyes are fixed on Jesus will leave all. He will die to selfishness. He will believe in all the Word of God, which is so gloriously and wonderfully exalted in Christ.[22]

1. McDermott, "The Physical Effects of the Scourging and Crucifixion of Jesus." The excerpt includes quoted material from Zugibe, *The Cross and the Shroud*, 66.

2. White, *The Desire of Ages*, 745.

3. C. Truman Davis, "The Crucifixion: A Medical View," *New Wine*, April 1982, 13, 14, accessed February 16, 2017, https://www.csmpublishing.org/wp-content/NewWineArchives/Full_Issues/1982/NewWineMagazine_Issue_04-1982.pdf.

4. White, *The Desire of Ages*, 753.

5. Ibid., 685, 687.

6. Ibid., 753.

7. White, *Steps to Christ*, 13, 14.

8. Ellen G. White, *Faith and Works* (Hagerstown, MD: Review and Herald® Pub. Assn., 2003), 95.

9. Ellen G. White, *Our High Calling* (Washington, DC: Review and Herald® Pub. Assn., 1962), 261.

10. White, *Faith and Works*, 70.

11. White, *The Desire of Ages*, 746, 749.

12. Ibid., 761.

13. Ibid., 764.

14. Ibid., 756.

15. Ibid., 753.

16. Ibid., 752.

17. Ibid., 753.

18. Ibid., 753, 754.

19. Ibid., 754.

20. Ibid., 758.

21. Ibid., 83.

22. Francis D. Nichol, ed., "Ellen G. White Comments," *The Seventh-day Adventist Bible Commentary*, vol. 6 (Washington, DC: Review and Herald® Pub. Assn., 1957), 1113.

CHAPTER 18

Jesus' Resurrection

Jesus' disciples were devastated by His crucifixion. They were sure He was the Messiah whom all the prophets had foretold would deliver Israel. They still clung to the notion that the Messiah's mission was to deliver Israel from the Romans. During Jesus' trial, they kept waiting for Him to flash forth His divinity and subdue the Sanhedrin, Pilate, and Herod. Even during the crucifixion they expected Him to overwhelm His persecutors with His glory, come down from the cross, and conquer the Romans. But He didn't do that. Instead, He allowed Himself to be beaten, condemned, crucified, and finally killed. Their hopes for a conquering Messiah were blasted—as they should have been, but they didn't understand that. The two disciples whom Jesus walked beside on the road to Emmaus expressed the feelings of all Jesus' disciples: "We had hoped that he was the one who was going to redeem Israel" (Luke 24:21). Old expectations die hard!

Once Jesus was dead, His disciples probably assumed that the Roman governor would order Him to be buried in an unmarked grave, and they were no doubt amazed when Nicodemus and Joseph of Arimathea—two members of the Sanhedrin, no less—asked Pilate's permission to take charge of Jesus' body and bury it in Joseph's exquisite new tomb, a man-made cave that had been cut out of the side of a cliff. The two men, probably with the aid of Mary Magdalene and Mary the mother of Joses, wrapped Jesus' body, along with about seventy-five pounds of spices, in strips of burial cloth and laid Him in the tomb. Then Joseph rolled a large stone in front of the entrance to the tomb (Matthew 27:57–60; Mark 15:42–47; John 19:38–42).

The next day the wily Jewish leaders, remembering that Jesus had foretold His resurrection from the dead, went to Pilate and asked that the tomb be secured with a seal on the stone and that a guard be posted in front of the tomb to prevent Jesus' disciples from coming at night, stealing the body, and claiming that Jesus had been raised from the dead. Pilate authorized them to carry out their wishes (Matthew 27:62–66).

So the rest of that Sabbath and early into Sunday, as Jesus lay in the tomb, He had a Roman guard to shield Him from grave robbers! How nice of

Pilate and the Jewish leaders to protect Him like that!

But they could have spared themselves the trouble, for beyond the view of human beings two groups of powerful angels were also surrounding the tomb. Ellen White says that "hosts of evil angels were gathered about the place." Satan exulted that he had triumphed. "He dared to hope that the Saviour would not take up His life again. He claimed the Lord's body, and set his guard about the tomb, seeking to hold Christ a prisoner."[1] He was determined to prevent Jesus from rising from His tomb!

But there was the other group: "A heavenly host surrounded the sepulcher. Angels that excel in strength were guarding the tomb, and waiting to welcome the Prince of life."[2] Please notice where each group of angels was located. Hosts of evil angels "were gathered about the place"; but closer in, "a heavenly host surrounded the sepulcher," and God's angels were "guarding the tomb." You would think that by now Satan would realize that he couldn't conquer heaven's angels, who with Michael (the one lying in the tomb, no less!) had cast him and his angels out of heaven several thousand years earlier. And the heavenly host had the powerful Creator of the universe on their side. Defeating that combination of divinity and loyal angels was an absolute impossibility. But such is the power of evil to distort one's thinking. The one thing I have to give Satan credit for is his dogged determination to persist in fighting a losing battle.

Jesus passed the Sabbath day resting in the tomb. There was no more sense of the loss of His Father's presence, no more agonizing pain from the stripes across His back, and no more excruciating pain and exhausting efforts to lift Himself up with His nail-pierced feet in order to breathe. Except for Ellen White's statement that "divinity did not die,"[3] neither the Bible nor Ellen White comment on Jesus' divine nature while He lay in the tomb. But that statement is enough. His divinity is the reason why He was able to rise from the dead by His own power. He Himself said, "I lay down my life—only to take it up again" (John 10:17). I'll paraphrase Jesus' words to say what I think He meant: "I lay down My human life in order for My divine nature to restore My humanity to life again."

This explains why He could pay the price for our sins *and* give us eternal life. Paul said that "the wages of sin is death" (Romans 6:23). It's possible for you and me to pay for our sins, and in fact, those people who are not saved *will* pay that wage in the lake of fire. Then they'll cease to exist for eternity. Only Jesus, the divine Son of God, could pay those wages in His human nature and then rise again from the grave by His own divine power.

Ellen White said that "in His divinity, Christ possessed the power to break the bonds of death."[4] And that's why He said, "I hold the keys of death and Hades [the grave]" (Revelation 1:18). With those keys, He can unlock the grave and reverse the death penalty of all those who repent of their sins, confess them, and by faith accept Him as their Savior. This is why Jesus' resurrection is as important to the plan of salvation as the painful cross: for without the resurrection, Jesus wouldn't hold the keys of death and the grave, and He couldn't bring us back to life. If He were still locked in His tomb, we would be locked in ours—for eternity!

Jesus' resurrection

It's early Sunday morning and the first day of the week. The sky is still as dark as midnight. The birds haven't started their chirping yet. The soldiers surrounding Jesus' tomb are keeping their watch, for to do otherwise would be to risk being executed. Suddenly, a light brighter than the sun at noonday illuminates the ground in front of the tomb. The soldiers fall to the ground and throw their arms over their eyes to shield them from the light. At the same time, the earth rolls like the sea in a violent storm. Matthew describes the scene: "There was a violent earthquake, for an angel of the Lord came down from heaven and, going to the tomb, rolled back the stone and sat on it. His appearance was like lightning, and his clothes were white as snow. The guards were so afraid of him that they shook and became like dead men" (Matthew 28:2–4).

Ellen White also described the scene:

> "And, behold, there was a great earthquake: for the angel of the Lord descended from heaven." Clothed with the panoply of God, this angel left the heavenly courts. The bright beams of God's glory went before him, and illuminated his pathway. . . .
>
> . . . This messenger is he who fills the position from which Satan fell. . . . The earth trembles at his approach, the hosts of darkness flee, and as he rolls away the stone, heaven seems to come down to the earth. The soldiers see him removing the stone as he would a pebble, and hear him cry, Son of God, come forth; Thy Father calls thee. They see Jesus come forth from the grave, and hear Him proclaim over the rent sepulcher, "I am the resurrection, and the life." As He comes forth in majesty and glory, the angel host bow low in adoration before the Redeemer, and welcome Him with songs of praise.[5]

Where were Satan and his host during these brief moments? Satan "was bitterly angry when his angels fled at the approach of the heavenly messenger. When he saw Christ come forth in triumph, he knew that his kingdom would have an end, and that he must finally die."[6]

Revelation's rejoicing

What a cause for rejoicing! Revelation depicts heaven's praise:

> "Now have come the salvation and the power and the kingdom of
>   our God,
>   and the authority of his Christ.
> For the accuser of our brothers,
>   who accuses them before our God day and night,
>   has been hurled down. . . .
> Therefore rejoice, you heavens
>   and you who dwell in them!" (Revelation 12:10, 12).

The conflict between the Kingdom of Light and the Kingdom of Darkness that had begun in heaven thousands of years earlier was finally settled. With Jesus' resurrection from the dead, the Kingdom of Light finally conquered the Kingdom of Darkness. Earth's history has continued for more than two thousand additional years, but the end of sin, suffering, and death is assured. And you and I have the privilege of living in a time when that promise is about to become a reality!

A brief reflection

It's an understatement to say that we see the principles of the two kingdoms in stark contrast in these chapters about the closing scenes in Christ's life. In all the vast crowd surrounding Jesus at His trial and crucifixion, He was the only one who truly reflected the principles of the Kingdom of Light, both because of His profound love and patience and because of His insight into the conflict between His kingdom and the Kingdom of Darkness. He understood what no one else who witnessed His trial and crucifixion understood: The issue was whether His Kingdom of Light would defeat Satan's Kingdom of Darkness. The issue was whether He would pay the death penalty for human sin and provide a way for every human being to be released from the death penalty that was imposed on the human race because of Adam and Eve's transgression.

The issue was also one of authority. Jesus had come, not merely as one of God's prophets, but as God Himself in human form. No prophet ever spoke with greater authority than Jesus. Yet the Jewish leaders, because of their personal ambitions and vain pride, refused to acknowledge His heavenly authority—the authority of God Himself, because He was God.

As the leaders of the Jewish nation, the priests and rulers acted on behalf of their entire nation. By rejecting the Son of God, these leaders closed their nation's probation, and less than forty years later the Romans destroyed Jerusalem and crushed out its life.

But we can praise God that Jesus Christ defeated the Kingdom of Darkness by His death and resurrection and assured you and me of eternal lives in His Kingdom of Light.

Summary of the Kingdom of Darkness in Jesus' life

Let's review the conflict between the Kingdom of Light and the Kingdom of Darkness up to this point. The Kingdom of Darkness rebelled against the Kingdom of Light in heaven thousands of years ago, but the Kingdom of Light cast the Kingdom of Darkness down to planet Earth. That was the first victory for the Kingdom of Light.

Unfortunately, the Kingdom of Darkness managed to get the first humans to join its rebellion against God, which was its first victory. The Flood was the second victory for the Kingdom of Darkness. This was followed by the third victory after the Exodus when the people worshiped the golden calf and the fourth victory with the Babylonian captivity.

The critical battle began when Jesus was born to the virgin Mary. The Kingdom of Darkness knew that this was the crucial battle, and it put forth the most desperate efforts to defeat Jesus. The Kingdom of Darkness was extremely successful in getting the leaders of God's chosen people to join its side. These leaders were utterly passionate about maintaining their position. Giving up every semblance of respect for God's law of love, which is the defining characteristic of the Kingdom of Light, they were filled with an intense hatred of Jesus. Making themselves slaves of Satan, they lost all their freedom to make right choices. As a result, they totally rejected the authority of God's chosen Representative to them. Instead, they got the Roman governor, Pilate, to crucify Him. It appeared that the Kingdom of Darkness had won round five.

However, praise God that on Resurrection morning Jesus rose from the dead, and by this act He defeated the Kingdom of Darkness! That was the second victory for the Kingdom of Light. There would still be more victories for the Kingdom of Darkness, but now the final victory of the Kingdom of Light was assured.

1. White, *The Desire of Ages*, 779, 782.

2. Ibid., 779.

3. White, *The Faith I Live By*, 51.

4. White, *The Desire of Ages*, 785.

5. Ibid., 779, 780.

6. Ibid., 782.

CHAPTER 19

Jesus' Church

J ust before Jesus returned to His Father in heaven, His disciples asked Him, "Lord, are you at this time going to restore the kingdom to Israel?" They still clung to their old expectation that Jesus would lead the Jewish nation to victory over the Romans! Jesus replied, "It is not for you to know the times or dates the Father has set by his own authority. But you will receive power when the Holy Spirit comes on you; and you will be my witnesses in Jerusalem, and in all Judea and Samaria, and to the ends of the earth" (Acts 1:6–8). Instead of answering their question, Jesus gave them a job to do: Go tell the world about My life, My crucifixion, and My resurrection. Spread the good news everywhere that because of Me men and women can have a new understanding of God's love for them, and because of My death and resurrection they have the hope of eternal life beyond the grave. Go tell it to the world!

I can assure you that the Kingdom of Darkness, which was already doomed to destruction because of Christ's death and resurrection, *was not pleased.* Now that there was no longer any possibility of defeating Christ, Satan turned his attention to Christ's church. Here he was much more successful, as we shall see. Revelation 12 describes Satan's attack in vivid language. He is represented by a great red dragon, and the church is represented by a woman. She's pregnant with a male Child, Jesus, whom the dragon, Satan, attempts to destroy the moment He's born. However, God delivers Jesus from the dragon by catching Him up to His throne (verses 1–5). When the dragon sees that he can no longer attack Jesus Himself, he pursues the woman, the church. And his efforts pay off marvelously.

From Sabbath to Sunday

During the first century (from A.D. 34 to about 100), the church was kept relatively pure thanks to the efforts of the apostles, especially Paul, Peter, and John. However, doctrinal divergence began shortly after the year A.D. 100. The first definite evidence of Christians meeting for worship on the first day of the week dates to about 135. It's found in a document titled *The*

First Apology, by Justin Martyr. Justin, an early Christian defender of the faith, wrote, "On the day which is called *Sunday* . . . we have a common assembly of all who live in the cities or in the outlying districts. . . . *Sunday*, indeed, is the day on which we hold our common assembly."[1]

Some fifty years later the church father Tertullian defended Sunday observance with a "biblical" argument. He began with Isaiah 1:13, in which God said, "New Moons, Sabbaths and convocations—I cannot bear your evil assemblies." In other words, according to Tertullian, God didn't like the Sabbath. Tertullian then went on to argue that Jesus agreed with Isaiah, because He condemned the Jewish leaders for their unbiblical and legalistic traditions about keeping the Sabbath. So, Tertullian argued, Jesus also despised the Sabbath! In his book *From Sabbath to Sunday*, Samuele Bacchiocchi reflected on Tertullian's reasoning. He pointed out that "in his attempt to defend the oneness of the God of the Old and of the New Testament, Tertullian reduces the Sabbath to an institution which God has always despised. He does so by equating arbitrarily Isaiah 1:13 . . . with Christ's attitude toward the Sabbath."[2]

As the centuries went by, the Sabbath was increasingly associated with fasting and asceticism, while Sunday was associated with celebration. In 325, the Roman emperor Constantine issued his famous Sunday law forbidding work on the first day of the week. Nevertheless, Sabbath observance continued here and there throughout the empire for another two hundred some years. However, it was a day of mourning and fasting. Sabbath observance kept diminishing until by the year 600 it had largely disappeared.

The rise of the papacy

The papacy didn't just show up overnight. It took more than a millennium following the apostolic era—from A.D. 100 to about 1200—for the papacy to reach the zenith of its political power over the kings of Western Europe, and it held that power for several hundred years. Much of what I say in the rest of this chapter is based on two books: Ellen White's *The Great Controversy* and *The Future of the Catholic Church With Pope Francis* by Garry Wills.[3] Wills is a Pulitzer Prize–winning author and historian. He's a Catholic who has specialized in the history of his church, and he's very candid about revealing the deception and religio-political manipulation that gave rise to the papacy.

The Emperor Constantine. For almost three centuries after Jesus returned to heaven, Christians were persecuted: first by the Jews during the thirty-seven years prior to the destruction of Jerusalem, and by the Roman Empire for nearly two and a half centuries after that. Persecution by the empire was sporadic but intense at times. Many Christians suffered martyrdom rather than give up their faith in Christ. One of the bitterest periods of persecution occurred during the ten years immediately preceding the reign of the emperor Constantine.

However, Constantine saw Christians as allies that he could use to enhance his rule, and shortly after he became the emperor, he legalized the Christian faith. Prior to that time, paganism had been the official religion of the empire, but within a hundred years Christianity replaced paganism as the dominant religion.

Constantine took an active role in church affairs and thus began a trend that for almost a thousand years saw the church increasingly dominating the empire. Constantine built churches in all of Christianity's sacred places and gave the bishops freedom from taxation.[4] Less than fifteen years after he took the reins of government, he chaired the Council of Nicea, which settled (or tried to settle) the dispute between the Trinitarians and the anti-Trinitarian doctrine of a bishop by the name of Arius.

Satan had offered Jesus dominion over the world in exchange for Jesus worshiping him. Jesus refused, but the Christian church under Constantine accepted the offer. As Wills put it, "What if Caesar becomes an ally, a patron, a partner? When does paying Caesar become obeying Caesar, and when does obeying Caesar slide into being Caesar?"[5]

Western culture today creates a clear distinction between church and state, but it's important to understand that seventeen hundred years ago the idea of keeping church and state separate was the furthest thing from anyone's mind, including Christians. The pagan Roman Empire considered the emperor to be a god of sorts, and everyone was supposed to pay him homage. Thus, it was easy for the Christian church to slip into a relationship with the state that would be totally unacceptable in Western nations today. This was especially easy for Christians to do, given the harsh persecution they had experienced immediately prior to Constantine's reign. And the church's bishops cultivated the emperor's favor and gladly accepted his attention.

The bishops decided what beliefs the church should hold, and then they turned enforcement over to Constantine. When the bishops felt that a particular one of their number was teaching heretical ideas, enforcing the church's doctrine on the defiant bishop was the emperor's responsibility.[6]

Wills said, "The church grew stronger under Constantine by using *him*, getting him (at least sometimes) to side with 'orthodoxy,' punish 'heretics,' strengthen and centralize the network of bishops, build churches, and sub-sidize the services inside them."[7] At this point, the state in many ways dom-inated the church, but a day would come when the church dominated the state—or at least thought it should and tried to do so.

Ellen White commented that "the nominal conversion of Constantine, in the early part of the fourth century, caused great rejoicing; and the world, cloaked with a form of righteousness, walked into the church. Now the work of corruption rapidly progressed. Paganism, while appearing to be vanquished, became the conqueror. Her spirit controlled the church. Her doctrines, ceremonies, and superstitions were incorporated into the faith and worship of the professed followers of Christ."[8]

How Peter became the first pope. Biblical evidence suggests that Peter may have labored for a while in Rome, because in the closing remarks of his first letter he wrote, "She who is in Babylon . . . sends you her greetings" (1 Peter 5:13). In the comments on this verse, *The Seventh-day Adventist Bible Commentary* says, "There is no evidence to support the idea that Peter ever labored in literal Babylon. On the other hand, tradition locates his closing labors and violent death at Rome. . . . It is known that early Christians often used the cryptic title 'Babylon' when speaking of the Roman capital, to avoid political reprisals."[9] It's reasonable, then, to conclude, that Peter worked in Rome for a period of time near the end of his life. However, there's absolutely no evi-dence to support the idea that he was a bishop in Rome, and there's certainly no evidence that he ruled over the entire Christian church from that city! It's significant that as part of the conclusion to his letter to the Christians in Rome Paul sent special greetings to twenty-five people, but Peter is not one of them (Romans 16:3–16).

So where did the popes come up with the idea that they were the succes-sors of "Bishop Peter," which would make Peter the first pope? Gary Wills answers the question:

> By the third century, bishops of Rome claimed to stand *vice Petri*, "in the place of" Peter, as ruler over the whole church, East and West. . . .
>
> . . . The Roman church, not having a bishop until the second century, could not have recorded a line of bishops before that, and was hazily sketched in after that. The list was confected in retrospect, as Eamon Duffy says, "based on scraps of half-remembered information, or simply invented." The aim was not history but symbol. . . . In short, where records were lacking, they were simply made up.[10]

So there you have it. The idea that the pope is a successor to Peter, the first pope, is an invention of the papacy and not a historical fact. Wills makes the significant comment that "the novelty of the claim to sole power in Peter seemed absurd on the face of it—that Jesus would rest the whole future of his disciples on one man, isolated from the other disciples. (Jesus, remember, had forbidden his followers to have any preeminence among them)—(Mk 9:33–37, Lk 14:7–11)."[11]

How did the pope become the vicar of Christ? That isn't the only question. Where did the idea come from that the pope is *vice Christi*—the "vicar of Christ"? Gary Wills answers that question too. "The title Vicar of Peter was meant to establish primacy over the other bishops."[12] "But institutional power [authority over all the bishops] did not satisfy the popes who wanted a more intimate access to *the consciences of all believers*, prescribing all belief and behavior. *Christ's own access to the believer* was more important than Peter's sway over the bishops, so the pope took on a new title: he was *vice Christi*, the Vicar of Christ."[13]

Wills then cites a paragraph from *The Papal Monarchy: The Western Church From 1050 to 1250*, a book by Colin Morris: "The first application to the pope of the precise title 'Vicar of Christ' seems to be early in the twelfth century in Honorius's *Jewel of the Soul* . . . , which makes its special character quite clear: 'The pope is the Vicar of Christ and all the bishops are the vicars of the apostles.' . . . The first pope to use the title was Eugenius III in 1153, and thereafter its acceptance was widespread."[14]

How did the pope become the emperor? Next, how did the pope reach the point, between A.D. 1200 and 1500, that he could tell kings and rulers what to do and they would do it (sometimes)? It was a trend that began when Constantine became a Christian of sorts and stopped the Roman Empire's persecution against Christians. I pointed out earlier that at that time in history nobody had ever thought of separating church and state, so it was natural for the church to allow itself to be involved in political affairs and for the emperor to be involved in church affairs. Thus, Constantine took an active role in managing the church. As I pointed out earlier in this chapter, he built churches, led out in settling theological conflicts, and disciplined heretical bishops. At this point, the emperor was in the driver's seat, and the church was in the passenger's seat. The church accepted that gladly. After all, it was a huge change from the emperor persecuting the church during some 250 years of its early history!

However, from about A.D. 1200 to 1700, the pope told kings what to do. This doesn't mean that the kings always obeyed the pope. It was more a matter of the pope believing himself to be the supreme political leader of the world as well as its religious leader. And he had ways to get his will enforced, as evidenced by Henry IV standing barefoot in the snow for three days at the pope's winter palace at Canossa, humbly pleading for the pope's forgiveness.

How did this huge switch come about—from the emperor dominating the church to the church dominating (or at least thinking it had the right to dominate) the emperor?

The Donation of Constantine, a fake document probably composed in the eighth century, gave the popes what they needed to make their claim to supremacy over emperors and kings. Wikipedia states,

> The text, purportedly a decree of Roman Emperor Constantine I dated 30 March, in a year mistakenly said to be both that of his fourth consulate (315) and that of the consulate of Gallicanus (317),* contains a detailed profession of Christian faith and a recounting of how the emperor, seeking a cure of his leprosy, was converted and baptized by Pope Sylvester I. In gratitude, he [Constantine] determined to bestow on the see of Peter [Rome] "power, and dignity of glory, and vigour, and *honour imperial*." . . . To Sylvester and his successors he also granted *imperial insignia*, the tiara, and "the city of Rome, and all the provinces, places and cities of Italy and the Western regions."[15]

From this forged document and others like it, popes in the Middle Ages claimed supreme authority over both church and state.

Ellen White recognized this deception. She wrote, "About the close of the eighth century, papists put forth the claim that in the first ages of the church the bishops of Rome had possessed the same spiritual power which they now assumed. To establish this claim, some means must be employed to give it a show of authority; this was readily suggested by the father of lies. Ancient writings were forged by monks. Decrees of councils before unheard of were discovered, establishing the universal supremacy of the pope from the earliest times. And a church that had rejected the truth greedily accepted these deceptions."[16]

The popes also realized that they needed a scriptural basis for their claim to have the authority to rule over kings, and they found at least three. The first and most important one is Luke 22:36–38. After Jesus and His disciples had celebrated the Passover and the first Communion service in the upper room, He said to them,

---

* Gallicanus was a senator of the Roman Empire.

"If you don't have a sword, sell your cloak and buy one. . . ."
The disciples said, "See, Lord, here are two swords."
"That is enough," he replied."

The papacy's rationale was that the two swords represented the two forms of governing authority in the world: the moral and the political. In a long letter to Pope Eugene III, Bernard of Clairvaux* interpreted this to mean that "both swords therefore belong to the church, the spiritual and the material sword—the one is to be used *for* the church, the other *by* the church. This latter sword is in the priest's hand, the former in a military hand, but only when directed by the priest who guides the emperor's hand."[17]

Wills made a significant comment about the two-swords interpretation: "This and all other interpretations make Jesus himself talk of two swords. Actually, he just mentioned one. . . . The disciples alone mention two, and they are acting foolishly (as usual)."[18]

Pope Boniface VIII came up with another "biblical" evidence in support of the papacy holding temporal power over kings and emperors. He said that this power was supported by the spiritual meaning of Noah's ark. There was just one boat (God's boat) and one pilot (Noah) who was inside the boat. Outside, "everything on earth was obliterated." Similarly, there was one church (symbolized by Noah's boat) with one pope (symbolized by Noah), and thus "every human creature . . . must to be subject to the Roman Pontiff."[19]

A third scriptural evidence for papal supremacy over the state—and a very weird one—focused on Christ's seamless garment. The soldiers gambled for His other pieces of clothing, but His seamless garment was left in one piece. The argument was that the pope wears this garment, spiritually, and therefore exercises "seamless" authority both spiritual and temporal.[20]

Such reasoning was the basis during the first half of the second millennium for the papal claim that popes had the right to lord it over secular governments and their leaders.

Control over people's consciences. Earlier in this chapter I quoted a statement by Wills, who said that the bishops and the popes "wanted a more intimate access to the consciences of all believers, prescribing all belief and behavior." How did they achieve that? By preventing the people from having access to

---

* Bernard of Clairvaux was a French abbot (the head of a monastery) who had a great deal of influence on the popes of the first half of the twelfth century. See *Wikipedia*, s.v. "Bernard of Clairvaux," last modified February 11, 2017, https://en.wikipedia.org/wiki /Bernard_of_Clairvaux.

the Bible. They did that by refusing to translate the Bible into the languages of the people. Wills writes, "For some, the great advantage of limiting knowledge of the truth by limiting the language in which it was transacted increased the value of that truth, even for those being kept in the dark. It was a blessing for them to be kept outside. It made them more reverent, and their reverence more meritorious. . . . The laity could sense the power of the Mass 'independent of any comprehension in the natural sense of the word.' Mystery is enhanced by inaccessibility."[21]

In other words, a feeling of mystery and awe was the essence of a sound religious experience, and rational knowledge of biblical truth would interfere with a Christian achieving that awe. That's nonsense, of course. It was in fact a strategy for the pope, his bishops, and his priests to maintain control of the people, for what they didn't know they couldn't object to. Ellen White wrote,

> Satan well knew that the Holy Scriptures would enable men to discern his deceptions and withstand his power. . . . In order for Satan to maintain his sway over men, and establish the authority of the papal usurper, he must keep them in ignorance of the Scriptures. . . . Therefore its sacred truths must be concealed and suppressed. This logic was adopted by the Roman Church. For hundreds of years the circulation of the Bible was prohibited. The people were forbidden to read it or have it in their houses, and unprincipled priests and prelates interpreted its teachings to sustain their pretensions. Thus the pope came to be almost universally acknowledged as the vicegerent of God on earth, endowed with authority over church and state.[22]

By the twentieth century, the papacy realized that it could no longer keep the Bible from the people, and it allowed them to read it—with the caveat that they must turn to the church for its interpretation.

Daniel's prophecy. The papacy of the Middle Ages is described in Daniel 7 and 8. The prophet said that the little horn, which symbolized the papacy, would "speak against the Most High and oppress his saints and try to change the set times and the laws" (Daniel 7:25). In its claim to be the vicar of Christ, the papacy spoke "against the Most High," because Jesus said very specifically that His personal representative on Earth after He left would be the Counselor, the Holy Spirit (John 14:16, 17). Jesus said that the Holy Spirit would guide His people into all truth (John 16:13), but the papacy usurped the role of the Holy Spirit by refusing the people the right to study the Bible for themselves. When it did relent, the people still had to trust the papacy for its interpretation.

Daniel further foretold the role of the papacy, which was symbolized by a little horn. Speaking of this little horn, Daniel said, "It set itself up to be as great as the Prince of the host; it took away the daily sacrifice from him, and the place of his sanctuary was brought low. Because of rebellion, the host of the saints and the daily sacrifice were given over to it" (Daniel 8:11, 12).

Let's analyze these verses a phrase at a time. "It set itself up to be as great as the Prince of the host." Note that the New International Version capitalizes the word *Prince*, indicating that He is a Divine Being; namely, Jesus. I agree with that conclusion. The papacy fulfilled this prediction by calling the pope the vicar of Christ. "It took away the daily sacrifice from him." The papacy fulfilled these words by giving the pope, bishops, and priests the right to forgive people their sins, which is the prerogative of Deity alone and a role that Christ especially carries out (1 John 1:9).

Three phrases in Daniel 8:12 are also relevant to our discussion. First, "because of rebellion." From our discussion so far in this chapter it's very obvious that the papacy was, and is, in rebellion against God. Second, "the host of the saints . . . [was] given over to it." Five hundred years of papal persecution—from about A.D. 1200 through 1700—is a direct fulfillment of that prediction. Third, "the daily sacrifice . . . [was] given over to it." The daily sacrifice in the Old Testament sanctuary symbolized Christ's death on the cross for our sins, and Hebrews 9:26 says that Christ "has appeared once for all at the end of the ages to do away with sin by the sacrifice of himself." Notice that Jesus died "once for all," but the Catholic Church denies that verse by its sacrifice of the Mass, in which Jesus is supposedly sacrificed thousands of times a day in Catholic churches all over the world. Furthermore, teaching the faithful to pray to the saints for intercession before God, especially Mary (whom the Catholic Church calls the co-redemptrix and co-mediatrix before God), totally goes against the biblical teaching that Christ is the "one mediator between God and men" (1 Timothy 2:5).

The demise of the papacy

Powerful political entities tend to rise slowly, and they also decline slowly. Usually, the decline begins some time before the political entity is aware of what's happening; but when it does become aware, it fights vigorously to maintain its dominance. The papacy is an excellent example of this phenomenon.

Two forces were instrumental in challenging the power of the papacy:

religion and secularism. On the religious side, John Wycliffe, one of the first Reformers, lived at about the time that the papacy had reached the height of its political power, and it retained that power for several more centuries. Huss and Jerome are two other examples of challengers to papal power during the height of its existence. Wycliffe was fortunate to live in England, which was some distance from Rome, and he managed to escape its persecution. (However, some years after his death the church condemned him as a heretic and had his corpse exhumed and burned to ashes.) Huss and Jerome lived on the European continent. They actually placed themselves under papal control in Rome itself and were martyred for their faith. The next prominent religious leader to challenge the papacy was Martin Luther. By his time, Europe's political leaders had grown weary of Rome's dominance in their affairs, and they protected Luther so that he also escaped martyrdom. And Luther, as we all know, started the very successful Protestant Reformation, which was one of the forces that broke the power of the papacy. The other was secularism. *Secularism* is a belief system that considers God and religion to be either irrelevant at best or harmful at worst. Secularism has especially been a part of Western culture during the past three hundred or four hundred years. Prior to that, it was alive but submissive to papal control. Secularism began its rise to dominance in society through what is known as the "scientific revolution"—a phenomenon that began in secret when Nicolaus Copernicus challenged the Ptolemaic theory that Earth is the center of the universe, which had been the accepted theory in Europe for about fifteen hundred years.*

A bit of background is necessary at this point. Keep in mind that our understanding of the universe is far different from what it was even one hundred years ago, and it's vastly different from what it was five hundred years ago. The Ptolemaic theory is based on the observation that the sun, moon, planets, and stars *appear* to revolve around the earth. Thus, the Ptolemaic theory that the earth is the center of the universe seemed reasonable, and, as I said, it was accepted by European society, including the church, for fifteen hundred years. Furthermore, the church saw biblical support for this idea in Psalm 93:1, which says, "The world is firmly established; it cannot be moved." The church interpreted this to mean that the earth is stationary,

---

* Ptolemy developed his theory in the second century A.D., but the idea that the stars and the planets revolved around the earth had been held for at least a thousand years before that. See *Wikipedia*, s.v. "Geocentric Model," last modified February 25, 2017, https://en.wikipedia .org/wiki/Geocentric_model.

thus supporting the Ptolemaic theory. It also saw this as elevating the earth and humanity to the center of God's creation.

However, during the fifteen hundred years that Ptolemy's theory was the accepted view, it kept encountering more and more problems scientifically. Finally, Copernicus determined to resolve the difficulties, and he developed what's known as the heliocentric theory; namely, that the *sun* is the center of the universe and that the earth, the stars, and the planets orbit the sun. This was such a powerful challenge to the church's accepted view—the Ptolemaic theory—that Copernicus, fearing papal reprisal, didn't publish his work until shortly before he died.

Galileo was born about twenty years after Copernicus died. He accepted Copernicus's theory, and he had a powerful instrument to support it that wasn't available to Copernicus: the telescope. With this, Galileo was able to establish visually what Copernicus had developed in theory. In spite of the fact that the church condemned Galileo's conclusions, the scientific revolution took off, and the result, five hundred years later, is the comfortable world of medicine, air conditioning, and global travel that we enjoy today.

In spite of that, it's important to understand the difference between the Christian religion and secularism. Christianity is based on the assumption that there is a God and that He has revealed Himself in the Bible. Secularism, in its modern form, is based on the assumption that the only acceptable reality to be considered is that which our five senses can perceive, either directly or through the instruments we've devised. However, for several hundred years, secularists were also religionists to one degree or another. Sir Isaac Newton was one of the most famous scientists of all time, but he was also a dedicated Christian who wrote commentaries on the Bible, including Bible prophecy. Even America's founding fathers, though very much secularists, believed there is a God who orders the universe and holds us morally accountable to Himself.

Protestantism began challenging papal supremacy; and by the mid-1600s, it was joined by secularism, which had begun to challenge religion in general. Over a period of about three hundred years, both Protestantism and secularism grew to the point that papal supremacy over kings and emperors was significantly curtailed. Its death knell came during the French Revolution, as it was a totally secular movement that all but destroyed the papacy in France, took over most of the papacy's lands, and executed a large number of priests and bishops. The stroke that put a final end to papal supremacy came in February 1798, when the French general Berthier entered the Vatican and took Pope Pius VI as prisoner. Thus was inflicted what Revelation 13:3 calls a "fatal wound" (KJV: "deadly wound"). The papacy had almost no influence over European politics for the next 130 years.

Through the papacy, the Kingdom of Darkness dominated Jesus' church for fifteen hundred years, but the time had come for the Kingdom of Light to rise again, break the fetters that had bound the church, and free it to proclaim God's end-time message to the world. Today we are in the final stages of that mission. Once it is accomplished, the Kingdom of Darkness will attack the Kingdom of Light in a final, fierce struggle that will be settled in favor of the Kingdom of Light at the battle of Armageddon.

Summary of the Kingdom of Darkness and Jesus' church

Following Jesus' ascension, Saul, who was one of the most prominent leaders of the Kingdom of Darkness, suddenly and dramatically defected to the Kingdom of Light and led the early church to a resounding victory over the Kingdom of Darkness. However, during the next millennium and a half the Kingdom of Darkness managed to get God's church almost totally on its side. It changed God's law and, claiming the title "Vicar of Christ" (vice Christ), assumed the authority of the Holy Spirit, whom Christ had appointed as His personal Representative on Earth during His absence. Losing its love, which is the basis of God's law and the founding principle of the Kingdom of Light, Christ's church developed an intense hatred for His true followers, putting thousands of them to death. Of the conflicts we've considered thus far in this book, this was the fifth victory for the Kingdom of Darkness. However, God's Kingdom of Light wasn't through. Armageddon, the final battle, was still to come.

1. Justin Martyr, *The First Apology*, chap. 67, quoted in Samuele Bacchiocchi, *From Sabbath to Sunday* (Berrien Springs, MI: Biblical Perspectives, 1999), 224, 225; emphasis in the original.

2. Bacchiocchi, *From Sabbath to Sunday,* 201n62.

3. Garry Wills, *The Future of the Catholic Church With Pope Francis* (New York: Penguin Books, 2015).

4. Ibid., 84.

5. Ibid.

6. Ibid., 88.

7. Ibid., 96; emphasis in the original.

8. White, *The Great Controversy*, 49, 50.

9. Nichol, *The Seventh-day Adventist Bible Commentary*, 7:589.

10. Wills, *The Future of the Catholic Church*, 102, 103.

11. Ibid., 101.

12. Ibid., 106.

13. Ibid., 107; emphasis added (except for the words *vice Christi*).

14. Colin Morris, *The Papal Monarchy: The Western Church From 1050 to 1250* (Oxford: Oxford University Press, 1989), 107, quoted in ibid., 107.

15. *Wikipedia*, s.v. "Donation of Constantine," last modified February 5, 2017, https://en.wikipedia.org/wiki/Donation_of_Constantine; emphasis added.

16. White, *The Great Controversy*, 56.

17. Bernard of Clairvaux, *De Consideratione*, quoted in Wills, *The Future of the Catholic Church*, 112; emphasis in the original.

18. Wills, *The Future of the Catholic Church*, 111.

19. Pope Boniface, *Unam Sanctam* (1302), quoted in ibid., 113.

20. Wills, *The Future of the Catholic Church*, 113.

21. Ibid., 16.

22. White, *The Great Controversy*, 51.

CHAPTER 20

Jesus' End-Time Church

Seventh-day Adventists have always thought of themselves as the "remnant." This concept comes from Revelation 12:17, which in the King James Version reads, "The dragon was wroth with the woman, and went to make war with the *remnant* of her seed, which keep the commandments of God, and have the testimony of Jesus Christ" (emphasis added). The Greek word for "remnant" is *loipoi*, which means "remaining ones," and which the New International Version and the New King James Version have both translated as "the rest of her offspring."

A brief overview of Revelation 12 will assist us in understanding the meaning of this "remnant." When the dragon (Satan) failed in his effort to destroy Jesus during His life on earth (verses 1–5), he attacked the woman; that is, the church (verses 6, 13). However, God provided a place in "the desert" (verses 6, 14), where He protected her for 1,260 days (verse 6).* Then the serpent (Satan) "spewed water like a river, to overtake the woman and sweep her away with the torrent" (verse 15). Adventists have always interpreted this as symbolizing the persecution against Christians who dissented from the papal teachings during the Dark Ages.

But God had a rescue plan, also expressed symbolically: *"The earth* helped the woman by opening its mouth and swallowing the river that the dragon had spewed out of his mouth" (verse 16; emphasis added). In some way, God would use planet Earth itself to free the woman, His church, from papal tyranny. And that is indeed what happened.

European sailors had always traveled east to reach India. But after concluding that the earth is a globe, Columbus sailed west in search of a new route to India. When he reached land, he assumed that he had arrived at India, which is how Native Americans got the name *Indians*. Columbus didn't realize it, but God had used him to open up a way of escape for persecuted Christians to find freedom from papal tyranny. That's how the earth opened its mouth and swallowed the flood of water that the serpent spewed out of its mouth.

---

* Verse 14 says "time, times, and half a time," which is the same wording used in Daniel 7:25 and which expresses the number 1,260 symbolically.

Verse 17, which immediately follows, gives us a snapshot of God's end-time church, "the remnant." Here is how it reads in the King James Version: "The dragon was wroth with the woman, and went to make war with the remnant of her seed, which keep the commandments of God, and have the testimony of Jesus Christ." Notice that this remnant church has two characteristics: it keeps God's commandments—all of them, including the Sabbath—and it has the testimony of Jesus, which according to Revelation 19:10 is "the spirit of prophecy," that is, the gift of prophecy. Seventh-day Adventists meet both of these criteria. We keep the biblical Sabbath, and we have the gift of prophecy in the ministry of Ellen White.

Verse 17 also says that Satan, the dragon, was "enraged" at the woman. Revelation 13, which we will discuss in a later chapter of this book, goes on to describe how the dragon will express that rage. But for now, let's find out more about God's end-time church. The first issue we need to address is the process God went through to set up His end-time church.

Setting up God's end-time church

God was very careful in setting up His church that would live during the final years of Earth's history. From start to finish, it took about 350 years—from the late 1400s to the mid-1800s.

A safe place. The first thing God had to do was to provide a safe place from which His end-time church could carry out its mission. The European continent with its rigid religions, both Protestant and Catholic, that persecuted dissenters, certainly was not that place! Instead, God opened up the New World. Columbus set out in 1492 to discover a new sea route to India, and that was right around the time that both the religious Reformation and secularism began asserting themselves against the papacy.

There are two reasons why it took more than 350 years for that new world to be ready for God's end-time church. First, the initial settlers in the early 1600s had to establish a government and a society that could support God's end-time church. God could hardly have set up His church as soon as the Pilgrims and the Puritans landed on the continent, nor could He have done so fifty or even one hundred years after that. The North American continent was still under British rule then, and God had to establish the United States as an independent nation with the Constitution and Bill of Rights that provided the political climate that would give His end-time church the freedom to carry out its work unimpeded by strict government regulations.

The second reason God had to wait about 350 years after 1492 to set up

His end-time church is that the Puritans, who came from England, where the state dominated the church, brought with them the Old World notion that it was the duty of their new government to enforce religious dogma. The result was the persecution of dissenters, especially smaller groups such as the Baptists, Quakers, and Mennonites. God's end-time church would definitely have been subjected to that same persecution. God had to create a safe place in which to set up His church that would proclaim the final warning to the world. He did that both by opening up the New World and by creating within it a new nation that was different from any other nation that had ever existed on the earth.* However, it took a bitter war to do it.

The American Revolution was, first of all, a rebellion against British rule. The British political philosophy of the time would not have permitted Jesus' end-time church to operate with the freedom it needed. Second, the American Revolution was a critical step in eliminating religious persecution. When the war was over, the new nation had a constitution, including a Bill of Rights; the first of those rights kept church and state separate and guaranteed citizens the freedom to think and believe whatever they pleased as long as their beliefs and their actions didn't harm others. Another important part of this first amendment was the freedom of speech. It gave God's end-time church the freedom to proclaim its message throughout the United States without interference from the government or from people who didn't like its message. People could debate with God's end-time church, but they could not interfere with its right to teach and preach its message—all of which would have been impossible during the medieval period in Europe or on the American continent prior to the establishment of the new nation.

Secularism. Religionists, however, were not the only moving force behind the push for religious freedom. Religious persecution by the dominant churches against the Mennonites, the Quakers, and the Baptists continued almost up to the adoption of the American Constitution. Because these smaller denominations were powerless against the dominant denominations, much of the moving force behind the demand for religious freedom came from secularists. Thomas Jefferson, Benjamin Franklin, and James Madison—three of the key leaders in setting up the new government—were secularists and mostly Deists, who believed in God but weren't particularly pious. These secularists had the political clout to rein in the dominant churches and stop their persecution.

---

* The closest thing to the American political experiment was Greek democracy a several hundred years before Christ, but even that was much different from the American Constitution and Bill of Rights.

It's also *very* important to note that, in spite of a bit of tension between religionists and secularists, they got along fairly well during the first two hundred years of American history. Both sides agreed on the importance of religious freedom, the separation of church and state, freedom of speech, and other principles of the Constitution and the Bill of Rights.

Over the years, most of the rest of the Western world—Canada, Europe, Australia, and many parts of Latin America—adopted the American experiment. With occasional exceptions, even Asia and Africa have become tolerant of Christianity. All this made it possible for God's end-time church to spread its message throughout the world.

Two spiritual revivals in the United States also helped to lay the foundation for God's end-time church. These revivals are known as the First and Second Great Awakenings. The First Great Awakening swept the Protestant world in Europe and America during the 1730s and 1740s, and John Wesley's Methodist Church sprang from it. Many of the Adventist pioneers, including Ellen White, were raised in the Methodist Church, and they brought their Methodist theology of free will into the Adventist Church.

The Second Great Awakening had an even greater impact on the establishment of God's end-time church. It began in the 1790s and continued through most of the first half of the 1800s. A great missionary movement began during this time. Several of those who pioneered in what we today would call the underdeveloped world are still fairly well known, at least in religious circles. David Livingstone pioneered in taking the Christian message to Africa, Hudson Taylor to China, and William Carey to India. Also during this time, several Bible societies were established, including the British and Foreign Bible Society and the American Bible Society, which continue to operate to this day.

It took time for God to *set up* His end-time church. He had to provide a safe place from which it could carry out its work, and the American Revolution contributed to that by breaking the power of the British Empire over the nation. With the aid of secularists, the new Constitution, with its Bill of Rights, broke the power of the dominant churches over the religious life of the nation, and two religious revivals created a spiritual climate in which God's end-time church could get its start.

God's end-time church

It was in this secular and spiritual context that God raised up His end-time church. He began with a man named William Miller, who was a farmer in upstate New York. Miller grew up a Christian, but in his early adult years he became a Deist—a religion of sorts that taught that there is a God who created the world, but then He abandoned it to take care of itself. However, Miller eventually converted back to Christianity, and his skeptical Deist friends challenged him about the reliability of the Bible. Not knowing how to respond, Miller set out to study the Bible for himself. Beginning with Genesis, he proceeded to read it through page by page. Anytime he encountered a problem, he stopped and, with the aid of a concordance, resolved it to his satisfaction before continuing.

In due time, Miller came to Daniel's prophecies, and he was particularly intrigued by Daniel 8:14: "Unto two thousand and three hundred days, then shall the sanctuary be cleansed" (KJV). Miller concluded that the sanctuary was the earth and the cleansing of the sanctuary represented the cleansing of the earth by fire at the second coming of Christ. Then, putting Daniel 8:14 together with the seventy-week prophecy in Daniel 9:24, 25, he concluded that Christ would come sometime in 1843 or at the latest by March 1844.

This seemed like astounding news, and Miller was convicted that he should begin preaching it! So, beginning in 1832, with some trepidation, he began to share with others his interpretation of Daniel 8:14, and it immediately caught on. It wasn't long before Miller had to give up farming to go into full-time preaching. In 1839, he began preaching his message in the large cities, such as New York, Boston, and Philadelphia, and his message became a movement. Tens of thousands of people joined it. Unfortunately, March 1844 came and went, and Jesus didn't return. The believers were discouraged, but many of them continued clinging to the hope that Jesus' coming was very near.

Then in August 1844, a man by the name of Samuel Snow proclaimed at a camp meeting in Exeter, Massachusetts, that, based on his calculation of the Jewish Day of Atonement, Jesus would return on October 22, which was less than three months away! The people left that camp meeting absolutely inspired and energized; the news spread like wildfire. Statistics are impossible to verify, but estimates of the number of people who joined what was known as the "seventh-month movement"* vary from 50,000 to 150,000. The population of the United States in 1844 was around 20 million. Splitting the difference between 50,000 and 150,000 comes to 100,000, which would be about half a

* Snow's interpretation was based on a comparison of Christ's second coming with the Old Testament feast days. Just as Christ's death occurred on the very day of Passover, and just as the Holy Spirit was poured out on the apostles on the very day of Pentecost, so Snow concluded that Christ's second coming would occur on the actual Day of Atonement, which in 1844 was October 22. The Old Testament Day of Atonement occurred on the tenth day of the seventh month. Hence the expression "seventh-month movement."

percent of the U.S. population at the time. That may not sound like a lot, but bring these statistics forward to our day. According to the U.S. Census Bureau, the American population at the beginning of 2015 was about 320 million. One half of one percent of that number would be 16 million people. Imagine a Christian revival today that was so powerful it garnered 16 million adherents in just a few years! Percentage-wise, that's what happened in 1844.

However, Miller's movement wasn't just a popular fanaticism in the way today's public can get worked up over a political campaign. It was a profoundly spiritual movement. Ellen White, who experienced it firsthand, said that as people realized that Christ's coming was near, "they approached this hour with calm solemnity. They rested in sweet communion with God, and [were] earnest of the peace that was to be theirs in the bright hereafter. None who experienced this hope and trust can forget those precious hours of waiting. For some weeks preceding the time, worldly business was for the most part laid aside. The sincere believers carefully examined every thought and emotion of their hearts as if upon their deathbeds and in a few hours to close their eyes upon earthly scenes."[1]

As we all know, Jesus did not return on October 22, 1844. Hiram Edson wrote that, after the clock passed midnight and the people realized that Jesus was not going to return, "Our fondest hopes and expectations were blasted. . . . We wept and wept, till the day dawn."[2] And Ellen White said, "Those who with sincere faith and love had looked for their Saviour, experienced a bitter disappointment."[3]

Why the Great Disappointment?

Ellen White went on to say, "The purposes of God were being accomplished; He was testing the hearts of those who professed to be waiting for His appearing. There were among them many who had been actuated by no higher motive than fear. Their profession of faith had not affected their hearts or their lives. When the expected event failed to take place, these persons declared that they were not disappointed; they had never believed that Christ would come. They were among the first to ridicule the sorrow of the true believers."[4] By the time everything settled out, there were only about a hundred people left who still believed that Miller's interpretation of the 2,300 days in Daniel 8:14 was correct. His mistake, they concluded, was not in the date 1844. His mistake was his misinterpretation of what was to happen in 1844. *God used this small band of disappointed believers to establish His end-time church.*

Some Christians still ridicule Seventh-day Adventists today because their expectation of Christ's return in 1844 failed to materialize. But please notice the similarity between the Great Disappointment of October 22 and the "great disappointment" that Jesus' disciples experienced in A.D. 33. Their false expectation of Christ leading the Jewish nation to victory over the Romans and establishing His own eternal kingdom were blasted. In both cases, the expectations of God's people were crushed, because their expectations were based on a misinterpretation of the Bible's prophecies. In the case of the disciples, their disappointment turned to joy within about a day and a half by Christ's resurrection, and less than two months later three thousand people were converted to Christ by Peter's energetic preaching under the power of the Holy Spirit on the Day of Pentecost (Acts 2:41). The resolution to the 1844 Great Disappointment was slower in coming.

In both A.D. 33 and 1844, God put His people through a severe crisis in order to rid them of their false expectations. People who come through a crisis with their faith intact, even if their numbers are few, are much more likely to be energized to carry forward God's work after they understand God's real purpose for them. God used the Great Disappointment in 1844 to weed out the insincere "believers" so that the true believers would not be hindered by the lukewarm Christian experience of their faithless brothers and sisters. All these reasons were part of God's plan to set up His end-time church for success in carrying out its mission.

Another way in which God prepared for His end-time church to carry out its mission was the appointment of a special messenger to His church, Ellen White, to whom He entrusted the gift of prophecy. He called her to her prophetic office about two months after the Great Disappointment. She was just seventeen years old when she received her first vision in December 1844, which she immediately related to the group of Advent believers in Portland, Maine, where she lived at the time. About a week later, God gave her a second vision, and this time He specifically instructed her to relate it to others, which she did with much fear and trembling.[5]

God's end-time church established

Now it was time for God's end-time church to begin its mission. But notice something interesting: the Great Disappointment and the establishment of God's end-time church took place in the middle of the nineteenth century, and these believers were absolutely certain that Jesus would come in their day—probably within no more than ten or fifteen years, twenty at the most. Yet here we are more than 165 years later, still carrying on the mission that they started, because Jesus still hasn't come. The problem for the early believers was that they had a very limited understanding of their mission. In the mid-1800s, there were people from all parts of Europe living in the United States, as well as a few from Asia, and our pioneers assumed that the mission God had given them would be fulfilled as these people accepted the message and then shared it with their friends and loved ones in their homelands. It took these early believers about thirty years after the Great Disappointment to begin to understand that *they* were to go *themselves* to these unreached lands and preach God's end-time message. In 1874, thirty years after 1844, the church sent J. N. Andrews to Switzerland as its first overseas missionary.

By the beginning of the twentieth century, Seventh-day Adventist mission work had spread to every continent except Antarctica. For the first hundred years after 1844, most Adventist missionaries were sent out from North America. However, around the mid-twentieth century, missionaries began going out from other countries, and today many missionaries from other countries are coming to North America.

Another development began during the second half of the twentieth century: church leadership in underdeveloped nations was increasingly appointed from within those nations. Today nearly all leadership positions in local conferences, unions, and divisions are filled by men and women from the regions where those entities exist. Western nations primarily send missionaries for specialized responsibilities, such as physicians, university professors, and others who can provide skills that are still unavailable in less developed parts of the world. Often one of the primary tasks of these missionaries is to train local people to carry out their work.

Yet another phenomenon developed during the last quarter of the twentieth century: independent Adventist organizations in the United States began sending out their own missionaries. These organizations are loyal to the church, its teachings, and its organization. Adventist Frontier Missions establishes indigenous Seventh-day Adventist church-planting movements among unreached people groups. Gospel Outreach is dedicated to extending the ministry of the Seventh-day Adventist Church in unreached areas of the world, with a special emphasis on the 10/40 Window. Maranatha International sends people from Western nations to build churches and schools all over the world. Western people who participate in these activities raise the funds for their own travel expenses and accommodations in the countries where they serve.

At the General Conference Session in 1990, the church adopted a five-year plan called One Thousand Days of Reaping, which had the objective of increasing global church membership by one million members during the following five years. And it happened! Since then, church members in the developing parts of the world have put forth energetic efforts at evangelism. The result is that, as I write these words at the beginning of 2017, the world membership of the Seventh-day Adventist Church stands at about twenty million, and it's growing.

We now understand what our pioneers could not—that God's plan was for His end-time church to develop an organizational structure that could support a global movement, and then He had to give His church time (172 years at the time I'm writing this book) to establish itself throughout the world so that it would be ready to proclaim the warning message when the final crisis breaks upon the world. Because that has not yet started, we still have time to keep growing until God allows the Kingdom of Darkness to initiate it.

The mission of the remnant

From the very beginning of the Advent movement, Seventh-day Adventists have viewed themselves as "the remnant" of Revelation 12:17 (KJV). We have looked at the reasons for this in the introductory pages of this chapter. Here I will share with you what Revelation 14:6–11 says about our mission. This passage describes three angels flying in midair with messages for the world. Of course, the point of these angels' messages is not that we can expect to see literal angels flying through the skies and shouting down their warnings to the people of the world. These angels symbolize God's end-time Seventh-day Adventist Church, and the messages they proclaim are the messages that God has commissioned *us* to proclaim to the world. So let's examine those messages.

The first angel's message has an introduction, which is followed by things that the angel actually proclaims. Revelation says that this first angel "had the eternal gospel to proclaim to those who live on the earth—to every nation, tribe, language and people" (verse 6).

This introduction is clearly a repetition of Christ's great commission, because Christ told His disciples to "go and make disciples of all nations" (Matthew 28:19). Thus, our most important responsibility as God's end-time church is to win souls to Jesus by teaching them about Christ's life and death, that He forgives their sins and covers them with His righteousness, and that He promises them eternal life in His kingdom. This is the gospel in a nutshell.

The second part of the first angel's message is that we should urge people everywhere to "fear God and give Him glory" (Revelation 14:7). This command is especially relevant in our secular age, when the fastest-growing religious group is the "nones"—those with no religious affiliation. We live in a culture that has rejected God, and He has given us the responsibility of calling all human beings back to God, regardless of the ridicule and hostility they may face for doing so.

The third part of the first angel's message is to proclaim that "the hour of his [God's] judgment has come" (verse 7). This is especially appropriate, because the pre-Advent judgment is taking place right now in heaven. People need to be aware that as affairs on Earth wind up, God's judgment is nearing its end, and they need to make a final decision to accept Jesus and His commandments before it's too late.

The fourth part of the first angel's message is to "worship him who made the heavens, the earth, the sea and the springs of water" (verse 7). This is almost a direct quote from the Sabbath commandment in the Decalogue (Exodus 20:11), which is a command to keep the seventh-day Sabbath as a memorial of God's creation of the world. And, as we shall see in the third angel's message, this command to observe the Bible Sabbath is *the* critical decision that each human being must make before the close of probation.

These four aspects of the first angel's message are part of God's mission for the remnant.

The second angel's message. The word *Babylon* in the second angel's message is a symbol of confusion, which is most appropriate in today's world with its thousands of branches of the Christian faith plus all of the world's non-Christian religions (Revelation 14:8). Before the final crisis ends, all religions throughout the world will unite into one super-religion under the leadership of the papacy, and that's what will constitute Babylon. The second angel is giving us—God's end-time remnant church—the responsibility to warn the world that this conglomerate, global religion is inspired by Satan, and we are to call human beings everywhere to come out of it (Revelation 18:1–4).

The third angel's message is the most fearsome description of God's anger in the entire Bible. It warns that anyone who "worships the beast and his image and receives his mark on the forehead or the hand, he, too, will drink of the wine of God's fury, which has been poured full strength into the cup of his wrath. . . . There is no rest day or night for those who worship the beast and his image or for anyone who receives the mark of his name" (Revelation 14:9–11).

Adventists understand that the mark of the beast is the observance of Sunday when that observance is enforced by law. For 160 years, we've been explaining this to as many people as we can get to listen to us. However, during the entire history of the remnant thus far, there has been almost no government activity in the U.S. Congress to enact a Sunday law.* Yet, the time is coming when the message of the third angel will be extremely relevant, because we understand that Protestants and Catholics will unite to proclaim Sunday as an official day of worship. The trigger for this to happen will be some form of calamity, perhaps a global financial collapse or a natural disaster of global proportions. It may also include military action.

The first angel's message is the most important one, because it proclaims "the eternal gospel." It would be impossible for unconverted people to come out of Babylon. Therefore, of all three of the messages, we must always keep our primary focus on the first one. The response of each individual on planet Earth will be determined by two things: first, by his or her decision regarding Jesus and the salvation He offers through His sacrifice on the cross; and second, by each person's decision whether to be loyal to God's commandments, including the fourth one, regardless of the consequences.

Between 1500 and 1844, God laid the foundation for His end-time church to proclaim the three angels' messages. This included moving a significant portion of Protestantism out of Europe and onto the North American continent and then establishing a government in which His church could operate unencumbered by laws that would restrict its activities.

Since then, our primary focus has been on the first angel's message. We've taught people *about* the second and third angels' messages, but the world still hasn't experienced them. In the next chapter, I will explain why I believe we're approaching the time when that will change.

---

1. White, *The Great Controversy*, 373.

2. Hiram Edson, quoted in Arthur L. White, *Ellen G. White*, vol. 1, *The Early Years* (Hagerstown, MD: Review and Herald® Pub. Assn., 1985), 53.

3. White, *The Great Controversy*, 374.

4. Ibid., 374.

5. This account of Ellen White's call to the prophetic office is based on information provided in Don F. Neufeld et al., *The Seventh-day Adventist Encyclopedia* (Washington, DC: Review and Herald® Pub. Assn., 1976), s.v. "White, Ellen Gould (Harmon)"; and Arthur L. White, *Ellen G. White*, 1:63, 64.

---

* In the early 1890s, the U.S. Congress gave serious consideration to enacting a national Sunday law, but Alonzo T. Jones was able to head it off by his carefully reasoned arguments.

Response to a Recent View of the Remnant

For a number of years, the idea has been growing among some Seventh-day Adventists that our claim to be the remnant is arrogant. "We're no better than other Christians," they say. "Who are we to think that we're so special?"

There's some truth to these statements, and there's also a significant misunderstanding. The truth is, of course, that we *aren't* any better than other Christians. I suspect that those who think that is what the word *remnant* implies came up with this understanding because some Adventists do talk that way, although I think that is less true today than in the past. Those who see the term *remnant* as denoting a misguided exclusiveness may have grown up in homes where that attitude was expressed, but as they grew older they came to realize that it was wrong, and they rejected the whole idea of the remnant. If we think we're better than other Christians, then we're like the Pharisees in Christ's day who thought that being God's special people made Jews superior to the Gentiles. But rejecting the whole idea of Adventists being the remnant is just as much a mistake as thinking that Adventists are better than other Christians.

We need to ask ourselves this: Do we believe the Bible teaches that the Sabbath of the fourth commandment still applies to God's people today? And do we believe that a global crisis is coming when the Sabbath will be the focus of Satan's effort to get Sabbath keepers to yield their convictions by enforcing Sunday as the only legal day of worship? If you answer Yes to these two questions, then you're acknowledging the reason Adventists exist as the "remnant."

The most terrible global crisis since the Flood is about to break upon the world. Daniel predicted it. He said that there is coming "a time of distress such as has not happened from the beginning of nations until then" (Daniel 12:1). Speaking of the months and perhaps years leading up to His second coming, Jesus said that "then there will be great distress, unequaled from the beginning of the world until now—and never to be equaled again. If those days had not been cut short, no one would survive, but for the sake of the elect those days will be shortened" (Matthew 24:21, 22).

The Sabbath won't be the only issue at stake. Jesus said that as the end approaches "false Christs and false prophets will appear and perform great signs and miracles to deceive even the elect—if that were possible. See, I have told you ahead of time" (verses 24, 25). Many of the false prophets that Jesus said would arise in the time of the end will convince people of their deceptive doctrines through spiritualism. So our Adventist teaching about the state of the dead will be as relevant during the final crisis as our teaching about the Sabbath. Ellen White wrote, "Through the two great errors, the immortality of the soul and Sunday sacredness, Satan will bring the people under his deceptions."[1] There are groups here and there warning about one or the other of these doctrines. Seventh-Day Baptists and a few others proclaim the Sabbath, and the Jehovah's Witnesses teach a concept of the state of the dead that is similar to ours. But only Seventh-day Adventists teach both ideas emphatically. We are the ones whom God has given the responsibility of proclaiming these truths to the world in order to prepare the human race for the final crisis.

The idea that Seventh-day Adventists are the remnant isn't arrogant. It's a solemn responsibility, because it involves preparing the world for Armageddon and all that must take place in the world before Armageddon can happen.

---

1. White, *The Great Controversy*, 588.

CHAPTER 21

Signs of the Times

My mother was born on March 13, 1905. When she was about twelve years old, she said to her mother, "Mama, I wonder who I'll marry someday. Maybe he's way down in Texas." Her mother replied, "Oh, honey, you'll never get married. Jesus will come before you're old enough to get married." My mother did indeed marry a Texan, and she had two children and six grandchildren. She died when she was ninety-one years old.

Before we are too hard on my grandmother for telling my mother that Jesus would come before she could get married, let's stop and think about the context in which she said that. World War I was in full swing, and by then the United States would have joined the fray or was about to do so. *Signs of the Times*® and the *Review and Herald* were both proclaiming loud and long that "Armageddon is just around the corner!"

As I write these words, it's been right at one hundred years since my mother and my grandmother had that conversation, so obviously, today the world is much closer to Jesus' return than it was in 1916 or 1917. And I believe the indications of the approaching final crisis and Jesus' return are far stronger today than they were back then. Nevertheless, the lesson we can learn from my grandmother's conversation with my mother still applies: we don't know the day or the hour of Jesus' return (Matthew 24:36).

With that caution, I'll also say that it's always important to pay attention to what's going on in the world around us, and that's my purpose in writing this chapter, because I see a number of trends in today's world that point in the direction of the final crisis and Christ's return. Please take note of the word I just used—*trends*. There will no doubt be a few single events in the future that have great prophetic significance. But I find it much more helpful to observe religious, political, and cultural *trends*. My purpose in this chapter is to share with you trends that I see leading to the final events of world history and the second coming of Jesus.

Secularism

I pointed out in the previous chapter that Thomas Jefferson, Benjamin

Franklin, James Madison, and other secularist political leaders had a profound influence on the establishment of religious freedom in the United States. There was a strong cooperative relationship between these politicians and the minority religions of the time—Baptists, Mennonites, Quakers, and others—who were being persecuted for their faith by the established religions—Anglican, Presbyterian, Congregational, and so on. Nicholas P. Miller, a professor in the Church History Department of the Seventh-day Adventist Theological Seminary in Berrien Springs, Michigan, commented about this cooperative relationship in his book *The Religious Roots of the First Amendment*. He wrote, "Dissenting Protestant religious ideals converged with Enlightenment [secularist] ideas about the proper roles of church and state. . . . The Enlightenment ideas of the elite thinkers were themselves influenced and shaped by religious insights. Thus, rather than a story that has a few, elite thinkers almost single-handedly changing the face of church and state, it becomes the more plausible story of cooperation between elite [secularist] and popular [religious] thought."[1] This cooperative relationship between religionists and secularists during the formative years of the American nation continued for about two hundred years of American history.

Unfortunately, this cooperative relationship began to break down in the 1970s and 1980s. That's when Jerry Falwell's Moral Majority began pushing back against secular trends, such as removing prayer and Bible reading from public school classrooms. The Moral Majority continued to have some influence in American politics up through about 1989, when it closed its doors. Then, in the early 1990s, the Christian Coalition stepped in to take its place, and that organization was much more successful. Generally, the members of the Moral Majority and the Christian Coalition have been Republicans. Where the Moral Majority had put its major political emphasis on electing members of Congress, the Christian Coalition went for the grassroots level. They organized political groups to influence the election of city and county officials, school-board members, and state legislators, and they rallied Christians to become politically involved. The strategy paid off marvelously.

To understand the significance of what happened, you need to be aware that for the previous sixty years the Democratic Party had held almost continuous control of Congress. However, the midterm election in 1994 changed that. In the Senate, the Democrats lost eight seats, giving the Republicans a four-seat majority. In the House of Representatives, the Democrats' catastrophe was even worse: they lost fifty-four seats to the Republicans, giving the Republicans a twenty-six-seat majority! At the time, it looked like the

Adventist prediction of Sunday laws would be brought about by the religious right's conservative political activism. I still believe that at some point in the future the religious right will be a significant factor in bringing about the religious control of American and global politics that Revelation 13 predicts. However, the two-plus decades following 1994 have brought about a massive change in the American culture.

In order to understand that change, we need to understand the principle that for every action there's an equal and opposite reaction. When the secularists saw the success of the religious right, they reacted, and they've been eminently successful. Today secularists are the dominant force in American culture and politics, and they're winning over a significant proportion of religious people, including many conservative religious people.

The word *nones* is a recent newcomer to the English vocabulary. It means the *non*religious. The fastest-growing "religion" in the United States today is the nonreligious, and it's being fueled by people who are leaving their churches. This phenomenon hit western Europe and Australia several decades ago, leaving the United States as the only significant bastion of religious commitment in the developed world. America remained highly religious through the 1990s, which accounts for the political power of the religious right during that decade. However, that changed in the first fifteen years of the twenty-first century. Today young people are abandoning the Christian faith of their fathers in droves, giving a huge impetus to the secular movement.

The homosexual movement

Nowhere is secularism more evident in the United States than in the rise of the homosexual movement. And the speed with which it arose is astounding. Albert Mohler Jr., the president of the Southern Baptist Theological Seminary in Louisville, Kentucky, explained how it happened in his book *We Cannot Be Silent: Speaking Truth to a Culture Redefining Sex, Marriage, and the Very Meaning of Right and Wrong.*[2] Mohler writes, "In the 2004 U.S. presidential election no fewer than eleven states held referendums to ban gay marriage." Those bans "were supported by vast majorities of the voters in each of the eleven states." However, just eight years later, in the 2012 U.S. presidential election,

four states considered measures that would have defined marriage, in one way or another, as exclusively the union of a man and a woman or, on the other hand, would have authorized the legalization of same-sex marriage.

To put the matter plainly, in 2004 not one state out of the eleven in play failed to pass a defense of traditional marriage by a vast margin. Just eight years later . . . in 2012 not one effort to define marriage as the exclusive union of a man and a woman succeeded. And as most pundits affirmed, this trend would not be reversed.[3]

Mohler goes on to point out that this sea change in American morality was the result of a well-organized strategy developed by Marshall Kirk and Hunter Madsen in a book titled *After the Ball: How America Will Conquer Its Fear and Hatred of Gays in the 90s*.[4] "I did not know it at the time," Mohler writes,

> but this book held the quintessential strategy for what became the gay rights revolution. . . .
> . . . Kirk and Madsen set out a program that, in retrospect, was likely even more successful than they had dreamed, largely because it focused on changing the culture, rather than just changing the laws.[5]

Kirk and Madsen's strategy began with the AIDS crisis, which to a great extent was a homosexual disease. They portrayed gays and lesbians as a mistreated and misunderstood minority who deserved to have society's special concern. Their strategy included reaching out to America's liberal churches for support, because "the only way specifically religious arguments could be countered in the public square was to have persons who appeared as religious 'experts' answering the arguments. These defeater arguments required, in their [Kirk's and Madsen's] words, 'publicizing support by moderate churches and raising serious theological objections to conservative biblical teachings.' "[6] And in 2015, about twenty-five years after Kirk and Madsen published their book, the Supreme Court legalized same-sex marriage!

Please note that two institutions came out of Eden: the Sabbath and marriage. Seventh-day Adventists have long expected that the Sabbath institution will be compromised during the end time, and I fully expect that to happen. However, what we now realize is that the other institution coming out of Eden—marriage—is the first of these two to be compromised. The Sabbath will be the second one.

Gender issues have also been getting a huge amount of attention in the United States in recent years. The lesbian, gay, bisexual, and transgender (LGBT) movement is demanding that public restrooms be open to people who consider themselves, mentally and emotionally, to be the opposite of their physical gender and the opposite of the one that appears on their birth certificates. Again, this trend is experiencing a huge and very rapid success. Genesis 1:27 says that God created two genders: male and female, and that's a distinction He expects us to maintain. In our broken world, many aspects of God's original creation have become distorted, and perhaps for some people this includes their sense of gender identity. I'm not disputing the fact that some men may feel like they are women in men's bodies or that some women may feel like they are men in women's bodies. But does this justify society in allowing men to use women's restrooms and vice versa? If society at large decides that the answer to that question is Yes, then so be it. Some churches may even accept that idea. This certainly isn't the only aspect of God's creation that's being distorted these days. But do churches that hold to the Bible have to go along with these ideas just because society—or even society's laws—tells them to?

I see this as a very significant indication that the final crisis and Armageddon are approaching. And there are other trends.

The papacy

Revelation 13 describes a fearsome beast that arose out of the sea. This beast had seven heads and ten horns. Adventists have always identified this beast as the papacy. A couple of chapters previously I described the papacy's powerful influence over kings and emperors between about 1200 and 1700. During this time, the papacy used its spiritual power to control the civil power, and it believed it had a God-given mandate to do so. This papal control over civil governments declined during the 1600s and 1700s, and it came to an abrupt end in February 1798 when, during the French Revolution, the French army took Pope Pius VI prisoner and exiled him to France. I pointed out in the previous chapter that this is what Revelation called "a fatal wound" (Revelation 13:3; KJV: "deadly wound") to one of the beast's heads—namely, the papacy. The popes spent the next 130-plus years fuming about their loss of power.

However, in 1929, the Italian dictator Benito Mussolini signed a concordat with the papacy that restored 108 acres of land in Rome to the church, making it once again an independent "nation." Many Adventists at the time proclaimed that the fatal wound had been healed. That reaction is understandable, but it was also incorrect. For the deadly wound to be healed, the papacy will have to regain significant control—or at least significant influence—over European governments, and that certainly did not happen in 1929. However,

Revelation 13:7 predicts that it will happen someday. It says that the beast from the sea "was given authority over *every tribe, people, language and nation*" (verse 7; emphasis added). In other words, during the final crisis, the papacy will regain political authority, not just over Europe, but over the entire world!

And that brings us to today.

The modern papacy. The September 28, 2015, issue of *Time* magazine featured an article with this headline: "Pope Francis and the New Roman Empire." The article goes on to say, "From Cuba to climate change, he [Pope Francis] has revitalized the Vatican's role in global diplomacy. Now he's bringing his activist agenda to the U.S."[7] It also gives the details of how Pope Francis negotiated the restoration of diplomatic relations between Cuba and the United States. The author, Elizabeth Dias, said that Francis "is leading the Vatican on the world stage 30 months into his reign." Speaking of the pope's role in negotiating the restoration of diplomatic relations between the United States and Cuba, Dias wrote, "Coaxing U.S.-Cuba reconciliation is just the start: the Pope is making the Holy See a player in the most pressing global issues in a way unseen since the early days of Pope John Paul II." Dias also pointed out that, according to a poll by the Pew Research Center, Francis is "viewed favorably by 84% of those polled in Europe, 78% in the U.S. and 72% in Latin America."[8]

Climate change. One of Francis's boldest initiatives after he became pope was dealing with the earth's degenerating climate. Scientists and government leaders have been increasingly concerned about changing climate patterns for the past several decades. Over the years, scientists have held numerous climate-change conferences that resulted in strong warnings and proposals for dealing with the problem, but nothing ever came of them. Then Pope Francis made climate change a major initiative of his papacy. He called for a meeting of the world's scientists and government leaders to deal with the problem, and the result was a climate-change conference in Paris in December 2015. Government representatives from 196 nations attended the conference; and at the conclusion, a unanimous vote was taken that these representatives would return to their home countries and push for their governments to take action "to keep warming well below 2 degrees Celsius" and "to pursue efforts to limit temperature increases to 1.5 degrees Celsius."[9]

This is an example of the growing political influence of Rome on global politics. Pope Francis was very shrewd. He and his church focused on an issue in which they were almost guaranteed to win. And it has significantly increased the world's respect for the papacy.

Ecumenism

In Revelation 17:1–5, the word *Babylon* is used as a symbol that represents two things: a union of the world's religions, and the influence they have on global politics. My understanding is that near the end of time the world's various religions—Catholicism, Protestantism, various Orthodox branches of Christianity, plus Islam, Hinduism, Buddhism, and others—will all join in a global super-religion with the papacy at its head. My reason for seeing the papacy as the head of this super-religion is twofold. First, Revelation 13 points to the geopolitical role of the papacy during the final crisis, and second, of all the various world religions, the papacy is the most logical one to head up the enterprise, because it's the only one that has a visible head in one man who is highly respected by the large majority of people around the world. And Pope Francis has been very active in promoting a union of Catholics, Protestants, and Orthodox Christians.

Uniting Catholics and Protestants. One of the early examples of Catholics and Protestants being united was a short talk that Francis gave before a national gathering of Pentecostal Christians at a Charismatic Evangelical Leadership Conference, sponsored by Kenneth Copeland Ministries, in January 2014. Francis himself was not present. His talk was recorded on an iPhone a week before the conference by Tony Palmer,* the pope's close friend. Francis looked straight into the camera and spoke slowly in a fatherly tone of voice. He said,

> We are kind of, permit me to say, separated. Separated because, it's sin that has separated us, all our sins. . . . Who is to blame? We all share the blame. We have all sinned. . . . I am nostalgic [yearning], that this separation comes to an end and gives us communion. I am nostalgic [yearning] of that embrace. . . . Let's pray to the Lord that He unites us all. Come on, we are Brothers. Let's give each other a spiritual hug and let God complete the work that He has begun. And this is a miracle; the miracle of unity has begun.[10]

Following the playing of the pope's video, the crowd of charismatic leaders applauded, and Copeland praised the Lord and spoke in tongues for two or three minutes. Then he said he would like to meet with Francis. The pope responded with an invitation for Copeland and other evangelical charismatic leaders to meet with him at the Vatican. That meeting took place on June

---

* Palmer, a bishop with the Communion of Evangelical Episcopal Churches, died in a motorcycle accident about six months later.

24, 2014. With Copeland were several prominent charismatic and evangelical leaders, including James and Betty Robison, the hosts of the *Life Today* TV program, Geoff Tunnicliff, then leader of the World Evangelical Alliance, and John and Carol Arnott, founders of Partners for Ministry in Toronto, Canada. The meeting lasted for three hours and included lunch with the pope. One Protestant turned Catholic commented that "what we are witnessing is the fruit of a historic realignment in Christianity."[11]

Uniting Catholics and Lutherans. The Christian world was already split into two major divisions—Catholic and Orthodox—when Martin Luther nailed his Ninety-Five Theses to the church door in Wittenberg, Germany, on October 31, 1517. I'm sure Luther had no idea that his simple protest would lead to a traumatic third division. Hundreds of years of bitter recrimination on both sides followed. But the division between Lutherans and Catholics is well on the way to healing. In 2013, the Vatican and the Lutheran World Federation released a joint document titled "From Conflict to Communion" that focused on the progress toward unity that had been achieved by the two churches.[12] On August 10, 2016, a church-wide assembly of the Evangelical Lutheran Church in America approved a document called "Declaration on the Way" by a vote of 931 to 9. The declaration includes thirty-two "Statements of Agreement" where Lutherans and Catholics no longer have church-dividing issues regarding matters of church, ministry, and the Eucharist.

October 31, 2017, marks the five hundredth anniversary of Luther's nailing his Ninety-Five Theses to the church door—the event that launched the Protestant Reformation. The Council of Trent (1545–1563) was called to deal with the growing Protestant challenge to Rome's authority; and for centuries, popes and prelates railed against the Reformation and persecuted its followers when it could get its hands on them. That all began to change with Vatican Council II (1962–1965), and it has advanced to the point that Francis is apologizing to Protestants for his church's role in the conflict, as noted in his video presentation to Protestant charismatic leaders cited above.

He's doing more than apologizing; he's commemorating. The twelve months leading up to October 31, 2017, is a year of commemoration, and to kick off that year, the Lutheran World Federation and the Catholic Church held a joint prayer service at the Lutheran cathedral in Lund, Sweden, on October 31, 2016. Pope Francis attended that prayer service. In making the announcement of his visit, Francis said that, as the leader of the Catholic Church he wanted to

"ask for mercy and forgiveness for the behavior of Catholics toward

Christians of other churches which has not reflected gospel values.

"We cannot erase what happened before, but we do not want to allow the weight of past wounds to continue to contaminate our relations" in the future.[13]

During this meeting, Pope Francis and Bishop Munib Younan, the president of the Lutheran World Federation, signed an agreement in which they pledged to remove the obstacles to full unity between their churches, with the objective of eventually being able to share the Eucharist. In Catholic theology, the Eucharist refers to the consecration of the bread and the wine at the time of the Mass, at which time they supposedly become the literal body and blood of Christ. So signing a pledge to that goal is a commitment to reach full unity between Lutherans and Catholics. It means that Lutherans are expressing their commitment to eventually participate in the Catholic Mass! I can assure you that Pope Francis doesn't have in mind joining the Lutheran understanding of the bread and wine in the Communion service! But apparently the Lutherans do, because Pope Francis and Bishop Younan said, "Today, we hear God's command to set aside all conflict. We recognize that we are freed by grace to move towards the communion to which God continually calls us."[14]

Uniting Catholics and Orthodox Christians. On February 12, 2016, Francis met with Russian Orthodox Church Patriarch Kirill (Cyril) at Cuba's José Martí International Airport in Havana. Kirill is the patriarch of Moscow and the primate of the Russian Orthodox Church. The Orthodox Church split from Rome in 1054, and that informal meeting over coffee at the Cuban airport is the first time in nearly a thousand years that the head of the Russian Orthodox Church has met with a Roman Catholic pope. The meeting lasted for two hours,[15] and at its conclusion, the pope and the patriarch signed a joint declaration that included a "call on the world community to unite against violence and terrorism." It concluded with this statement: "we are not rivals, but brothers. We urge Catholic and Orthodox believers of the world to learn to live in peace, love and harmony."[16]

Uniting all religions. Assisi, a town in central Italy, is the birthplace of Saint Francis of Assisi, Pope Francis's namesake. On September 20, 2016, Pope Francis met in Assisi with more than five hundred people, including Muslim refugees, four Nobel laureates, United Nations emissaries, and the representatives of nine religions, such as Christians, Jews, Muslims, and Hindus. The day was devoted to preaching and prayer. In his message, Francis urged his listeners to practice tolerance and gentleness.[17] One of the news reports said, "The representatives of nine religions had a clear message: to denounce fundamentalism as an instrumentality of God." The report also said, "The current pontiff's visit and encounter with the leaders of other religions, gives a firm message of unity in diversity in a world unable to communicate."[18]

Francis truly is an ecumenical pope!

I'm reminded of Ellen White's statement, "When the leading churches of the United States, uniting upon such points of doctrine as are held by them in common, shall influence the state to enforce their decrees and to sustain their institutions, then Protestant America will have formed an image of the Roman hierarchy, and the infliction of civil penalties upon dissenters will inevitably result."[19]

Violence

In Matthew 24:37, Jesus said, "As it was in the days of Noah, so it will be at the coming of the Son of Man" (see also Luke 17:26). So one of the ways we can know what the time of the end will be like is to look at the Bible's record of what was happening in the world in the days leading up to the Flood.

I pointed out in chapter 9 that one of the most significant characteristics of the days before the Flood was violence. Genesis 6:11–13 says, "Now the earth was corrupt in God's sight and was full of *violence*. God saw how corrupt the earth had become, for all the people on earth had corrupted their ways. So God said to Noah, 'I am going to put an end to all people, for the earth is filled with *violence* because of them. I am surely going to destroy both them and the earth' " (emphasis added).

You don't have to tune your TV to the news for very long these days in order to realize the truth of Jesus' words that "as it was in the days of Noah, so it will be at the coming of the Son of Man." Violence is coming into prominence in today's world. The third millennium had barely gotten its start when, on September 11, 2001, the most horrifying example of violence in recent times took place in New York City with the destruction of the Twin Towers of the World Trade Center that took almost three thousand lives. More recently, ISIS (the Islamic State of Iraq and Syria, or ISIL, the Islamic State of Iraq and the Levant) has brutally assassinated hundreds of people in the Middle East, and it's spreading its tentacles into Europe and the United States. Twice terrorists have attacked in Paris (and they may do so again). The first time was on January 7, 2015, when gunmen invaded the *Charlie Hebdo* editorial offices, after the editors had published derogatory cartoons of the prophet Muhammad. The second attack on November 13, 2015, was even more brutal and widespread. Terrorists struck at several locations around Paris, killing 130 people from twenty-six countries and injuring more than 350 people.[20] Then there is the ISIS attack in Brussels on March 22, 2016, that resulted in 35 deaths (including the suicide bombers) and caused more than 300 injuries.[21] Who knows how many more of these brutal massacres will have happened by the time you are reading this book.

I wish I could tell you that attacks by Muslim extremists from groups such as ISIS and al-Qaeda in the Middle East and Boko Haram in Africa are the primary evidence of violence in today's world. Unfortunately, I can't. At the time I write these words, we're hearing almost daily about the senseless murders of individuals and groups in the United States. Some of the most tragic are those of children, such as when Adam Lanza murdered 20 children and 6 adult staff members at the Sandy Hook Elementary School in Newtown, Connecticut, on December 14, 2012. And on June 12, 2016, Omar Mateen, a Muslim with ties to ISIS, entered a gay nightclub in Orlando, Florida, carrying a semiautomatic rifle and a semiautomatic pistol, and began opening fire. Before the carnage was over, 50 people were dead, including Mateen, and 53 were injured—some critically.[22]

Violence "as it was in the days of Noah" is happening again in our world, and this is yet another indication of the approaching final crisis and Christ's second coming.

The rise of secularism and the homosexual movement, the growing influence of the papacy in global political affairs, the emerging ecumenical movement, and the dramatic increase in violence in today's world are four very significant indications that we are approaching the final crisis and the second coming of Jesus. And there's more. One of the most alarming trends that is leading to the final crisis and Armageddon is the decline of respect for religious freedom, especially in the United States. That will be the topic of the next chapter, "Religious Freedom Under Fire."

---

1. Nicholas P. Miller, *The Religious Roots of the First Amendment: Dissenting Protestants and the Separation of Church and State* (New York: Oxford University Press, 2012), 7.

2. R. Albert Mohler Jr., *We Cannot Be Silent: Speaking Truth to a Culture Redefining Sex, Marriage, and the Very Meaning of Right and Wrong* (Nashville, TN: Nelson Books, 2015).

3. Ibid., 33, 34.

4. Marshall Kirk and Hunter Madsen, *After the Ball: How America Will Conquer Its Fear and Hatred of Gays in the 90s* (New York: Doubleday, 1989).

5. Mohler, *We Cannot Be Silent*, 36, 37.

6. Ibid., 38.

7. Elizabeth Dias, "Pope Francis and the New Roman Empire," Faith, *Time*, September 17, 2015, 40–46.

8. Ibid. See also "Pope Francis' Image Positive in Much of World," Pew Research Center, December 11, 2014, http://www.pewglobal.org/2014/12/11/pope-francis-image-positive-in-much-of-world/.

9. "Climate Change: The Paris Agreement," The Nature Conservancy, http://www.nature.org/ourinitiatives/urgentissues/global-warming-climate-change/the-paris-agreement-what-does-it-mean.xml.

10. "Pope Francis Sends Video Message to Kenneth Copeland—Lets Unite," YouTube video, 45:56, posted by "Prove All Things," February 21, 2014, https://www.youtube.com/watch?v=uA4EPOfic5A.

11. Dwight Longenecker, "Pope Francis, Evangelical Catholic: We Are Witnessing the Fruit of a Historic Realignment in Christianity," *Aleteia*, July 1, 2014, http://aleteia.org/2014/07/01/pope-francis-evangelical-catholic/.

12. "From Conflict to Communion: Lutheran-Catholic Common Commemoration of the Reformation in 2017," Vatican, accessed February 21, 2017, http://www.vatican.va/roman_curia/pontifical_councils/chrstuni/lutheran-fed-docs/rc_pc_chrstuni_doc_2013_dal-conflitto-alla-comunione_en.html.

13. Pope Francis, quoted in Rosie Scammell, "Pope Will Visit Sweden for Reformation Anniversary," Religion News Service, January 25, 2016, http://religionnews.com/2016/01/25/catholic-pope-will-visit-Lutheran-sweden-reformation-anniversary.

14. Austen Ivereigh, "Catholic and Lutheran Churches Pledge to Work for Shared Eucharist," *Crux,* October 31, 2016, https://cruxnow.com/papal-visit/2016/10/31/catholic-lutheran-churches-pledge-work-shared-eucharist/.

15. "Russian Patriarch Kirill and Pope Francis Meet in Cuba, Sign Declaration," *Moscow Times*, February 15, 2016, https://themoscowtimes.com/articles/russian-patriarch-kirill-and-pope-francis-meet-in-cuba-sign-declaration-51831.

16. Ibid.

17. Associated Press, "Pope Meets Religious Leaders and Refugees at Assisi Peace Day," *Catholic Herald*, September 20, 2016, http://catholicherald.co.uk/news/2016/09/20/pope-francis-greets-religious-leaders-at-assisi-peace-day/.

18. "Meeting of Assisi: A Mosaic of Religions and Nationalities. All United for Peace," *Rome Reports,* September 20, 2016, http://www.romereports.com/2016/09/20/meeting-of-assisi-a-mosaic-of-religions-and-nationalities-all-united-for-peace.

19. White, *The Great Controversy*, 445.

20. See *Wikipedia*, s.v. "November 2015 Paris Attacks," last modified December 13, 2016, https://en.wikipedia.org/wiki/November_2015_Paris_attacks.

22. *Wikipedia*, s.v. "2016 Brussels Bombings," last modified February 18, 2017, https://en.wikipedia.org/wiki/2016_Brussels_bombings#Victims.

22. *Wikipedia*, s.v. "2016 Orlando Night Club Shooting," last modified December 16, 2016, https://en.wikipedia.org/wiki/2016_Orlando_nightclub_shooting.

How Should Christians Relate to Homosexuals?

A common saying among Christians when talking about homosexuals is that we should "love the sinner but hate the sin." Christians have had no problem hating the sin, but as a culture we've almost universally ostracized homosexuals. In extreme cases, we've publicly hated them.* It's easier to push gays and lesbians out of our minds than it is to respect them as human beings, become friends with them, and, insofar as possible, try to understand them.

I've read several Christian books or parts of books about homosexuality, and I have come to understand that in most cases homosexuality is not a choice. It's an orientation. There are two primary explanations about where this orientation comes from: genetics and early childhood influences. I don't care to debate that point here. What we have to keep in mind is that in the large majority of cases the homosexual did not choose to be a homosexual. He discovered that orientation as he grew out of childhood. In many cases—probably most—this was an extremely painful discovery, especially because of the social contempt for their orientation. How would you feel if you knew that society hated you for *who you are*?

I'm a conservative Seventh-day Adventist Christian who holds to a biblical view of homosexuality—namely, that it is a sinful lifestyle. However, as a Christian, I also have to treat practicing sinners the way Jesus treated them, and my Bible says that He associated with them (Luke 15:1, 2), sympathized with their frailty and pain, and encouraged them to live in harmony with biblical principles (John 8:1–11). And finally He died for them.

If you would like to adopt a genuinely Christian attitude toward gays and lesbians, I recommend that you read the book *People to Be Loved: Why*

---

* An extreme example of this is the Westboro Baptist Church in Topeka, Kansas, which has publicly demonstrated at homosexual funerals with antigay signs that say such things as "God hates fags." See *Wikipedia*, s.v. "Westboro Baptist Church," last modified December 16, 2016, https://en.wikipedia.org/wiki/Westboro_Baptist_Church.

Homosexuality Is Not Just an Issue, by Preston Sprinkle. Sprinkle, a conservative Christian who adheres to a biblical view of human sexuality, decided to make an in-depth study of homosexuality. In the preface to his book, he says, "As I began researching for this project, I made it a point to spend half my time in books and the other half in the lives of gay people. And my life will never be the same. I have made many unexpected friends whose stories have seeped down into my bones."[1]

I don't have all the answers as to how the *church* should relate to homosexuals in terms of membership and holding office, but I do have the answer to how Christians should relate to homosexual people. If we're serious about hating the sin but loving the sinner, then we must *truly love* the sinner and not just mouth the cliché.

Some homosexuals and lesbians may say the mere fact that I consider homosexuality to be a sinful lifestyle is in itself homophobic. However, I have to be true to what I understand the Bible to say on this issue. I included this addendum to chapter 21 because, while I recognize the unbiblical trend in today's Western society, I don't want what I felt needed to be said regarding signs of the end to contribute to the extreme prejudice against homosexual people that has existed in Christian culture for almost two thousand years. I want my readers to understand "the other side of the story"—that as followers of Jesus, we must always treat people with whom we disagree, including people who we think are engaged in an unbiblical lifestyle, with understanding and respect. I believe the following statement by Ellen White is a guide to how Christians should relate to homosexuals:

> Even those who had fallen the lowest He [Jesus] treated with respect. It was a continual pain to Christ to be brought into contact with enmity, depravity, and impurity; but never did He utter one expression to show that His sensibilities were shocked or His refined tastes offended. . . .
>
> . . . No one was ever reclaimed by reproach.[2]

---

1. Preston Sprinkle, *People to Be Loved: Why Homosexuality Is Not Just an Issue* (Grand Rapids, MI: Zondervan, 2015), 9.

2. Ellen G. White, *The Ministry of Healing* (Mountain View, CA: Pacific Press® Pub. Assn., 1942), 165, 166.

CHAPTER 22

Religious Freedom Under Fire

Back in February 1887, Adventist evangelist Dudley Canright renounced his affiliation with the Seventh-day Adventist Church, and two months later he was ordained as a Baptist minister.[1] Two years after that he published a 416-page book, titled *Seventh-day Adventism Renounced.*[2] The introduction to Canright's book was written by the Reverend Theodore Nelson, LLD, who was a former president of Kalamazoo College in Kalamazoo, Michigan.

In his introduction, Nelson wrote,

> Seventh-Day Adventists believe and teach that before the second coming of Christ the United States will form a union of church and state, and, like France and Spain in the seventeenth century, will become a persecuting power. . . . They believe and teach that the Seventh-Day Adventists are to be especially tried in this ordeal that is being prepared by the civil government; that they are to be the chief victims of the fiery persecutions that will be waged against the "Saints of the Most High." . . . Indeed, they stake their whole system of doctrine upon this meaning of the Word of God, and they regard these momentous events, which they claim the Bible forecasts, as much a reality as though those events had already transpired. . . . To one who is fairly acquainted with the spirit of the age and country in which we live, this ostentatious martyr-spirit of our Adventist friends seems quite absurd.[3]

Then Nelson added, "Such a change would be a greater miracle than for God to grow a giant oak in an instant. The trend of our civilization, the most powerful currents of public opinion, are all in the opposite direction."[4]

Nelson was correct that religious liberty is one of the foundational principles of Western society. He was also correct that Adventists believe a day is coming when religious freedom will end in the United States. And that's what he thought was foolish. His problem was that he was writing about 125 years too soon.* Today, Seventh-day Adventists aren't the only Americans who are concerned about threats to religious freedom in the United States. A study published by Barna Group in 2015 stated that "41 percent of Americans believe that the state of religious freedom in the U.S. is worse today than it was a decade ago. This is up from 33 percent who believed the same thing when a study was conducted in 2012."[5] The study also reported that the statistics on evangelical (conservative Christian) Americans are even more startling: 77 percent of evangelicals believe that religious freedom in the nation is worse than it was a decade ago—up from 60 percent in 2012!

Had Nelson read Revelation 13 carefully, he could have known that religious freedom would be compromised, not just in the United States but globally, before the second coming of Jesus.

Based on what Jesus' apostle John wrote in Revelation, Adventists have historically predicted that religious freedom will indeed disappear during the final crisis. The first half of Revelation 13 says that the whole world will worship the beast from the sea, which we understand to be the papacy, and that this beast will persecute God's people who refuse to go along with that worship (verses 4–7). In the second half of the chapter, the beast that rises from the land, which we understand to be the United States of America, will enforce the worship of the sea beast with the threat of death against anyone who dares to refuse that worship (verse 15).

In the same vein, Ellen White wrote, "Our country [the United States] shall repudiate every principle of its Constitution as a Protestant and republican government."[6] In the context of our understanding of the end time, she meant that a day is coming when religious freedom in the United States will end.

Adventists have always expected that this rejection of religious freedom will come about through governmental legislation of Sunday observance, and we still believe this will happen. But it's happening first through laws protecting homosexual marriage and gender identity.

Homosexual issues and religious liberty

In the previous chapter, I discussed the rapid rise in the United States of the cultural acceptance of homosexuality as an appropriate lifestyle. Here I will share with you the profound impact this is having on religious freedom. My guess is that you're already well aware of this issue, and by the time you read this there will certainly be much more evidence than what I'm able to present

---

* Canright's book was published in 1889 and 125 years later was 2014.

here. But let's take a look at the situation in the United States in late 2016 and early 2017.

The LGBT community is insisting that religious convictions against gay marriage are not valid reasons for photographers, bakers, and florists to refuse services for gay weddings. In the past, such situations were typically settled by a compromise. For example, for quite some time, pharmacists who, for reasons of conscience, objected to filling abortion prescriptions could refer customers to another pharmacist in their pharmacy or to a nearby pharmacy that had no objection to filling these prescriptions.* However, the LGBT community isn't interested in accommodation. They insist that their civil rights take precedence over the religious rights of the people they ask to serve them.

In Oregon, Aaron Klein, the owner of the Sweet Cakes by Melissa bakery in the Portland area, ended up paying more than $135,000 in fines for his refusal to bake a cake for a lesbian couple.[7] And in 2012, a gay couple asked Jack Phillips, the owner of Masterpiece Cakeshop in Lakewood, Colorado, to bake a wedding cake for them. Because of his religious convictions, Phillips declined their request. The couple filed a complaint with the Colorado Civil Rights Commission, which ordered Phillips to change his policy. The Colorado Court of Appeals also ruled against him, and on April 25, 2016, the Colorado Supreme Court refused to take the case, which allowed the lower court's ruling to stand.[8]

However, it isn't just conservative Christian bakers, photographers, and florists who are being targeted. What about artists and designers who object for religious reasons to preparing gay and lesbian illustrations and Christian printers who object to printing gay wedding announcements? Must they be forced to violate their consciences in order to obey the law? What if a Christian university student wants to enroll in a counseling program at a public university? Can he be denied entry into the program just because of his belief that homosexuality is sinful? In fact, a variation on this theme has already happened. Andrew Cash, who was pursuing a master's degree in counseling at Missouri State University, was close to graduating when the dean of the program learned of his conservative Christian views about homosexuality and expelled him. In a lawsuit against the university, Cash said that the turn of events caused him "daily emotional suffering." The outcome of Cash's legal action against the university remains to be seen.[9]

Along the same lines, in late April 2016, Tennessee's governor, Bill

---

* This accommodation may not have been available in every state in the United States.

Haslam, signed a bill into law that allows a mental-health professional in private practice to refuse to treat patients based on the therapist's religious or personal beliefs, provided the counselor refers the patient to a counselor who is willing to accept him or her. The reaction of the homosexual community and the counseling industry was angry condemnation.[10]

In an effort to protect Christian bakers, florists, and photographers, a number of states have proposed, and in some cases enacted, laws allowing these small-business owners to discriminate for religious reasons. Indiana was one of the first to enact such a law. Its Religious Freedom Restoration Act allowed small businesses the right to refuse wedding services to homosexual couples if carrying out those services would violate the business owner's sincerely held religious beliefs. Governor Mike Pence signed the law on March 26, 2015, and defended it, saying that it was not intended to discriminate but to protect religious freedom.

Then there's the case of the California legislature's bills AB 1888 and SB 1146.* These bills, had they passed, would have stipulated that students at any college or university in the state could receive Cal Grants (student aid for college or university students in California) only if their school had certified that it would not discriminate "on the basis of, among other things, sex, sexual orientation, gender identity, or gender expression."[11] However, the bills were dropped because of intense pressure on the state's legislature by Christian higher-education institutions both in California and the rest of the nation.

Public institutions of higher learning would have had no problem meeting the requirements the bills imposed, but think of what it would have meant for Christian colleges and universities had these bills been enacted into law. These Christian schools would have had to remove from their handbooks any requirement that faculty and students agree to abide by biblical standards of sexual morality. Any school that refused to employ a prospective faculty member based solely on the fact that the individual was in a homosexual relationship (whether married or living together) would be discriminating, and students at that school would no longer have received Cal Grants. Christian colleges and universities would have also had to eliminate any requirement that students abide by biblical standards of sexual morality in order to receive Cal Grants. And Christian colleges and universities would no longer have been able to maintain dormitories exclusively for men and women if they wanted their students to be eligible for these grants. Christian schools would have had to allow their students to live in the dormitory of the gender they

---

* AB means Assembly Bill; SB means Senate Bill.

identified with, regardless of whether it was their physical gender.

AB 1888 and SB 1146, had they actually become state law, would have gutted the religious freedom of California's Christian colleges and universities to operate according to their biblical moral standards. And there's a very real possibility that similar laws may yet be enacted in California and other states.

Gender issues and religious liberty

Gender identity has become a huge issue in the United States since roughly 2010. In the previous chapter, I briefly discussed the increasing trend toward people claiming to be mentally and emotionally of a different gender than the gender they were born with. Stemming from this is a question of increasing public debate—whether such people should have the right to use the public restrooms of the gender with which they identify or whether they must be required to use the restroom of their physical gender. Gender identity is increasingly being considered a civil right; this has the potential to bring it into conflict with religious rights, especially if conservative churches and religious institutions such as schools whould be required to accommodate the restroom "rights" of transgender individuals.

The most significant example of treating gender identity as a civil right is the case of Massachusetts Senate Bill 2407, which bans transgender discrimination in public accommodations, allowing people to use the restrooms that correspond to their chosen gender identity. The bill was enacted into law in 2015 and went into effect on October 1 of that year. Governor Baker, who signed the bill into law, said, "No one should be discriminated against in Massachusetts because of their [chosen] gender identity."[12]

Religious leaders are concerned that they may be required to accommodate gender identity in the restrooms of their churches, and this is a real possibility. Exactly one month before the gender law went into effect, the Massachusetts Commission Against Discrimination (MCAD), which is the state's civil rights agency, issued a document titled "Gender Identity Guidance." The document states that "all persons, regardless of gender identity, shall have the right to full and equal accommodations, advantages, facilities and privileges of any place of public accommodation," including "any place, whether licensed or unlicensed, which is open to and accepts or solicits the patronage of the general public." The document goes on to say that "even a church could be seen as a place of public accommodation if it holds a secular event, such as a spaghetti supper, that is open to the general public."[13] Of course, every Sabbath or Sunday School and every church worship service I've ever attended is open to the general public! Indeed, we openly welcome guests from the general public to these services.

I don't think it takes a PhD to recognize the challenge that Massachusetts Senate Bill 2407 and the MCAD guideline pose to churches and other religious institutions. In fact, four churches and their pastors in the Boston area filed a lawsuit against the Massachusetts attorney general, asking the U.S. District Court for the District of Massachusetts, Eastern Division, to issue a decision declaring that the law violates the First and Fourteenth Amendments of the U.S. Constitution for all pastors and churches in the state. Their challenge argues that as a result of "forcing Churches and Pastors to self-censor their speech and violate their religious beliefs, the Churches and Pastors suffer and will continue to suffer irreparable harm to their constitutional liberties."[14]

When no one can buy or sell

Previously, I shared with you the effort by Indiana and several other states to enact laws that would protect the religious freedom of small businesses, such as bakers, florists, and photographers, to refuse service to homosexuals for their weddings if the owners had religious and/or conscientious reasons for their refusal.

The reaction to Indiana's law from the business community was swift and furious. Angie's List canceled a forty-million-dollar expansion in the state, and various other major businesses in the country registered their disapproval, including Apple, Eli Lilly, Nike, and NASCAR. And several government entities around the country banned all city- and state-funded travel to Indiana until the law was changed, including the mayors of San Francisco; Portland; Washington, DC; and Seattle and the governors of Connecticut, Washington, Vermont, and New York.[15] Within a week, the Indiana legislature enacted Senate Bill 50 as an amendment to the law, which provided protection for LGBT customers, and the governor signed it.[16]

On March 23, 2016, North Carolina's governor, Pat McCrory, signed into law a bill that banned cities and counties from approving gender-neutral restroom ordinances. Again the repercussion from businesses was swift. PayPal canceled its plans to establish a plant in Charlotte that would have generated four hundred jobs for the city, and Google and Apple registered their displeasure. The NBA refused to hold its All-Star Game in Charlotte in 2017, moving it instead to Toronto, Canada. And a motion picture producer refuses to film in the state as long as the law is left standing.[17]

What's the take-away message from all these business threats? Revelation 13:16, 17 says that the beast that arises from the land will force everyone to receive a mark on his right hand or on his forehead and that no one can buy or sell unless he has that mark. That's basically what today's large businesses are doing. They're using their economic power to force their LGBT views onto cities and states. Revelation is simply telling us that during the final crisis this very same strategy will be used against individuals, and this time it will be on a global scale. Either you will worship on the government-approved day, or you'll be shut out from carrying on any economic activity.

So how will governments enforce that edict? Obviously, we don't know, because it hasn't happened yet. But a good guess would be that your bank account and mine will be closed, our credit cards will be canceled, and stores will refuse to accept our cash—if cash is even being used anymore. There is currently a strong movement that supports the idea of all financial transactions becoming digital.

Religious rights versus civil rights

As these issues have developed over the past few years, I've become increasingly aware that the bottom-line issue is civil rights versus religious rights. Which one has the priority? A middle ground that both sides can agree on is not likely to be found anytime soon. A poll conducted by the Pew Forum in 2016 found that 51 percent of American adults "say transgender people should be allowed to use restrooms of the gender with which they currently identify, compared with 46 percent who say members of this community should use restrooms that correspond to their gender at birth." Only 18 percent of U.S. adults "say they have at least some sympathy for both arguments in debates over transgender bathroom use or wedding services."[18]

I pointed out in the previous chapter that for more than two hundred years religionists and secularists got along fairly well because they respected each other and were willing to accommodate each other's needs. But the days of mutual respect and accommodation are over. Today it's a tug-of-war over which one will dominate the other. At this point, secularists hold the winning edge.

Nowhere is this more obvious than in a report by the United States Civil Rights Commission (USCRC) that was released on September 7, 2016. The commission's position is summarized in the following statement: "Religious exemptions to the protections of civil rights upon classifications such as race, color, national origin, sex, disability status, sexual orientation, and gender identity, when they are permissible, significantly infringe upon these civil rights."[19]

That's a list of seven civil rights that the government protects, and the USCRC is complaining that religious exemptions to these protections is bad. My first comment is that, to my knowledge, religion has requested an exemption to only two of the civil rights on the list: sexual orientation and gender identity. And these are deeply held religious beliefs that do not arise from the religious people's prejudices and bigotry.*

Are churches that require their members to order their lives in harmony with the biblical guidelines on sexual relationships being bigoted and intolerant? I don't think so. Unless one twists the words of the Bible to mean something they don't say, the Bible condemns homosexual activity in very strong language, and the Christian understanding of gender identity arises from the Creation story: "God created man in his own image, . . . male and female he created them" (Genesis 1:27).

In a letter introducing the USCRC's report to President Barack Obama, the commission's chairman, Martin R. Castro, went on record saying, "The phrases 'religious liberty' and 'religious freedom' will stand for nothing except hypocrisy so long as they remain code words for discrimination, intolerance, racism, sexism, homophobia, Islamophobia, Christian supremacy or any form of intolerance."[20] In one sense, I can agree with Chairman Castro's statement. The religious convictions of Christians should never be code words for intolerance and discrimination. However, Castro ignores the fact that beliefs that are based on Scripture aren't motivated by intolerance. They're based on moral conviction. Some people may use their moral convictions to justify attitudes of intolerance. Unfortunately, that has too often happened. But that doesn't mean that all opposition to homosexuality and gender change is based on intolerance. The fact is that Castro and others like him are as intolerant of Christian ideals as some Christians are of secular ideals.

Evangelicals take a stand

During the past few years, evangelical Christians in the United States have become increasingly alarmed at the trend toward public acceptance of secular sexual morals, especially the fact that more and more states have enacted laws compelling those who have conscientious objections against

---

* Unfortunately, these clear biblical commands have too often led Christian conservatives to hold intolerant attitudes toward gays and lesbians, and that's unfortunate. It means that Christians have some housecleaning of their own to do.

gay marriage to participate in these ceremonies by photographing them, preparing flowers for them, or baking wedding cakes for them. In response to this trend, on Sunday, September 25, 2016, a group of prominent evangelicals published a one-page advertisement in the *New York Times*, titled "Declaration of Dependence." The declaration reiterated their objection to abortion and gay marriage and pledged to "commit to conducting our churches, ministries, businesses, and personal lives in accordance with our Christian faith and choose to obey God rather than man." To put it plainly, these religious leaders are committed to breaking the law of the land if necessary rather than compromise their consciences. Among the signers of the declaration were James Dobson, the founder of Focus on the Family; Jerry Boykin, the vice president of the Family Research Council; and televangelist Kenneth Copeland.[21]

This is a bold statement that's similar to the position God's people will have to take with respect to Sunday observance during the final conflict.

Who are fundamentalists?

In November 2015, Pope Francis visited Kenya, Uganda, and the Central African Republic. During his time there, while visiting a mosque in the Central African Republic, he made a significant statement about religious extremism. He said, "Together we must say no to hatred, to revenge and to violence, particularly that violence which is perpetrated in the name of a religion or of God himself." I think we can all agree with what the pope said. But he put a different slant on his views in a conversation he had with journalists who were accompanying him on his plane ride back to Rome. He said that "fundamentalism is always a tragedy. It is not religious; it lacks God; it is idolatrous."[22] Continuing on, he stated, "It is a disease of all religions. We Catholics, we have a few, even many fundamentalists. They believe they know absolute truth and corrupt others. I can say this because this is my church."[23]

The question is, what is an *extremist*? Pope Francis said that it's someone who believes he or she knows absolute truth. I have some questions for Pope Francis: Does he still believe that his church is the only true church? Does he believe that Mary is a co-redemptrix with Christ? Does he believe in the confessional and in indulgences? Is he convinced that these are valid spiritual truths? Then according to his own definition, he, too, is a fundamentalist.

I find it significant that President Barack Obama used the same "fundamentalist" language in the last speech he made before the United Nations on

September 20, 2016. He said, "Alternative visions of the world have pressed forward both in the wealthiest countries and in the poorest: Religious fundamentalism; the politics of ethnicity, or tribe, or sect; aggressive nationalism; a crude populism—sometimes from the far left, but more often from the far right—which seeks to restore what they believe was a better, simpler age free of outside contamination." Later in his speech, the president said, "We must reject any forms of fundamentalism, or racism, or belief in ethnic superiority that makes our traditional identities irreconcilable with modernity. Instead we need to embrace the tolerance that results from respect of all human beings."[24]

Again I think we can surely agree with President Obama that we must "embrace the tolerance that results from respect of all human beings." But what about his statement that "we must reject any forms of fundamentalism . . . that makes our traditional identities irreconcilable with modernity"? By "modernity" I understand him to mean today's culture, today's dominant worldview, and today's majority opinions about truth and error, right and wrong. What if the biblical teachings about right and wrong, truth and error, differ from "modernity"? And what about his statement that it's "the far right" that promotes these fundamentalist ideals? I'm reasonably certain that the evangelicals who signed the "Declaration of Dependence" that I mentioned previously would be considered far right, at least by Obama and his crowd. I also think most Adventists would agree with the evangelicals.

Fortunately, our evangelical friends *are* taking a stand with respect to abortion and marriage that differs from "modernity." And Adventists believe that a day is coming when our "fundamentalist" views about the Sabbath will conflict with what's considered "modernity" at the time. Will we also take a stand to violate the law rather than compromise our biblical convictions? Fortunately, the answer is Yes, many will.

At the time I'm writing these words, Pope Francis has been making some very critical remarks about people who keep the law, meaning the Ten Commandments. He said that these people "appear good because they follow the Law; but behind there is something that does not make them good. Either they're bad, hypocrites or they are sick. They suffer!"[25] I can easily see that kind of reasoning being used against Sabbath keepers someday!

Summary of the Kingdom of Darkness, signs of the end, and freedom

This chapter and the previous one have dealt with current trends in the

United States and in the world that are leading toward the final crisis and Armageddon. The rise of the "nones"—the nonreligious—reminds us of the situation before the Flood when the descendants of Seth "saw that the daughters of men were beautiful, and they married any of them they chose" (Genesis 6:2). In other words, young people—the age when humans most often get married—were abandoning the moral principles of their fathers. As we today sometimes put it, they were "giving up on organized religion." They were defying God's authority and ordering their lives according to their own moral judgments about right and wrong. That's precisely what Lucifer and his angels were doing in heaven, and it's what the descendants of Seth were doing before the Flood. And it's what a large number of Americans and other Westerners are doing today.

What's most concerning is that secularists, in their demand for the protection of their civil rights, are challenging the religious freedom of those who are loyal to God's moral principles of marriage and sexuality. But this is the condition that has to exist in order for the world's final events to occur as described in the Bible and the writings of Ellen White.

Jesus' end-time church began so small as to be hardly recognizable—about a hundred people! Very early in its history this church recognized the authority of God's law, especially the fourth commandment, which the Kingdom of Darkness and its church had rejected for almost two thousand years. God blessed His remnant church with a prophetic voice, which it continues to accept, even though its members often fall short of its prophetic ideals. Jesus' end-time church has recognized His purpose for it—that it is to prepare the world for the final conflict over the law of God, especially the Sabbath. The Kingdom of Darkness has done its best to hinder the progress of God's end-time church, but God has provided it with the freedom to proclaim its message, and it continues to grow. However, that freedom is closing down in various parts of the world, and it will soon end in the Western world, especially the United States, as we've seen in this chapter.

However, signs in the world indicate that the final conflict—the period of the most intense struggle between the Kingdom of Light and the Kingdom of Darkness since Jesus returned to heaven—is about to break upon the world. During this time, "Satan [the leader of the Kingdom of Darkness] will work his miracles to deceive; he will set up his power as supreme. The church [Jesus' end-time church] may appear as about to fall, but it . . . [will] not fall. . . . This is a terrible ordeal, but nevertheless it must take place."[26] To put it in terms we've used before in this book, it will appear that the

Kingdom of Darkness has gained another victory, but the victor will actually be the Kingdom of Light. And that, of course, is exactly what happened at the time of the cross.

The conflict that lies just ahead will be the last great struggle between the Kingdom of Light and the Kingdom of Darkness on earth. Then will come Armageddon.

I pointed out in a previous chapter that during most of American history religionists and secularists got along fairly well. Each side respected the other, even if they didn't always agree with each other. However, since the 1960s there's been a growing hostility between the two sides to the point that today (2017) they despise each other. And I don't believe that development can be reversed. If anything, it will continue to grow stronger.

So here's a significant question: which side will predominate during the final crisis? And the answer is quite simple. It's evident from Revelation 13 that it will be religion. The sea beast (the papacy) and the land beast (the United States) will unite to enforce their form of worship on the entire world. I have no doubt that secularism will still be a strong cultural force at that time, especially in the Western world, but religion will dominate, requiring secularists to accept the mark of the beast "on the hand" (Revelation 13:16).

So is Donald Trump's surprise rise to the presidency of the United States, which was brought about largely with strong support from the Religious Right, the beginning of that trend in the United States?

Wait and see.

---

1. Neufeld et al., *The Seventh-day Adventist Encyclopedia*, s.v. "Canright, Dudley Marvin."

2. Dudley M. Canright, *Seventh-day Adventism Renounced* (New York: Fleming H. Revell, 1889).

3. Theodore Nelson, introduction to *Seventh-day Adventism Renounced*, 22, 23.

4. Ibid.

5. Veronica Neffinger, "Study Reveals More Americans Are Concerned About Religious Freedom Rights," Christian Headlines.com, http://www.christianheadlines.com/blog/study -reveals-more-americans-are-concerned-about-religious-freedom-rights.html.

6. Ellen G. White, *Testimonies for the Church*, vol. 5 (Mountain View, CA: Pacific Press® Pub. Assn., 1948), 451.

7. "Oregon Bakery That Rejected Lesbian Couple Pays Fine After All," *Huffington Post*, December 28, 2015, http://www.huffingtonpost.com/entry/oregon-bakery-gay-fine_us _5681ff01e4b014efe0d91e33. It's important to note that sympathetic donors gave the bakery's owners between four hundred and five hundred thousand dollars.

8. Associated Press, "Colorado Court Rules That Baker Cannot Cite Religion in Refusal to Make Same-Sex Cake," April 26, 2016, GOPUSA, http://gopusa.com/?p=9096?omhide =true.

9. Michael F. Haverluck, "Univ. Denies Student Degree Over Same-Sex Stance," GOPUSA, April 26, 2016, http://www.gopusa.com/?p=9036?omhide=true.

10. Sheila Burke and Erik Schezig, "Tennessee Governor Signs Religious Counseling Bill Into Law," AP, April 27, 2016, http://bigstory.ap.org/article /672be8831855413096b03db90af7b172/tennessee-governor-signs-religious-counseling-bill -law.

11. "Assembly Bill No. 1888," California Legislative Information, last amended May 2, 2016, http://leginfo.legislature.ca.gov/faces/billNavClient.xhtml?bill_id =201520160AB1888.

12. Billy Hallowell, comp., "Massachusetts Government Issues Transgender Guidance— and What It Says About Churches Has Some Worried," *Deseret News*, September 15, 2016, http://www.deseretnews.com/article/865662492/Massachusetts-government-issues -transgender-guidance-2-and-what-it-says-about-churches-has-some-.html?pg+all.

13. Ibid.

14. Dominic Holden, "Massachusetts Churches Sue to Avoid Transgender Bathroom Rules," BuzzFeed News, October 12, 2016, https://www.buzzfeed.com/dominicholden /massachusetts-churches-sue-to-avoid-transgender-bathroom-rul?utm_term =.vmw4Kd466#.te6g3Ognn.

15. Libby Hill, "Some Call It Religious Freedom, Others Call It Anti-gay. Here's a Look at the Battle in Some States," *Los Angeles Times*, April 5, 2016, http://www.latimes.com /entertainment/la-et-states-antigay-battle-20160325-snap-htmlstory.html.

16. *Wikipedia*, s.v. "Religious Freedom Restoration Act," last modified November 24, 2016, https://en.wikipedia.org/wiki/Religious_Freedom_Restoration_Act_%28Indiana%29.

17. Hill, "Some Call It Religious Freedom."

18. Kelsey Dallas, "Pew Survey Finds No Middle Ground in Religious Freedom Debates," *Deseret News*, September 28, 2016, http://deseretnews.com/article/print/865663485/Pew -survey-find-no-middle-ground-in-religious-freedom-debates.html.

19. Billy Hallowell, "U.S. Civil Rights Commission Chairman Says Religious Freedoms 'Stand for Nothing Except Hypocrisy,' " Recordnet.com, September 20, 2016, http://www .recordnet.com/news/20160920/us-civil-rights-commission-chairman-says-religious -freedoms-stand-for-nothing-except-hypocrisy.

20. Ibid.

21. Miranda Blue, "Religious Right Leaders Vow to Defy Laws on Abortion, 'Sexual Perversion' in 'Declaration of Dependence Upon God,' " Right Wing Watch, September 26, 2016, http://www.rightwingwatch.org/content/religious-right-leaders-vow-defy-laws -abortion-sexual-perversion-declaration-dependence-upon-god.

22. AFP, "Pope Says Fundamentalism Is 'Disease of All Religions,' " *Express Tribune*, December 1, 2015, http://tribune.com.pk/story/1001637/pope-says-fundamentalism-is -disease-of-all-religions/

23. Anthony Joseph, "Fundamentalism Is 'a Disease of All Religions': Pope Says It Is Not Just Islam That Has Extremist Factions," *Daily Mail*, December 2, 2015, http://www

.dailymail.co.uk/news/article-3343363/Fundamentalism-disease-religions-says-Pope.html.

24. Office of the Press Secretary, "Address by President Obama to the 71st Session of the United Nations General Assembly," White House, September 20, 2016, https://www .whitehouse.gov/the-press-office/2016/09/20/address-president-obama-71st-session-united -nations-general-assembly.

25. Pope Francis, quoted in Edward Pentin, "Pope Francis: Rigid People Are Sick," *National Catholic Register*, October 24, 2016, http://www.ncregister.com/blog/edward-pentin/pope -francis-rigidity-is-something-pathological.

26. Ellen G. White, *Selected Messages*, bk. 2 (Washington, DC: Review and Herald® Pub. Assn., 1958), 380.

CHAPTER 23

About Face!

Ten years ago Pacific Press® published my book *Could It Really Happen?* In that book, I addressed the issue of how the Adventist prediction that the United States will become a persecuting power could be fulfilled, and my basic answer was that America's religious right would cooperate with the papacy in leading the nation and the world into that persecution. At the time my book was published, George W. Bush, who was very much a supporter of the religious right, was still the president of the United States, and it seemed that the religious right and the papacy would work together to bring about religious legislation in America.

Could It Really Happen? was published in 2007. This book, which you are reading now, was published in 2017. What a difference ten years has made! For the eight years of the Obama administration, secularism dominated the American culture, and the religious right was increasingly on the defensive. As the nation approached the election on November 8, 2016, secularists looked forward to holding their dominance for at least another four years and possibly eight under Hillary Clinton. The future looked grim for conservative Christians, who were scrambling to maintain their religious freedoms against the hostility of the left. The religious right was struggling to survive in the American culture war. As previously mentioned, they even published a defiant, full-page advertisement in the *New York Times*, declaring that they would hold fast to their values regardless of the political consequences.

This was the political climate in the United States when I turned over the completed manuscript for this book to Pacific Press® during the first week of October 2016, and, as I said, it appeared that the secular dominance in American politics would continue under Clinton. But then came Donald Trump's stunning election to the U.S. presidency in the 2016 election. One of the major factors contributing to his election was the still very powerful religious right's dissatisfaction with Obama's presidency and their concern that Clinton would perpetuate his policies. Everything I said in the previous two chapters is still valid, but I would like to take a moment to reassess it in light of the changed political climate.

In a previous chapter, I said that I look more to *trends* than single *events* as indicators of prophetic fulfillment. I'm sure there will be *events* in the future that are significant indicators of prophetic fulfillment. Is Donald Trump's election one of these? It most certainly was a stunning political event. But in terms of Bible prophecy, I see Trump's election more as a reemergence of the trend during the late 1990s and the early 2000s in which the religious right held significant political power. That trend, which was interrupted by the Obama presidency, has now been reinstated—or at least that's how it appears at the time I'm writing these words. Secularists may still try to challenge religious conservatives who refuse to supply homosexual couples with wedding cakes, flowers, and photographs, and they may continue to press for transgender rights for public bathrooms. But they won't have the powerful political support that a Democratic president and his government gave them during the previous eight years. Also, as time goes on, Donald Trump will probably appoint politically conservative judges to the Supreme Court and lower federal courts, which will make it more difficult for LGBT activists to achieve their objectives.

From a prophetic standpoint, one of the significant statements that Donald Trump made during his campaign was his pledge to give more power to the churches. What he especially meant by that was that he would work to rescind the Johnson Amendment to the Internal Revenue Code. The Johnson Amendment, named after former president Lyndon B. Johnson, prevents churches from campaigning on behalf of individual politicians. They can urge parishioners to vote one way or another on political and moral *issues*, but they cannot openly support candidates for public office. Obviously, if Trump succeeds in eliminating the Johnson Amendment, churches will have a more powerful voice in future American politics. It will be much easier for them to get their favorite political leaders voted into office, which will make it more difficult for secularists to get their preferred leaders elected.

I've devoted much of the previous two chapters to analyzing current events in the light of end-time events. Several trends seem to be moving the world in that direction, especially the ecumenical movement, the increase of violence in the world, the growing political influence of the Vatican on global issues, and the secular rejection of biblical moral values. So does the recent dramatic political shift in American politics fit into that scenario? I believe the answer is Yes. It brings us back to one of the main points I made in my book *Could It Really Happen?*—namely, that it continues the trend toward powerful religious forces dominating the world at the end of time. Revelation 13 is very clear on this. The beast that rises out of the sea represents the papacy, and the beast that rises from the earth represents the United States. And Revelation says that these two powers will join hands to enforce a false form of worship. Revelation 13:8 states that "all inhabitants of the earth will worship the beast," save for God's loyal people.

Secularism is still a powerful player, and it may again dominate U.S. politics at some time in the future. There may be some seesawing back and forth between secularism and religion. However, Adventists understand Revelation 13 to predict that religion will emerge as the dominant force in American and global politics during the final days of Earth's history, and the election on November 8, 2016, appears to move the United States, and ultimately the world, in that direction.

The world is moving toward Armageddon!

CHAPTER 24

The Coming Global Crisis

A careful examination of the various New Testament discussions about the end time reveals a significant reality: we can expect that the months and years leading up to the second coming of Christ will be a time of great global upheaval. We sometimes refer to this crisis as "the time of trouble," which we further divide into a "little time of trouble" before the close of probation and a "great time of trouble" after the close of probation, just before the second coming of Christ. In this chapter, we're going to examine the time of trouble that occurs before the close of probation, which will bring a terrible crisis on the world. This crisis will consist of calamities, which can include natural disasters, military action, a global financial meltdown, and terrorist violence of an even greater degree than we've already seen. Ellen White said that these calamities will spark the initial demand for Sunday laws: "Satan puts his interpretation on events, and they [Sunday-law advocates] think, as he would have them, that the calamities are the result of Sunday breaking. Thinking to appease the wrath of God these influential men make laws enforcing Sunday observance."[1] "The class that have provoked the displeasure of Heaven will charge all their troubles upon those whose obedience to God's commandments is a perpetual reproof to transgressors. It will be declared that men are offending God by the violation of the Sunday sabbath; that this sin has brought calamities which will not cease until Sunday observance shall be strictly enforced."[2]

Ellen White didn't indicate the nature of these calamities, but it could be any of the ones I mentioned earlier—natural disasters, wars, a global financial meltdown, or terrorism. The global economy is on very shaky ground as I write these words, and it wouldn't surprise me if the first calamity was a financial crisis that affects the entire world. Note, however, that Ellen White spoke of calamities, plural, bringing on Sunday legislation. So it could be any combination of the calamities I've mentioned above and perhaps some I didn't mention.

Be that as it may, I expect the coming global crisis to begin with more "mild" calamities, which will be followed by events of increasing magnitude.

As we shall see, the most dire calamities will threaten the survival of the human race. These are the calamities that will lead the world to persecute God's people the most severely, including martyrdom in some cases. However, in order to provide you with a complete understanding of what I mean, we need to take a short detour into Revelation 13.

The two beast powers in Revelation 13

You're no doubt aware that in Bible prophecy a beast represents a political entity—a nation. Revelation 13 introduces us to two beasts; both of which are end-time powers. One emerges from the sea and the other from the earth. These beast powers are intimately associated with the coming global crisis.

The beast from the sea. Almost from the beginning of our movement, Seventh-day Adventists have identified the beast that rises from the sea to be the same power as the little horn on the dragon in Daniel 7, and I agree with that conclusion. Daniel's little horn describes the papacy during the medieval period, whereas in Revelation 13 the beast from the sea describes the papacy during the final global crisis. So let's examine Revelation 13 to see what it says about the papacy during this critical period of Earth's history.

The first thing to notice is that this beast, the papacy, is controlled by Satan, because verse 2 says, "The dragon [Satan] gave the beast his power and his throne and great authority." So the beast from the sea is an agent of Satan, who is the leader of the Kingdom of Darkness. Verse 3 goes on to say that one of the beast's seven heads "seemed to have had a fatal wound." Adventists have always understood this fatal wound to have been inflicted in 1798, during the latter part of the French Revolution, when the French army took Pope Pius VI prisoner and exiled him to Valence, France. At that point, the papacy totally lost its influence in European political affairs. The popes seethed with rage and complained bitterly over this loss of their political influence, but it did no good. The European nations, having become secular in their governmental affairs, went cheerfully about their business and let the popes rant and rave to their hearts' content.

I mentioned in an earlier chapter that this turn of events gave God's church a reprieve from the persecution of the Middle Ages for more than two hundred years, and God designed it to be that way. He knew that His people needed these two centuries to establish a global organization that could proclaim His final message, which would prepare the world for the coming global crisis. Thus, the reprieve was to be only temporary, which verse 3 affirms when it says that the fatal wound was healed. By this, Revelation is telling us that the papacy is destined to regain its former political power over the world. And, as I pointed out in a previous chapter, this resurrection of papal political power has already begun.

The papacy still has not fully regained the political power it had during the Middle Ages, but that *will happen.* Verse 7 tells us that the beast from the sea "was given authority over every tribe, people, language and nation." In other words, when the fatal wound is fully healed, the papacy won't have political control over just the European nations; it will have political authority over every nation on planet Earth! Most people today, looking at the current rise in the pope's popularity, wouldn't think it would come to that, but Revelation assures us that it will.

And there's more. The papacy will repeat its persecution of God's people, because verse 7 informs us that not only will the papacy be given authority over the entire world, it will also be given "power to make war against the saints and to conquer them." In other words, at the height of the final crisis, God's people will be powerless at the hands of the papacy. They will have absolutely no protection from Earth's governments.

The beast from the earth. Almost from the beginning of our movement, Seventh-day Adventists have identified the United States of America as the beast that rises out of the earth in Revelation 13.

The first thing to notice about this beast power is that it "exercised all the authority of the first beast on his behalf" (verse 12). In other words, the land beast will be the enforcer of the sea beast's authority. That's how it was during the medieval period. The papacy had no army. It used the police and the military power of the various nations of Europe to enforce its dogmas and decrees. Revelation tells us that this will also be true of the relationship between the papacy and the United States during the coming global crisis.

This concept is further confirmed by a statement in verse 14, which says that the land beast "ordered [the inhabitants of the earth] to set up an image in honor of the beast who was wounded by the sword and yet lived." The *Seventh-day Adventist Bible Commentary* says, "Among the principles by which the first beast [the medieval papacy] operated was the use of the secular arm to support religious institutions. In imitation the second beast [the United States] will repudiate its principles of freedom. The church will prevail upon the state to enforce its dogmas. State and church will unite, and the result will be the loss of religious liberty and the persecution of dissenting minorities."[3]

The United States will enforce the dogmas of the papacy with an iron fist, for verses 15–17 say that the beast from the earth "was given power to give breath to the image of the first beast, so that it could speak and cause all who refused to worship the image to be killed. He also forced everyone, small and great, rich and poor, free and slave, to receive a mark on his right hand or on his forehead, so that no one could buy or sell unless he had the mark, which is the name of the beast or the number of his name."

Obviously, the persecution of dissenters during the final crisis will be brutal. Revelation's description sounds like ISIS, not like the United States that you and I know. I pointed out in a previous chapter that some restrictions on religious liberty are already occurring in today's world, but not even the most rabid of today's secularists would kill people who disagree with them, nor would they refuse such people the freedom to buy and sell goods and services.

So here's a question that begs for an answer: How can this happen in today's world? How can the United States and the papacy become like ISIS? Under normal circumstances, it would take decades, perhaps even centuries, for the United States to become involved in this kind of persecution of dissenters. Revelation 13 only says that this *will happen*. It doesn't so much as hint at the circumstances that will *lead* to this sort of despotic behavior on the part of the papacy and the United States. *However, I propose that something will be going on in the background that Revelation 13 doesn't tell us about, something that will motivate these two powers to clamp down viciously on religious dissenters.*

Fortunately, other parts of the New Testament do provide us with the necessary background information.

Global calamities

I pointed out a few pages back that during the early stages of the coming global crisis the calamities will be more mild—an international financial meltdown, perhaps, or increased terrorist attacks and multiplying natural disasters. However, during the most intense part of this global crisis the natural disasters will be so overwhelming that if God didn't intervene, they would threaten the survival of the human race. John hinted about this in Revelation, and Jesus was quite specific about it in His sermon on signs of the end that was recorded by both Matthew and Luke. I'll begin with John.

What John said. In Revelation 7:1, John described "four angels standing at the four corners of the earth, holding back the four winds of the earth to prevent any wind from blowing on the land or on the sea or on any tree." Please notice two things that John said. First, the angels are holding back the winds—that is, the calamities—that will usher in the coming global crisis. And second, he said that when the angels do release the winds, they will harm the earth, the sea, and the trees. You can interpret these words symbolically if you wish, such as the sea representing multitudes and peoples. However, I take John's words very literally. I believe he means that terrible natural disasters will come upon the world that will wreak havoc on the global ecology. After all, the deterioration of the earth, sea, and vegetation are three of the various areas of our ecology that are causing environmental scientists grave concern today.

A fifth angel that came flying in from the east echoed this conclusion. He "called out in a loud voice to the four angels who had been given power to harm the land and the sea: 'Do not harm the land or the sea or the trees until we put a seal on the foreheads of the servants of our God' " (verses 2, 3). So again we see that the world's ecology will be severely damaged when the angels release the four winds

But what will these global calamities consist of? What can we expect to happen that will severely damage the global ecology? John didn't elaborate, but Jesus gave us some clues.

What Jesus said. In His comments in Matthew 24 about the signs of His second coming, Jesus made a very startling statement. He said, "Then there will be great distress, unequaled from the beginning of the world until now—and never to be equaled again. If those days had not been cut short, no one would survive, but for the sake of the elect those days will be shortened" (verses 21, 22).

Please note two details about these verses. First, this will be the worst time of trouble the world has ever known. Jesus said it would be "unequaled from the beginning of the world." His words echo those of Daniel, who said that when Michael stands up "there will be a time of distress such as has not happened from the beginning of nations until then" (Daniel 12:1).

Second, Jesus said that "if those days had not been cut short, *no one would survive*" (Matthew 24:22; emphasis added). In other words, if God didn't intervene to stop the natural disasters causing the final global crisis, the human race would become the next extinct species!

Signs in the heavens in Matthew. Jesus was very specific about the nature of the disasters that will come close to wiping out our human race. In Matthew 24:29, He said,

"Immediately after the distress of those days

" 'the sun will be darkened,

and the moon will not give its light;
the stars will fall from the sky,
and the heavenly bodies will be shaken.' "

Adventists have traditionally understood these signs in the heavens as having been fulfilled by the Dark Day on May 19, 1780, and the falling of the stars on November 13, 1833—I can understand why they did that. These events were fresh in the minds of William Miller and our early Adventist pioneers. They saw them as dramatic indicators that Jesus was coming soon. However, two hundred years later the Dark Day and the falling of the stars that our pioneers found so meaningful have lost most of their dramatic impact. Fortunately, Luke also reported on Jesus' prediction of signs in the heavens, and when we put his account alongside Matthew's, we gain a much more complete understanding of what Jesus had in mind.

Signs in the heavens in Luke. There's a significant difference between Matthew's account and Luke's. Matthew tells us only *what* will happen: falling stars and a darkened sun and moon. He gives no indication of the effect these signs will have on the human race. But that's precisely what Luke emphasizes. All he says about the events themselves is that there will be signs in the sun, moon, and stars. He doesn't say a word about falling stars or a darkened sun and moon. Instead, he focuses on the human reaction to those events. He says, "On the earth, nations will be in anguish and perplexity at the roaring and tossing of the sea. Men will faint from terror, apprehensive of what is coming on the world, for the heavenly bodies will be shaken" (Luke 21:25, 26).

Please notice two things about Luke's description of the human response to the signs in the heavens. In verse 25, Jesus says that "nations will be in anguish and perplexity"; and in verse 26, He says that "men will faint from terror."

I'll begin with what Luke 21:25 says—that "nations will be in anguish and perplexity." *Nations* refers to the governments into which people organize themselves, and Luke describes these governments as being "in anguish and perplexity." *Anguish* means "This hurts a lot," and *perplexity* means "What do we do now?" So these signs in the heavens will involve major natural disasters that leave the world's leaders at a loss to know how to meet the emergency. It could be something like Hurricane Katrina in 2005, the earthquake that devastated Haiti in 2010, the tsunami that hit Japan in 2011, and half a dozen similar disasters all happening within one month. The world's nations can deal with these tragic events when they're spread out over time, but they would be overwhelmed were all of them to happen at once.

In verse 26, Jesus said that "men [the human race] will faint from terror, apprehensive of what is coming on the world, for the heavenly bodies will be shaken." People all over the world will panic over the shaking of the heavenly bodies; that is, the falling of the stars and the darkened sun and moon.

Now let me ask you a couple of simple questions: Did the Dark Day in 1780 throw the world's leaders into anguish and perplexity? Did the falling of the stars in 1833 cause a global panic? Of course not. This doesn't mean that the events in the late 1700s and the early 1800s had no prophetic significance. It simply means that they were precursors to what is coming. They were a type, while the antitype is still future. And every antitype is always much greater than its type (see, for example, Hebrews 8:3–6; 9:1, 11).

This still doesn't tell us why the falling of the stars and the darkening of the sun and moon will cause this dramatic human reaction. But something else Jesus said gives us a good clue. He said that the "nations will be in anguish and perplexity at the roaring and tossing of the sea" (Luke 21:25). At first glance, there doesn't seem to be any relationship between the dark day and the falling of the stars on the one hand and the roaring and tossing of the sea on the other, but there is. The falling of the stars in 1833 was caused by meteorites, as our pioneers clearly understood. Asteroids are simply huge meteorites, and today's scientists know that an asteroid impact in the ocean would create a huge tidal wave that, depending on the size of the asteroid and the geography of the nearby coastland—whether mountainous or flat— could wash inland anywhere from ten to one thousand miles.

Ellen White made an interesting comment about Luke's words that I believe supports this conclusion. After quoting the part of verse 25 about "the sea and the waves roaring" (KJV), she said, "Yes, they [the sea and the waves] shall pass their borders, and destruction will be in their track."[4] The seas passing their borders is a perfect description of a tidal wave.

Now let's return to Matthew's account. He said that "the sun will be darkened, and the moon will not give its light" (Matthew 24:29). An asteroid striking on land would cast dust and pulverized rock into the upper atmosphere that would indeed darken the sun and the moon for several months, causing a dramatic global climate change and huge crop failures. It's no wonder that the human race will "faint from terror, apprehensive of what is coming on the world" (Luke 21:26)! It's no wonder that the survival of the human race will be threatened if God doesn't cut short this time of distress! I propose that it will require these type of natural disasters to cause the ecological devastation that the four angels in Revelation 7 are holding back at the present time. It's these kinds of catastrophic events that will lead to a global worship of the beast from the sea and the persecution of God's people by both the sea beast and the land beast.

Ellen White made another startling statement that may apply to what I've been sharing with you. She wrote, "Transgression has almost reached its limit. Confusion fills the world, and a great terror is soon to come upon human beings. The end is very near. We who know the truth should be preparing for what is soon to break upon the world as an *overwhelming surprise*."[5]

Ellen White didn't say what this "overwhelming surprise" would consist of, but an asteroid impact such as we've been considering here would certainly match her words. Ellen White also spoke about "a sudden and unlooked-for calamity" that "brings the soul face to face with death."[6] Again she didn't tell us what that calamity will be, but it's significant that she said it will confront God's people with death. You'll recall that both beasts in Revelation 13 will persecute God's people, and the beast that rises from the earth will threaten to kill them if they don't worship the beast from the sea (verse 15).

In conclusion, I need to remind myself and you that we always have to be careful when we talk about how unfulfilled prophecy will work out. The big mistake the Jews of Christ's time made their expectation that when the Messiah came He would lead the armies of Israel to defeat the hated Romans. They weren't expecting the Messiah they got, so when He showed up, they rejected Him. I've seen some elaborate charts outlining the fulfillment of the predictions of the Bible and Ellen White about the final crisis, and perhaps you have too. I believe we need to be careful not to define the future too precisely because the more detailed we get, the more likely we are to be wrong.

However, we also know that both the Bible's writers and Ellen White made some very specific statements about the final crisis, and these things were revealed to them to share with us, because God wants us to know what's coming so we can prepare spiritually and physically to deal with what lies ahead. The chief problem with the Jews two thousand years ago wasn't their false expectations. Jesus' disciples held these same false expectations, which is why they were continually debating among themselves about which one of them would hold the top positions in the coming kingdom. But the Jewish leaders rejected Christ when He came, whereas the disciples accepted Him. The difference lay in the spirituality of the two groups. Christ's disciples were willing to submit to Him and learn from Him, even though they were very slow learners sometimes. The Jewish leaders were so concerned about maintaining their authority that they weren't willing to listen and learn.

So whatever false expectations about the end time that you and I may hold—and I'm sure we have some—if we're loyal to the message Christ has given us in the Bible and in the writings of Ellen White, we will make it through the final crisis on His side.

What I've described in this chapter is the calamities that will bring the world to eventually give global political power to religion. This will set the stage for the final conflict between the Kingdom of Light and the Kingdom of Darkness. It is to this conflict that we will now turn.

---

1. Ellen G. White, *Last Day Events* (Boise, ID: Pacific Press® Pub. Assn., 1992), 129.

2. White, *The Great Controversy*, 590.

3. Nichol, *The Seventh-day Adventist Bible Commentary*, 7:821, 822.

4. Ellen G. White, *Selected Messages*, bk. 3 (Washington, DC: Review and Herald® Pub. Assn., 1980), 417.

5. Ellen G. White, *Testimonies for the Church*, vol. 8 (Mountain View, CA: Pacific Press® Pub. Assn., 1948), 28; emphasis added.

6. White, *Christ's Object Lessons*, 412.

CHAPTER 25

The Final Conflict

Armageddon is the final battle on planet Earth between the Kingdom of Light and the Kingdom of Darkness. At this point in our story, and in the context of the entire history of evil on our planet, it's "just around the corner." However, there must first be a final conflict between these two kingdoms *before* the close of probation to determine who on planet Earth will stand on the side of the Kingdom of Light and who will be on the side of the Kingdom of Darkness *after* the close of probation. Once every human being has made that final choice, probation will close, and the seven last plagues will begin to be poured out.

Revelation 12:12 says that following Jesus' death and resurrection Satan was "filled with fury," because he knew that his time was short. Two thousand years later his time is almost up, and he's absolutely enraged. He's desperate to get the whole world on his side, because he hopes that if he can accomplish this, there's a chance that God might give up the conflict and let him keep his world.*

Unfortunately for Satan, there will be a few people—a small number compared to the global population—who will be loyal to God and Christ, and they will stand in his way. That's why Revelation 12:17 says that "the dragon was enraged at the woman and went off to make war against the rest of her offspring." Satan will be absolutely furious with God's end-time people, because they will block his efforts to rule the world, and he will do his absolute best to destroy them. There are two ways he can accomplish this. One is to kill them—and there will be martyrs. But Satan will also have accomplished his purpose if he can get those of God's people who aren't martyred to give up their loyalty to Jesus. He will use torture, imprisonment, the inability to buy or sell, and threats of death in his effort to get them to

---

* I'm not aware of any Bible text or Ellen White comment suggesting that Satan hopes that God might permit him to continue dominating our planet if he could just get rid of all God's people. But it seems consistent with some of the other foolish hopes he's held, such as the one mentioned in the *The Desire of Ages*: if God had destroyed the world rather than redeeming it, he (Satan) could "carry out his plan for securing to himself the allegiance of heavenly beings." White, *The Desire of Ages*, 37.

yield their convictions. He'll be as desperate to tempt God's people to give up their faith as he was to get Jesus to give up the great controversy during His trial and crucifixion. Unfortunately, he will get a large number of God's people to yield their faith—but not all!

However, for the most part, Satan won't do these things in person. He'll inspire human beings to carry out his purposes. Revelation says that the beast from the sea—the papacy—will "make war against the saints and . . . conquer them." It says that the beast that rises out of the earth—the United States—will "cause all who refused to worship the image to be killed" (Revelation 13:7, 15). This seems impossible as I write these words, but Revelation assures us that it *will* happen. And one of the major driving forces contributing to Satan's efforts to coerce God's people to yield their convictions will be the calamities that are coming upon the world.

By this time, religion will have regained its dominance in Western society (it has never lost that dominance in Eastern and Middle Eastern societies). As I pointed out in the previous chapter, religious leaders will proclaim that God is displeased with Sabbath keepers over their disrespect for Sunday and that is the reason why He's bringing calamities on the world. Thus, they'll demand that laws be enacted requiring the observance of Sunday as the officially designated day for rest and worship. Think of how secularists today jeer and condemn God's people who hold to the biblical teaching about homosexuality and gender identity issues. That's how the world will treat God's people during the final conflict, only multiplied many times over.

God's end-time message

One of the things that will most infuriate Satan during this time is that God's people are proclaiming His end-time message in an effort to win as many people as possible to the Kingdom of Light before probation closes. So, in addition to getting God's people to abandon their faith, Satan will also put forth desperate efforts to try and stop them from proclaiming the three angels' messages, especially the third one.

I shared these messages with you in the chapter on Jesus' end-time church. What's critical to note here is that the primary issue in the message God's people proclaim is the eternal nature of God's law. Revelation 12:17 and 14:12 both call attention to the fact that during the final conflict God's people will obey His commandments. Ellen White wrote that "the last great conflict between truth and error is but the final struggle of the long-standing controversy concerning the law of God. Upon this battle we are now entering."[1] In proclaiming this law, God's people will place special emphasis on the fourth commandment, which calls for the observance of the Sabbath on the seventh day of the week instead of on Sunday, the first day. Satan's agent, the papacy, changed the day from the seventh to the first day of the week, and Protestants have acquiesced to that change. During the final conflict, Satan will use both the papacy and the Protestant world to try to stop the proclamation of the Sabbath. The dividing line will be drawn between those who keep the Sabbath and those who keep Sunday.

There's a common question Sunday keepers ask that demands a biblical answer: What difference does it make which day one keeps so long as we keep one day out of seven? The quick answer is that in both the Creation account and in the fourth commandment God specifically designated the seventh day of the week as the Sabbath, not any one of the other seven days of the week that we might choose. That certainly is a valid answer, and it has persuaded a lot of people to keep the Sabbath on the seventh day of the week. But that answer doesn't say *why* God set aside the seventh day. There are two good answers to that question.

First, as both Genesis and the fourth commandment say so clearly, the Sabbath is a memorial of Creation: "For in six days the LORD made the heavens and the earth, the sea, and all that is in them, but he rested on the seventh day. Therefore [for this reason] the LORD blessed the Sabbath day and made it holy" (Exodus 20:11). The idea of the Sabbath being a memorial seems to be so ingrained in our human minds (or at least our Christian minds) that even Sunday keepers accept it. They simply switch the memorial from Creation to Christ's resurrection. Now I will be the first to concede that Christ's resurrection is worthy of a day for celebration. The problem is that nowhere does the New Testament state that the Sabbath was changed from the seventh day to the first day in honor of Christ's resurrection. The idea is simply imposed on the first day to provide a justification for observing it instead of the seventh day.

This brings us to the second reason for keeping the seventh day, which is the real reason why God set aside the seventh day as the Sabbath. While I explained this in chapter 5, I'll give you a brief review here.

Why God set aside the seventh day

Everything God created during the first six days of Creation week was made out of matter—stuff. But the Sabbath was made out of immaterial time. Why? Because God loved us, His human creations, and He made the Sabbath as a special time in which He could have a special weekly relationship with us and we with Him. So the Sabbath is both a memorial of Creation and a time when we can spend time together with God. To ensure that the seventh-day Sabbath would be respected throughout all time, "God blessed the seventh day and made it holy" (Genesis 2:3). The fourth commandment says exactly the same thing with a slight difference in wording (Exodus 20:11).

So what does it mean to make something holy? It means that once something has been declared holy, it is supposed to be treated with much more care than ordinary things. When Moses approached the burning bush, God told him to take off his shoes because he was standing on holy ground. At Sinai, God had the Israelites "put limits" around the base of the mountain, and He warned the people that anyone who touched the mountain would be killed—because His presence made it holy (Exodus 19:12). Then there's the case of Aaron's sons, Nadab and Abihu, who were priests. God had instructed the priests that anytime they approached the Most Holy Place—which was the holiest place in the Israelite culture—they were to put fire in their censers *from the altar of incense*. However, Nadab and Abihu put *their own fire* in their censers, contrary to God's instruction, and fire came out from God and killed them (Leviticus 10:1, 2; 16:12).

God is very strict about His requirements regarding the way we treat holy things. Our actions around holy objects, times, and places must be in strict harmony with His instructions, and any violation is worthy of death. Thus, technically, anyone who violates God's holy Sabbath on the seventh day of the week is worthy of death.

Why no punishment for two thousand years?

So why didn't God punish the deviation from the seventh-day Sabbath, which occurred about one hundred years after Jesus returned to heaven? Keep in mind that God gave Satan the freedom to tempt the Israelites into drifting from His instructions during the fifteen hundred years before Christ, but He eventually brought the nation to account through Christ. The Jews closed their probation when they rejected Christ; they were no longer His people. The very same thing happened to the church after Christ returned to heaven. He allowed Satan to introduce numerous errors into His church; one of which was substituting the first day of the week for the seventh as the Sabbath. And, as with the Israelites, He didn't immediately punish His church. He allowed Satan to pervert the church just as He had allowed him to pervert the Jewish nation.

But just as God eventually brought the Jewish nation to account through Christ's life and death, so He will bring His church to account over the many doctrinal errors it has developed. During the final conflict, the Sabbath will be the focal point of that accounting. This will demonstrate who treats God's holy Sabbath with respect and enters into the relationship with Him that He longs for—and who doesn't. Those who refuse to respect His holy day also refuse to enter into that special relationship with Him, and they are no longer worthy to be called His sons and daughters. They will receive the mark of the beast; they will suffer the wrath of God during the seven last plagues; and they will be slain with the brightness of Christ's second coming.

It's our responsibility as God's end-time church to warn the world about this terrible emergency! It has been our responsibility for more than 150 years to proclaim the Sabbath message and to build up a worldwide church that can proclaim the Sabbath truth to the world during the final crisis. Most of the world will reject our message, and as God allows natural disasters to occur that will threaten the survival of the human race, His people will be criticized bitterly and persecuted ferociously. Regardless of the consequences, we must proclaim the message that "if anyone worships the beast and his image and receives his mark on the forehead or on the hand, he, too, will drink of the wine of God's fury, which has been poured full strength into the cup of his wrath" (Revelation 14:9, 10).

Ellen White wrote,

Those who honor the Bible Sabbath will be denounced as enemies of law and order, as breaking down the moral restraints of society, causing anarchy and corruption, and calling down the judgments of God upon the earth. Their conscientious scruples will be pronounced obstinacy, stubbornness, and contempt of authority. They will be accused of disaffection toward the government. Ministers who deny the obligation of the divine law will present from the pulpit the duty of yielding obedience to the civil authorities as ordained of God. In legislative halls and courts of justice, commandment keepers will be misrepresented and condemned. A false coloring will be given to their words; the worst construction will be put upon their motives.[2]

This attitude is already evident in the way secular societies, businesses, and governments condemn and jeer at conservative Christians who hold biblical convictions about social issues, such as abortion and homosexuality, that are contrary to the secular understanding. That's why today we can understand that the attitude toward God's people, which Ellen White described, *really could happen in America.* Indeed, it *will* happen in America. The difference between then and now is that when this happens, religion will have replaced secularism as the dominant force in society. In light of the calamities that I shared with you in the previous chapter, it has already started to happen with the election of Donald Trump as president of the United States.

Sharing God's message with the world during the final conflict will not be easy. Revelation 13:7, 15 says that the saints will be conquered and threatened with death. Ellen White wrote, "The power attending the message [about the Sabbath] will only madden those who oppose it. The clergy will put forth almost superhuman efforts to shut away the light lest it should shine upon their flocks. . . . The church appeals to the strong arm of civil power, and, in this work, papists and Protestants unite. As the movement for Sunday enforcement becomes more bold and decided, the law will be invoked against commandment keepers. They will be threatened with fines and imprisonment."[3]

Spiritualism

Prior to the final conflict, God has permitted Satan to manifest himself openly only to a very few people who give themselves up totally to his control—people such as spirit mediums and clairvoyants. However, as the conflict increases in its intensity, Satan and his demons will be given more and more access to the people who reject God's message.

Jesus foretold this development in His sermon on signs of the end. He said, "At that time if anyone says to you, 'Look, here is the Christ!' or, 'There he is!' do not believe it. For false Christs and false prophets will appear and perform great signs and miracles to deceive even the elect—if that were possible" (Matthew 24:23, 24).

Paul affirmed the same development: "The coming of the lawless one will be in accordance with the work of Satan displayed in all kinds of counterfeit miracles, signs and wonders, and in every sort of evil that deceives those who are perishing" (2 Thessalonians 2:9, 10).

John said that the beast that rises out of the earth "performed great and miraculous signs, even causing fire to come down from heaven to earth in full view of men. Because of the signs he was given power to do on behalf of the first beast, he deceived the inhabitants of the earth" (Revelation 13:13, 14).

Ellen White said that "many will be confronted by the spirits of devils personating beloved relatives or friends and declaring the most dangerous heresies. These visitants will appeal to our tenderest sympathies and will work miracles to sustain their pretensions."[4] She went on to say that "except those who are kept by the power of God, through faith in His word, the whole world will be swept into the ranks of this delusion."[5]

Spiritualism will be the other falsehood, along with Sunday sacredness, that Satan will perpetrate upon the world. As Ellen White put it, "Through the two great errors, the immortality of the soul and Sunday sacredness, Satan will bring the people under his deceptions."[6]

In fact, I believe that spiritualism will be one of the primary influences in bringing secularists and religionists together during the final conflict. Today, secularism is dominated by naturalism and science, which claim that the only reality we can depend on is what we can see with our five senses and the instruments that help us to extend those five senses. Athiests deny the supernatural because it violates the natural order of things that they're so accustomed to. However, during the final crisis Satanic forces will manifest themselves openly to secularists, and they'll believe in the supernatural because it will satisfy their naturalistic assumptions. They can see it with their eyes and hear it with their ears. And religionists, who believe in the immortality of the soul, will be easily duped into believing the proclamations of these seducing spirits. That's how spiritualism will be one of the primary influences in bringing secularists and religionists together during the final conflict.

The mark of the beast

Adventists have taught for more than 150 years that the mark of the beast will be placed on those who refuse to observe God's holy Sabbath. Ellen White said a lot about that in her book *The Great Controversy*; but what is the biblical basis for that conclusion? It's actually fairly simple to understand. It has to do with the words *worship* and *worships*, which together appear eight times in Revelation 13 and 14 (Revelation 13:4 [twice], 8, 12, 15; 14:7, 9, 11). In seven of these instances, the word refers to false worship; in one reference, Revelation 14:7, it refers to true worship, and the key to understanding the mark of the beast is found in that verse. It says, "Worship him who made *the heavens, the earth, the sea* and the springs of water" (emphasis added). These words are almost a direct quote from the last verse of the fourth commandment: "In six days the LORD made *the heavens and the earth, the sea*, and all that is in them, but he rested on the seventh day" (Exodus 20:11). Revelation adds the words "And the springs of water."

Both Sabbath keepers and Sunday keepers recognize that both days are about worship. So in saying "worship him who made the heavens, the earth, the sea and the springs of water," Revelation is speaking about Sabbath observance according to the commandment. That's what true worship is like. Because true worship is about observing the Sabbath on the seventh day, and since the worship of the beast is the opposite of the worship of God, the worship of the beast is about observing the first day, contrary to the fourth commandment.

When a human being, with full knowledge of the facts on both sides of the issue, makes a deliberate choice to observe the first day of the week, that person will receive the mark of the beast. However, it's important to also understand that

> not one is made to suffer the wrath of God until the truth has been brought home to his mind and conscience, and has been rejected. There are many who have never had an opportunity to hear the special truths for this time. The obligation of the fourth commandment has never been set before them in its true light. He who reads every heart and tries every motive will leave none who desire a knowledge of the truth, to be deceived as to the issues of the controversy. The decree is not to be urged upon the people blindly. Everyone is to have sufficient light to make his decision intelligently.[7]

However, "with the issue thus clearly set before him, whoever shall trample upon God's law to obey a human enactment receives the mark of the beast."[8]

The latter rain

Today many people reject our message, as they will in the future. It's the responsibility of God's remnant church to proclaim the message about the mark of the beast and Sabbath observance even now so that as many people as possible will be forewarned. Before the close of probation, during the final conflict, God will make one more effort to warn the world, and He will use one additional means that He hasn't so far. We call it the "latter rain." This latter rain will be similar to the power of the Holy Spirit that was poured out in the early rain power on the apostles on the Day of Pentecost. Acts 4:33 says that in spite of fierce opposition from the Jewish leadership, "with great power the apostles continued to testify to the resurrection of the Lord

Jesus." The result on the Day of Pentecost was that some three thousand people joined the infant church and were baptized (Acts 2:41).

This manifestation of divine power will be repeated during the final conflict. John said that near the end of time he saw "another angel coming down from heaven. He had great authority, and the earth was illuminated by his splendor" (Revelation 18:1). That's the latter rain. John went on to say that "with a mighty voice he [the angel] shouted: 'Fallen! Fallen is Babylon the Great. She has become a home for demons and a haunt for every evil spirit' " (verse 2). That's a description of the Kingdom of Darkness during the final conflict. John continued, "I heard another voice from heaven say: 'Come out of her, my people, so that you will not share in her sins, so that you will not receive any of her plagues' " (verse 4). That's God's call for His people to leave the Kingdom of Darkness and join His Kingdom of Light. However, there won't be a literal angel making this proclamation. Rather, as with the three angels in Revelation 14, this angel is a symbol of God's people who will do the proclaiming.

Our responsibility during this time will be to surrender to the power of the Holy Spirit's outpouring of the latter rain. This will give us the ability and courage to face the onslaught of contempt and persecution that will confront us while we proclaim God's message to a dying world. And our message will succeed in accomplishing its purpose. Ellen White wrote, "As the question of enforcing Sunday observance is widely agitated, the event so long doubted and disbelieved is seen to be approaching, and the third message will produce an effect which it could not have had before."[9]

During this time, "multitudes will receive the faith and join the armies of the Lord."[10]

> Souls that were scattered all through the religious bodies answered to the call, and the precious were hurried out of the doomed churches, as Lot was hurried out of Sodom before her destruction. . . .
>
> There are many souls to come out of the ranks of the world, out of the churches—even the Catholic Church—whose zeal will far exceed that of those who have stood in rank and file to proclaim the truth.[11]

The close of probation

I used to wonder why the close of probation prior to Christ's second coming wasn't mentioned in the Bible. But instead of accepting this as a fact, I started searching, and I soon found what I was looking for. It's in Revelation

15. In verse 5, John said, "I looked and in heaven the temple, that is, the tabernacle of the Testimony, was opened." That's the first indication of the close of probation. When Jesus died on the cross, the veil in the temple was torn from top to bottom, exposing the Most Holy Place. This was an indication that the ceremonial services that God had given to Moses fifteen hundred years earlier had ended because Jesus' death fulfilled them. Similarly, the temple that John saw *opened* in heaven suggests that Christ's mediatorial ministry in the heavenly sanctuary will come to an end.

There's more. "The temple was filled with smoke from the glory of God and from his power, and no one could enter the temple until the seven last plagues of the seven angels were completed" (verse 8). The statement that no one could enter the temple would include Jesus, and therefore His mediatorial ministry will end. This is confirmed by what happened after the ark of the covenant was brought into Solomon's temple and set down in the Most Holy Place. "The temple of the LORD was filled with a cloud, and *the priests could not perform their service because of the cloud, for the glory of the LORD filled the temple of God*" (2 Chronicles 5:13, 14; emphasis added). Second Chronicles 7:2 also says that "*the priests could not enter the temple* of the LORD because the glory of the LORD filled it" (emphasis added).

Revelation 15:8, which is almost a direct quotation of these two verses, confirms that our heavenly High Priest will not enter His temple in heaven and that His priestly ministry in the sanctuary above therefore will come to a close. This is further confirmed by the fact that in Revelation 16:1—the very next verse—God commands the seven angels to begin pouring out the seven last plagues, which are the full wrath of God unmixed with mercy that was predicted in the third angel's message (Revelation 14:9–11). The wicked, who refused to listen to the warnings of God's end-time church, now receive the consequence of their decision, and this can't happen until after probation has closed.

Conclusion

The final conflict will be a fearful time and a glorious time. It will be the most intense period of spiritual conflict that the world has ever known, and this will require God's people to have a very deep spiritual experience. How to obtain that spiritual experience is the topic of the next chapter.

---

1. White, *The Great Controversy*, 582.

2. Ibid., 592.

3. Ibid., 607.

4. Ibid., 560.

5. Ibid., 562.

6. Ibid., 588.

7. Ibid., 605.

8. Ibid., 604.

9. Ibid., 606.

10. White, *Last Day Events*, 211.

11. Ibid.

CHAPTER 26

How to Prepare
for the Final Conflict

After reading the previous two chapters, I think you can understand that the coming global crisis and the final conflict will require that you and I have a very intimate relationship with God. The question is, how do we develop such a relationship with Him? The foundation of the Christian faith and of our Adventist faith is the Bible, so Bible study and prayer are the two primary ways we grow into a more intimate spiritual relationship with God.

The Bible

There are two ways to study the Bible: one is devotional, and the other is doctrinal. These two need to be in balance with each other.

Devotional Bible study. Devotional Bible study is one of the primary ways we develop our relationship with Jesus, especially as we focus on His life, death, and resurrection. Ellen White advised, "It would be well for us to spend a thoughtful hour each day in contemplation of the life of Christ. We should take it point by point, and let the imagination grasp each scene, especially the closing ones. As we thus dwell upon His great sacrifice for us, our confidence in Him will be more constant, our love will be quickened, and we shall be more deeply imbued with His spirit. If we would be saved at last, we must learn the lesson of penitence and humiliation at the foot of the cross."[1]

One of the best ways I've found for conducting devotional Bible study is to write out my thoughts as I study. I find that as I write, I gain a better understanding about the verse or verses I'm studying than if I simply read the words and reflect on them in my mind. I also find that Ellen White's comment about letting the imagination "grasp each scene" is greatly aided by writing down my thoughts. I experienced one of the most intense spiritual times of my life while writing the three chapters in this book on Christ's agonizing experience in Gethsemane, His trial, and His crucifixion. I wholeheartedly recommend writing—another word for it is *journaling*—as you read the Bible. You won't go through nearly as many verses with each sitting, but you will get much more out of what you do cover.

One of the most vital parts of your devotional life should be a prayer that God will reveal your character defects to you. Jesus told His disciples, "When he, the Spirit of truth, comes, he will guide you into all truth" (John 16:13), and I propose that some of the most important truths He will reveal to you are your character defects and the sins these defects have caused you to commit. Paul said that a primary reason that the wicked will be lost is that "they refused to love the truth and so be saved" (2 Thessalonians 2:10). I believe that one of the most significant truths they refuse to believe is the truth about themselves. Thus, asking God to reveal your character defects to you and the sins they have led you to commit should be one of the most important parts of your devotional life.

When God does reveal this to you and you recognize where these character defects have led you into sin, it's imperative that you confess those sins. This is fairly easy to do when the confession is to God. The hard part is when you need to confess to a fellow human being. Don't be discouraged if you feel that you simply cannot bring yourself to confess to someone a wrong you committed against that person. When I've faced this difficulty in the past, I kept praying this simple prayer: "God, I can't bring myself to confess my sin to this person, but I'm willing for You to lead me to be willing." Keep repeating that prayer until God leads you to be willing. If your prayer is sincere, *you will become willing to approach this person and make the confession.*

There's an important reason why confession of sin is a significant part of your preparation for the final conflict and the close of probation. Ellen White, in her chapter "The Time of Trouble" in *The Great Controversy*, wrote, "Though God's people will be surrounded by enemies who are bent upon their destruction, yet the anguish which they suffer is not a dread of persecution for the truth's sake; they fear that every sin has not been repented of."[2] So ask God to reveal to you any character defects and the sins they've caused you to commit so you won't have to face them during the time of trouble.

Doctrinal study. The first thing I want to say about doctrinal study is that it needs to be done within a community of believers. (I will include the study of Bible prophecy as a part of doctrinal study.) This doesn't mean that you can't study doctrine and prophecy by yourself, but it does mean that you should check your conclusions with others who are also serious students of doctrine and prophecy. The easiest way to do that is to read widely on the aspects of doctrine and prophecy you are studying, especially from Adventist sources. This is especially true of the study of prophecy, because there are so many interpretations out there in the Christian world, including Adventists who promote extreme ideas about prophecy, especially perfectionism.

You may not sense as much of the spiritual component in doctrinal Bible study as you do in devotional study, but you will gain a much broader understanding of God's Word that will enhance your spirituality. And it's absolutely essential that you do this kind of study as you prepare for the end time because you will be repeatedly challenged to support your beliefs from the Bible when it comes. One of Ellen White's most provocative statements to this effect is found in the first paragraph of her chapter "The Scriptures a Safeguard" in *The Great Controversy*: "The last great delusion is soon to open before us. Antichrist is to perform his marvelous works in our sight. So closely will the counterfeit resemble the true that it will be impossible to distinguish between them except by the Holy Scriptures. By their testimony every statement and every miracle must be tested."[3] That's why we need to be fortifying our minds with these doctrinal truths today.

The two most important doctrinal truths you need to focus on are the Sabbath and the state of the dead. Quoting Ellen White again: "Through the two great errors, the immortality of the soul and Sunday sacredness, Satan will bring the people under his deceptions."[4] And repeating a quotation that I shared with you a couple of chapters previously, the great deceiver "will persuade men that those who serve God are causing these evils. . . . It will be declared that men are offending God by the violation of the Sunday sabbath; that this sin has brought calamities which will not cease until Sunday observance shall be strictly enforced; and that those who present the claims of the fourth commandment, thus destroying reverence for Sunday, are troublers of the people, preventing their restoration to divine favor and temporal prosperity."[5] I can assure you that you will need a strong biblical defense of the Sabbath when that time comes. Bear in mind that some of those who hear you will be convicted of the truth and join with God's people in keeping the Sabbath holy. That's another reason why it's vital that you fortify your mind with the biblical evidences for these truths now.

Then there's the state of the dead and spiritualism. During the final conflict, the false beliefs of the leaders in the Sunday movement will be supported by satanic deceptions. "Communications from the spirits will declare that God has sent them to convince the rejecters of Sunday of their error, affirming that the laws of the land should be obeyed as the law of

God. They will lament the degree of wickedness in the world and second the testimony of religious teachers that the degraded state of morals is caused by the desecration of Sunday. Great will be the indignation excited against all who refuse to accept their testimony."[6] That's why it's critical that you are prepared to give a biblical response when that time comes.

Righteousness by faith. For your Bible study, I recommend that you familiarize yourself thoroughly with the concept of righteousness by faith; in your prayer time, ask God to guide you into an understanding of this important topic. Why? Because you need to develop your assurance of acceptance by God, which this will provide. I mentioned previously Ellen White's statement that one of the primary struggles God's people will experience during the time of trouble after probation's close is the "fear that every sin has not been repented of."[7] A clear understanding of the biblical teaching about righteousness by faith will help to alleviate that fear. I've written two books that deal with righteousness by faith: *Forever His* and *Conquering the Dragon Within.* I strongly recommend that you avail yourself of these books.

Having emphasized the importance of Bible study, there's a danger I must warn you about: fanaticism, especially about the end time. Some people propose that in order for God's people to be prepared for the close of probation they must be sinless. They support this idea by pulling certain statements by Ellen White out of the overall context of her writings about righteousness by faith. Often their emphasis is on the *behaviors* that God's people must develop in order to be ready for the close of probation. I don't believe God will require sinlessness after the close of probation, because we will continue to possess sinful natures until we are transformed at the Second Coming. And 1 John 1:8 says, "If we claim to be without sin, we deceive ourselves and the truth is not in us." So even if sinlessness is what God will require of us after the close of probation, we won't know when or whether we have achieved it; therefore, we can't claim it. Making a big point out of something that is impossible for us to know is detrimental to our spiritual lives because it keeps us from focusing on the real issues we need to be dealing with in order to prepare for the final crisis and the close of probation. In the next chapter, I will discuss two of Ellen White's most significant statements that are advanced by those who support the idea of sinless perfection after the close of probation.

Ellen White emphasized the seriousness of the time that's coming and the importance of making a spiritual preparation for it *now*:

The season of distress and anguish before us will require a faith that can endure weariness, delay, and hunger—a faith that will not faint though severely tried. The period of probation is granted to all to prepare for that time. . . . Those who are unwilling to deny self, to agonize before God, to pray long and earnestly for His blessing, will not obtain it. Wrestling with God—how few know what it is! How few have ever had their souls drawn out after God with intensity of desire until every power is on the stretch. When waves of despair which no language can express sweep over the suppliant, how few cling with unyielding faith to the promises of God.[8]

Prayer

Daily prayer is an absolute necessity in order for you to prepare for the coming global crisis and the final conflict. And it *must* be more than a quick prayer in the morning before you rush off to work or in the evening just before you crawl into bed. Preparing for the end time will require that you devote significant amounts of time to Bible study and prayer. I know how hard it can be in our hurried world to set this time aside, but it's essential that you *make* the time. I consider an hour a day divided between Bible study and prayer to be a good starting point.

I can hear you say, "There's no way I can do that!" I understand. So don't try to go from five minutes a day to an hour in one big jump. If you normally spend five minutes a day in your devotional time, increase it to ten, or if you've been spending ten minutes between morning and evening, add five minutes at each end and keep at it until you're comfortable with it for a few weeks. Then add another five minutes until you're comfortable with that. Keep adding these minutes until you reach twenty minutes, then settle with that for a while. Then start adding five minutes at a time until you reach forty minutes and so on until you reach that hour of Bible study and prayer. Also keep in mind that this hour doesn't have to be in one big chunk. For starters, divide it up between morning and evening,. If your schedule will accommodate it, spend some time during the day. If your job gives you a ten-minute break during the morning and/or afternoon, spend some of those minutes in prayer.

Next ask yourself, *What can I cut out of my day that could be time better spent on my devotional life?* For starters, how much time do you spend watching TV each day? How much time do you spend browsing the Internet? I don't mean that you should cut out all TV and Internet. But ask yourself whether some of it is in fact a waste of time that would be better devoted to your devotional time. You can probably think of other activities you can cut out entirely or partially in order to have more time with God.

In this regard, Ellen White's somber words from page 622 of *The Great Controversy* are worth reading:

> Those who exercise but little faith now, are in the greatest danger of falling under the power of satanic delusions and the decree to compel the conscience. And even if they endure the test they will be plunged into deeper distress and anguish in the time of trouble, because they have never made it a habit to trust in God. The lessons of faith which they have neglected they will be forced to learn under a terrible pressure of discouragement.
>
> We should now acquaint ourselves with God by proving His promises. Angels record every prayer that is earnest and sincere. We should rather dispense with selfish gratifications than neglect communion with God. The deepest poverty, the greatest self-denial, with His approval, is better than riches, honors, ease, and friendship without it. We must take time to pray. If we allow our minds to be absorbed by worldly interests, the Lord may give us time by removing from us our idols of gold, of houses, or of fertile lands.

The seal of God. Revelation 7:1–4 tells of a special relationship with God that 144,000 of His people will receive prior to the coming global calamity and the final conflict.* John wrote,

> After this I saw four angels standing at the four corners of the earth, holding back the four winds of the earth to prevent any wind from blowing on the land or on the sea or on any tree. Then I saw another angel coming up from the east, having the seal of the living God. He called out in a loud voice to the four angels who had been given power to harm the land and the sea: "Do not harm the land or the sea or the trees until we put a seal on the foreheads of the servants of our God." Then I heard the number of those who were sealed: 144,000 from all the tribes of Israel.

What is this seal? In ancient times, a king or other government official had either a signet ring or a cylindrical cone with a design that could be impressed on clay or other soft materials that indicated the ownership or authority of

---

* I believe this number is symbolic of many more than a literal 144,000 people. However, for our purpose here it doesn't matter whether the number is symbolic or literal.

the individual to whom the seal belonged. In Ephesians 4:30, Paul said that God's people are sealed by the Holy Spirit "for the day of redemption." In other words, they are His possession and have submitted to His authority.

However, the seal of God that is placed on the foreheads of the 144,000 is in an end-time setting, because when the winds are released they will harm the world's ecology—the land, the sea, and the trees. Therefore, I understand these winds to refer to the natural disasters that will come upon the world during the coming global crisis. Note that the fifth angel ordered the other four angels not to release these winds "until we put a seal on the foreheads of the servants of our God" (Revelation 7:3). In other words, the 144,000 will receive this seal *prior* to the coming global disasters that I discussed in chapter 24, and it will prepare them to stand through the terrible time of trouble and the persecution that's associated with it.

I can't prove this biblically, but I believe the seal of God that's placed on the foreheads of God's people prior to the coming global calamities means that He has closed their probation. While Ellen White doesn't use the word *probation* in the following quotation, she clearly suggests it: "Are we striving with all our God-given powers to reach the measure of the stature of men and women in Christ? Are we seeking for His fullness, ever reaching higher and higher, trying to attain to the perfection of His character? When God's servants reach this point, they will be sealed in their foreheads. The recording angel will declare, 'It is done.' They will be complete in Him whose they are by creation and redemption."[9]

If my conclusion is correct—that the seal of God that the 144,000 receive on their foreheads constitutes the close of their probation—this means their probations will be closed prior to the coming global calamities. If my conclusion that we are approaching the final crisis is also correct, that means the 144,000 are very likely being sealed *right now*, as I write these words and as you are reading them. And Ellen White asked, "Are we striving with all our God-given powers to reach the measure of the stature of men and women in Christ? Are we seeking for His fullness, ever reaching higher and higher, trying to attain to the perfection of His character?"

That's how important it is that we set aside every possible worldly advantage and focus our attention now *on preparing to receive God's seal.*

Having said this, I don't think the 144,000 represent *all* God's faithful Sabbath keepers who will live immediately prior to the final conflict. Many who are not among the 144,000 will nevertheless live through the final conflict successfully and will go home with Jesus when He comes. However,

I can't advise you to take comfort in this and think you can continue with business as usual and hope to spend more time developing your close relationship with Jesus *after* the coming global crisis and the final conflict begin. That would be an almost fatal mistake. That's why diligent spiritual preparation right now is absolutely essential.

Physical preparation

The spring of 1863 found James and Ellen White and several of their friends in Otsego, Michigan, which is a town about thirty miles northwest of Battle Creek. They were there to support a series of evangelistic meetings being conducted by two Adventist evangelists, M. E. Cornell and R. J. Lawrence. As the group met for prayer in the home of Brother A. Hilliard, Ellen White was asked to lead in prayer. While she was praying, her voice suddenly changed, and she exclaimed, "Glory to God!" She was in vision. The subject was health, and it became one of Ellen White's most significant visions. From this vision came counsel for church members on the health principles that Adventists still proclaim today.[10]

Ellen White received this vision two weeks after the organization of the General Conference on May 20–23, 1863.[11] I find this to be extremely meaningful. Ellen White considered medical missionary work to be the "right arm of the third angel's message"[12] and as vital to "the work of God as the hand is to the body"[13]—and for good reason. Seventh-day Adventists, as God's end-time church, are to prepare the world for the final crisis, which will be the most spiritually challenging period in the history of the world. In order to pass through that time successfully, we must be in the best possible physical health. More than that, we are to maintain the best possible health as we *prepare* for the final crisis. Why? Because the condition of our bodies has a profound influence on our minds, emotions, and spirituality. A mind that is dull from intemperate physical habits cannot possibly understand fully the truths for this time, nor can it develop the most intimate spiritual relationship with Jesus. If we expect to be ready to pass through the coming global crisis, the final conflict, and the time of trouble, it's imperative that we maintain the best possible physical health today. Some of the best advice on healthful living that you can find anywhere is in Ellen White's books on the topic, including *The Ministry of Healing*, *Counsels on Health*, and *Counsels on Diet and Foods*.

Conclusion

God's Kingdom of Light and Satan's Kingdom of Darkness are preparing to engage each other in the final battle for the control of the human race and the world. This battle will have two phases: one before the close of probation, which I shared with you in the previous two chapters, and the time of trouble after the close of probation, which I will share with you in the next chapter. This will be the most intense spiritual battle the world has ever seen, exceeded only by Satan's conflict with Christ from Gethsemane to His crucifixion.

I will close this chapter with the following warning from Ellen White: "Could the curtain be rolled back, could you discern the purposes of God and the judgments that are about to fall upon a doomed world, could you see your own attitude, you would fear and tremble for your own souls and for the souls of your fellow men. Earnest prayers of heart-rending anguish would go up to heaven. You would weep between the porch and the altar, confessing your spiritual blindness and backsliding."[14]

1. White, *The Desire of Ages*, 83.

2. White, *The Great Controversy*, 619.

3. Ibid., 593.

4. Ibid., 588.

5. Ibid., 590.

6. Ibid., 591.

7. Ibid., 619.

8. Ibid., 621.

9. White, *Selected Messages*, bk. 3, 427.

10. See Arthur Spalding, *Origin and History of Seventh-day Adventists* (Washington, DC: Review and Herald® Pub. Assn., 1961), vol. 1, 345; and Arthur L. White, *Ellen G. White*, vol. 2, *The Progressive Years* (Hagerstown, MD: Review and Herald® Pub. Assn., 1986), 17.

11. See Spalding, *Origin and History of Seventh-day Adventists*, 1:307.

12. Ellen G. White, *Counsels on Health* (Mountain View, CA: Pacific Press® Pub. Assn., 1951), 331.

13. White, *Testimonies for the Church*, 8:160.

14. Ellen G. White, *Counsels for the Church* (Nampa, ID: Pacific Press® Pub. Assn., 1991), 343.

CHAPTER 27

The Time of Trouble

The third angel in Revelation 14 proclaims a fearful warning to the inhabitants of the earth: "If anyone worships the beast and his image and receives his mark on the forehead or the hand, he, too, will drink of the wine of God's fury, which has been poured full strength into the cup of his wrath" (verses 9, 10). I explained in chapter 25 that the worship of the beast and his image is the observance of the first day of the week when it's enforced by law. During this final conflict, God's people will proclaim to a bitterly hostile world the importance of observing the true Sabbath of the fourth commandment. They will do this under severe persecution by those who are in rebellion against God's law, and God's people will come even to the point of martyrdom in some cases. Yet the wicked, who will be the vast majority of the world, will take the easy way out; observe the first day, Sunday; and receive the terrible mark of the beast. In God's eyes, they will be marked men and women—candidates, by their own choice, for receiving the horrible wrath of God that will be poured out during the time of trouble.

This time of trouble will immediately follow the close of probation. Ellen White describes this time in her chapter "The Time of Trouble" in *The Great Controversy*.[1] In the following quotation, I have selected the most relevant sentences from two fairly long paragraphs near the beginning of the chapter:

> When the third angel's message closes, mercy no longer pleads for the guilty inhabitants of the earth. . . . Every case has been decided for life or death. . . .
>
> When He [Jesus] leaves the [heavenly] sanctuary, darkness covers the inhabitants of the earth. . . . Satan has entire control of the finally impenitent. . . . Satan will then plunge the inhabitants of the earth into one great, final trouble. As the angels of God cease to hold in check the fierce winds of human passion, all the elements of strife will be let loose. The whole world will be involved in ruin more terrible than that which came upon Jerusalem of old.[2]

The time of trouble in Revelation

Revelation 16 describes this horrible time of trouble in broad strokes. The chapter begins with these ominous words: "Then I heard a loud voice from the temple saying to the seven angels, 'Go, pour out the seven bowls of God's wrath on the earth' " (verse 1). This is the wrath of God that the third angel in Revelation 14 warned about. It will consist of seven terrible plagues:

1. Ugly and painful sores will break out on everyone who has received the mark of the beast (Revelation 16:2).
2. The sea will turn to blood, and all creatures in the sea will die (verse 3).
3. The rivers and springs of water will turn to blood (verse 4).
4. The sun will scorch Earth's inhabitants with fire (verses 8, 9).
5. The kingdom of the beast will be plunged into darkness (verse 10).
6. The way will be prepared for the battle of Armageddon (verses 12–16).
7. A terrible earthquake will devastate the earth, and huge hailstones will fall from the sky (verses 17–21).

Are these plagues literal or symbolic? Ellen White describes them quite literally, and Adventists throughout our history have pretty much adopted that interpretation.

A number of years ago a friend asked me the purpose of these plagues. "Probation has closed," this person said, "and the decision about the eternal destiny of every human being has been made. So why will God send these plagues, and what's the purpose of the time of trouble?"

That's a very good question, and much of the answer is found in Revelation 16 itself. In verses 5 and 6, an angel says,

> "You are just in these judgments,
>   you who are and who were, the Holy One,
>   *because you have so judged*;
> for they have shed the blood of your saints and prophets,
>   and you have given them blood to drink *as they deserve*" (emphasis added).

These words take us back to the pre-Advent judgment, when the angels review God's decisions about the eternal destiny of both the righteous and the wicked. Now the angel who pours out the third plague acknowledges the justice of God's judgments, and in verse 7, a voice from the altar backs him up: "Yes, Lord God Almighty, *true and just are your judgments*" (emphasis added). Revelation 14:9–11 warns of the coming wrath of God, and once it has started, the angel from heaven who describes these plagues and who has participated in the pre-Advent judgment acknowledges what all the angels have agreed on: God is fully justified in both His anger at the wicked and in punishing them for their evil deeds. *They deserve it!*

Another reason for inflicting these seven plagues on the wicked is found in verses 9 and 11. In both verses, the wicked curse God because of the pain they are suffering from the plagues, but they refuse to repent. Throughout history, one of the purposes of God's judgments—the calamities that He allows—has been to lead people to repent of their sins and turn to Him for salvation. Often this strategy has worked. But God's purpose in bringing the seven last plagues on the world is different. He wants to demonstrate to the universe that no amount of calamities will move the wicked to repent. And the wicked, by their refusal to repent, provide conclusive evidence that the decision of the judgment in their case is fully justified.

While Revelation 16 doesn't mention a third reason for the seven last plagues, there is another reason that parallels with God's justification in His punishment of the wicked. It's this: loyalty to God by the righteous in the face of the most intense persecution by the wicked is conclusive evidence that they, too, deserve the destiny of eternal life that the judgment has conferred upon them.

Two or three times people have approached me with another question: Will we lose the presence of the Holy Spirit during the time of trouble? The answer is an absolute *No!* Through the power of the Holy Spirit in their minds and hearts, God's people will be able to prepare for the close of probation and the time of trouble! Why would God remove His Spirit from them then? Remember Jesus' words to His disciples that He would "ask the Father, and he will give you another Counselor *to be with you forever*—the Spirit of truth" (John 14:16; emphasis added). And remember His departing words to His disciples shortly before He returned to heaven: "Surely I am with you always, *to the very end of the age*" (Matthew 28:20; emphasis added). If the Holy Spirit were to leave God's people during the time of trouble, He would break these promises. Furthermore, it's *because* God's people will have the presence of the Holy Spirit in their minds and hearts that they will have the spiritual power to endure the persecution by the wicked and the spiritual assaults of Satan during the time of trouble.

Ellen White on the time of trouble

I have devoted the rest of this chapter to Ellen White's description of the time of trouble, and her depiction is so vivid that at certain points I can do no better than to quote fairly long passages from her chapter. Describing this time of trouble, she wrote,

> As the angels of God cease to hold in check the fierce winds of human passion, all the elements of strife will be let loose. The whole world will be involved in ruin more terrible than that which came upon Jerusalem of old. . . .
>
> Those who honor the law of God . . . will be regarded as the cause of the fearful convulsions of nature and the strife and bloodshed among men that are filling the earth with woe. . . . Satan will excite to still greater intensity the spirit of hatred and persecution.[3]

The death decree. Ellen White predicted that, at some point during the time of trouble, the wicked will enact a global death decree against God's people: "As the Sabbath has become the special point of controversy throughout Christendom, and religious and secular authorities have combined to enforce the observance of . . . Sunday, the persistent refusal of a small minority to yield to the popular demand will make them objects of universal execration. . . . A decree will finally be issued against those who hallow the Sabbath of the fourth commandment, denouncing them as deserving of the severest punishment and giving the people liberty, after a certain time, to put them to death."[4]

Describing this same development in her book *Early Writings*, Ellen White wrote, "I saw the leading men of the earth consulting together, and Satan and his angels busy around them. I saw a writing, copies of which were scattered in different parts of the land, giving orders that unless the saints should yield their peculiar faith, give up the Sabbath, and observe the first day of the week, the people were at liberty after a certain time to put them to death."[5]

There's bad news and good news in these last two statements. Revelation 12:12 says that Satan "is filled with fury, because he knows that his time is short"; the bad news is that the death sentence he inspires against God's people just prior to Christ's second coming will be the ultimate high point of that fury. The good news is that when this death decree is issued, specifying "a certain time" to go into effect, God's people can know that Jesus will return to deliver them shortly before that date!

An intensely spiritual challenge to God's people. However, the very knowledge of this death decree will plunge God's people

> into those scenes of affliction and distress described by the prophet as the time of Jacob's trouble [see Jeremiah 30:7]. . . .
>
> Jacob's night of anguish, when he wrestled in prayer for deliverance from the hand of Esau (Genesis 32:24–30), represents the experience of God's people during the time of trouble.[6]

This will be a period of intense spiritual conflict for God's people.

> [Satan] has an accurate knowledge of the sins which he has tempted them [God's people] to commit, and he presents these before God in the most exaggerated light. . . .
>
> As Satan accuses the people of God on account of their sins, the Lord permits him to try them to the uttermost. Their confidence in God, their faith and firmness, will be severely tested. As they review the past, their hopes sink; for in their whole lives they can see little good. They are fully conscious of their weakness and unworthiness. Satan endeavors to terrify them with the thought that their cases are hopeless, that the stain of their defilement will never be washed away. He hopes so to destroy their faith that they will yield to his temptations and turn from their allegiance to God.[7]

During this time, it will be vitally important that God's people have a clear understanding of the biblical teaching about righteousness by faith so that they can have the assurance that their sins have been covered with the robe of Christ's righteousness and claim the promise, "Christ's character stands in the place of your character, and you are accepted before God just as if you had not sinned."[8] This is what will give God's people the courage not to give up.

> Jacob's history is also an assurance that God will not cast off those who have been deceived and tempted and betrayed into sin, but who have returned to Him in true repentance. While Satan seeks to destroy this class, God will send His angels to comfort and protect them in the time of peril. The assaults of Satan are fierce and determined; his delusions are terrible; but the Lord's eye is upon His people, and His ear listens to their cries.

Their affliction is great, the flames of the furnace seem about to consume them; but the Refiner will bring them forth as gold tried in the fire. God's love for His children during the period of their severest trial is as strong and tender as in the days of their sunniest prosperity; but it is needful for them to be placed in the furnace of fire; their earthliness must be consumed, that the image of God may be perfectly reflected.[9]

In the previous chapter, "How to Prepare for the Final Conflict," I stressed the importance of making the spiritual preparation that can carry us through the time of trouble both before and after the close of probation. Ellen White also emphasized the necessity of this preparation. In a statement that I shared with you in the previous chapter, she wrote,

> The season of distress and anguish before us will require a faith that can endure weariness, delay, and hunger—a faith that will not faint though severely tried. The period of probation is granted to all to prepare for that time. . . .
>
> Those who exercise but little faith now, are in the greatest danger of falling under the power of satanic delusions [then] and the decree to compel the conscience. And even if they endure the test they will be plunged into deeper distress and anguish in the time of trouble, because they have never made it a habit to trust in God. The lessons of faith which they have neglected they will be forced to learn under a terrible pressure of discouragement.
>
> *We should now acquaint ourselves with God by proving His promises.*[10]

What about sinlessness?

While I discussed the issue of sinlessness in the previous chapter, Ellen White makes two statements in her chapter "The Time of Trouble" that suggest God's people will have to be sinless and absolutely perfect during this time. I have already quoted the first statement, but I will repeat it here: "It is needful for them [God's people] to be placed in the furnace of fire; their earthliness must be consumed, that the image of Christ may be perfectly reflected."[11]

The other statement is considerably longer:

> Now, while our great High Priest is making the atonement for us, we should seek to become perfect in Christ. Not even by a thought could our Saviour be brought to yield to the power of temptation. Satan finds

in human hearts some point where he can gain a foothold; some sinful desire is cherished, by means of which his temptations assert their power. But Christ declared of Himself: "The prince of this world cometh, and hath nothing in Me." John 14:30. Satan could find nothing in the Son of God that would enable him to gain the victory. He had kept His Father's commandments, and there was no sin in Him that Satan could use to his advantage. *This is the condition in which those must be found who shall stand in the time of trouble.*[12]

I will begin by stating again what I said in the previous chapter: even if we should be sinless, we couldn't claim it. First John 1:8 says, "If we claim to be without sin, we deceive ourselves and the truth is not in us." So the one who claims to be sinless during the time of trouble (or at any other time) will, in fact, be the worst sinner, not the most righteous saint! Furthermore, even if God should want us to be sinless during the time of trouble, we wouldn't know when we had attained that lofty estate. Ellen White put a stop to all claims of sinlessness when she said, "We cannot say, 'I am sinless,' till this vile body is changed and fashioned like unto His glorious body."[13]

How we become sinless. Both of these "sinless" quotations need to be understood in the light of Ellen White's understanding of how God's people become perfect. Note the following statement: "When it is in the heart to obey God, when efforts are put forth to this end, Jesus accepts this disposition and effort as man's best service, and He makes up for the deficiency with His own divine merit."[14] In other words, when we *want* to obey God and are doing *our best* to obey God, Jesus recognizes that at this moment in our lives we've done the best we possibly can, and He covers our sinful actions and attitudes with His perfect, sinless life.

Ellen White further confirmed this with the following short sentence: "Christ's character stands in place of your character, and you are accepted before God just as if you had not sinned."[15] Notice that Christ attributes His *character* to us. *Character* is what we are like on the inside, in our minds and emotions. So Christ covers our sinful *characters*, including all our wrong thoughts and feelings, with His perfect thoughts and feelings. And when that transaction is completed, God accepts us as if we were just as perfect as Jesus!

Now let's come back to the two perfectionist statements from *The Great Controversy.* My first comment is that, at the very least, they mean that we must have a very high level of Christian maturity in order to endure the fiery trials of the time of trouble.

The first perfectionist statement says that God's people must be "placed in the furnace of fire; their earthliness must be consumed, *that the image of Christ may be perfectly reflected.*" The italicized words can be interpreted to mean sinlessness, but reflecting the image of Christ doesn't necessarily require sinlessness. We can reflect the image of Christ today without being sinless. We do that by being totally committed to Him and doing our very best to serve Him. If we stumble and fall, then confess our sin and claim His righteousness to cover that sin, we have reflected His image. A reflection is obviously secondary to that which it reflects. As the moon reflects the light of the sun, so we reflect the sinless character of Jesus. But we can't achieve it.

The following sentences in Ellen White's second quote from above will take a bit more analyzing:

- "Now, while our great High Priest is making the atonement for us, we should seek to become perfect in Christ."
- "Not even by a thought could our Saviour be brought to yield to the power of temptation."
- "Satan could find nothing in the Son of God that would enable him to gain the victory. He had kept His Father's commandments, and there was no sin in Him that Satan could use to his advantage."
- *"This is the condition in which those must be found who shall stand in the time of trouble."*

At first glance, these words do seem to suggest that God's people must be sinless between the close of probation and Christ's second coming. However, we must keep in mind the principle of context in our interpretation of the Bible and the Spirit of Prophecy. There are two contexts that we need to pay careful attention to. One is the overall teaching of the Bible and Ellen White on the subject of righteousness by faith. We obviously can't probe into that topic in any depth in this short chapter; but I did give you a brief review a few paragraphs previously, and it's this: when we come to Jesus, repenting of our sins and confessing them, He covers these sins with His righteousness, and we stand perfect before God.[16] And this will be just as true during the time of trouble as it is at any time prior to the close of probation.

Remember Ellen White's quotation that I shared with you previously: "We cannot say, 'I am sinless,' till this vile body is changed and fashioned like unto His glorious body." At that point, I didn't share with you the next fairly long sentence: "But if we constantly seek to follow Jesus, the blessed hope is ours of standing before the throne of God without spot or wrinkle, or any such thing; complete in Christ, robed in His righteousness and perfection."[17] So it's Christ's sinlessness attributed to us—not our own righteousness—that will qualify us to stand perfect during the time of trouble.

Now let's return to Ellen White's long quote on page 623 of *The Great Controversy*. The very first sentence in this quote makes it clear that she is speaking of perfection through Jesus covering our sins with His righteousness, because she says, "Now, while our great High Priest is making the atonement for us, we should seek to become perfect *in Christ*" (emphasis added). I cannot say it strongly enough: our perfection after the close of probation will be only through Christ's righteousness covering us, not within ourselves.

Even a casual examination of the context following Ellen White's statement about our perfection after the close of probation bears this out. I have italicized the key phrases: "It is in this life that we are to separate sin from us, *through faith in the atoning blood of Christ*. Our precious Saviour invites us to join ourselves to Him, to unite our weakness with His strength, our ignorance to His wisdom, *our unworthiness to His merits*."[18] So it's *Christ's* righteousness that will provide us with the perfect, sinless "condition in which those must be found who shall stand in the time of trouble."

This is not to minimize the fact that God's people who live *after* the close of probation must develop a very deep spiritual connection with Him *before* the close of probation. That is an absolute essential, and I hope you're setting aside time each day, day after day, right now to develop your deep spiritual life with Jesus. If you aren't, I urge you to begin today. Read again the previous chapter, "How to Prepare for the Final Conflict."

The final great deception

Revelation 13:13 says that the beast that rises from the land "performed great and miraculous signs, even causing fire to come down from heaven to earth in full view of men." I've heard it suggested that this is a reference to atomic bombs. While atomic bombs have certainly been inspired by Satan, we can hardly call them miraculous signs, because they were created by humans, and they've been a part of our world for more than seventy years. A statement on page 624 of *The Great Controversy* comes closer to matching John's words in Revelation 13: "Fearful sights of a supernatural character will soon be revealed in the heavens, in token of the power of miracle-working demons." Immediately following the paragraph about these "fearful sights of a supernatural character" is another long paragraph in which Ellen White describes

Satan's great final deception. I will quote it in its entirety:

> As the crowning act in the great drama of deception, Satan himself will personate Christ. The church has long professed to look to the Saviour's advent as the consummation of her hopes. Now the great deceiver will make it appear that Christ has come. In different parts of the earth, Satan will manifest himself among men as a majestic being of dazzling brightness, resembling the description of the Son of God given by John in Revelation. Revelation 1:13-15. The glory that surrounds him is unsurpassed by anything that mortal eyes have yet beheld. The shout of triumph rings out upon the air: "Christ has come! Christ has come!" The people prostrate themselves in adoration before him, while he lifts up his hands and pronounces a blessing upon them, as Christ blessed His disciples when He was upon the earth. His voice is soft and subdued, yet full of melody. In gentle, compassionate tones he presents some of the same gracious, heavenly truths which the Saviour uttered; he heals the diseases of the people, and then, in his assumed character of Christ, he claims to have changed the Sabbath to Sunday, and commands all to hallow the day which he has blessed. He declares that those who persist in keeping holy the seventh day are blaspheming his name by refusing to listen to his angels sent to them with light and truth. This is the strong, almost overmastering delusion. Like the Samaritans who were deceived by Simon Magus, the multitudes, from the least to the greatest, give heed to these sorceries, saying: this is "the great power of God." Acts 8:10.[19]

But Ellen White goes on to say that "the people of God will not be misled. The teachings of this false Christ are not in accordance with the Scriptures. His blessing is pronounced upon the worshipers of the beast and his image, the very class upon whom the Bible declares that God's unmingled wrath shall be poured out."[20]

The persecution that follows

Can you imagine the hatred this will generate against the few in the world who are loyal to the Sabbath? In the pages following Ellen White's account of Satan impersonating Christ, she describes in vivid language the persecution that God's people will endure during this time.

As the decree issued by the various rulers of Christendom against commandment keepers shall withdraw the protection of government and abandon them to those who desire their destruction, the people of God will flee from the cities and villages and associate together in companies, dwelling in the most desolate and solitary places. Many will find refuge in the strongholds of the mountains. . . . But many of all nations and of all classes, high and low, rich and poor, black and white, will be cast into the most unjust and cruel bondage. The beloved of God pass weary days, bound in chains, shut in by prison bars, sentenced to be slain, some apparently left to die of starvation in dark and loathsome dungeons. No human ear is open to hear their moans; no human hand is ready to lend them help.[21]

However, God's people will not be left to suffer alone, for "while persecuted and distressed, while they endure privation and suffer for want of food they will not be left to perish. . . . Angels will shield the righteous and supply their wants."[22] And angels will protect them from enemies who want to kill them before the date of their execution: "Though a general decree has fixed the time when commandment keepers may be put to death, their enemies will in some cases anticipate the decree, and before the time specified, will endeavor to take their lives. But none can pass the mighty guardians stationed about every faithful soul. Some are assailed in their flight from the cities and villages; but the swords raised against them break and fall powerless as a straw. Others are defended by angels in the form of men of war."[23]

To all earthly appearances, God's people will be in great peril just before the second coming of Jesus. However, the situation will be the same as it was thousands of years ago when Syrian armies surrounded the city of Dothan in Israel one night. When Elisha's servant saw the armies the next morning, he was terrified and cried out. "Oh, my lord, what shall we do?" Elisha calmly replied, "Don't be afraid. . . . Those who are with us are more than those who are with them." Having said this, Elisha prayed, " 'O LORD, open his eyes so he may see.' Then the LORD opened the servant's eyes, and he looked and saw the hills full of horses and chariots of fire all around Elisha" (2 Kings 6:15–17). It will take courage and a very strong faith for God's people, just before Jesus returns, to trust that the same "chariots of fire" are surrounding them. *But the angels will be there!*

Ellen White's chapter on "The Time of Trouble" closes with these encouraging words: "If the blood of Christ's faithful witnesses were shed at this time, it would not, like the blood of the martyrs, be as seed sown to yield a harvest for God. Their fidelity would not be a testimony to convince others of the truth. . . . If the righteous were now left to fall a prey to their enemies, it would be a triumph for the prince of darkness."[24]

When the protection of human laws shall be withdrawn from those who honor the law of God, there will be, in different lands, a simultaneous movement for their destruction. As the time appointed in the decree draws near, the people will conspire to root out the hated sect. It will be determined to strike in one night a decisive blow, which shall utterly silence the voice of dissent and reproof.

The people of God—some in prison cells, some hidden in solitary retreats in the forests and the mountains—still plead for divine protection, while in every quarter companies of armed men, urged on by hosts of evil angels, are preparing for the work of death. It is now, in the hour of utmost extremity, that the God of Israel will interpose for the deliverance of His chosen.[25]

Before closing this chapter, I want to share with you one difference between Christ's experience in Gethsemane, His trial, and His crucifixion on the one hand and the experience of God's people during the final crisis on the other hand. It's this: in Gethsemane, Jesus pleaded with God to deliver Him, if at all possible, from the wrath of His enemies, but it was not possible. He had to go through with death at their hands. God's people will also be pleading for deliverance from their enemies, and by His second coming Jesus *will* deliver them. God will not permit the wicked to kill them, because, as Ellen White wrote, "If the righteous were now left to fall a prey to their enemies, it would be a triumph for the prince of darkness."[26]

There will be one great similarity between Christ's experience during His trial and crucifixion and the experience of God's people during the time of trouble, both before and after the close of probation. It's this: one of the things that made it possible for Jesus to endure the ferocious attacks of wicked humans and demons was His understanding of the conflict between good and evil, the great controversy, which has been the theme of this book. No one else in all the crowds surrounding Him understood this—not the Jewish rulers, not the Romans, not even His own disciples! But Jesus understood that these hours were an utterly critical period in the conflict between good and evil. I propose that this knowledge is one of the things that made it possible for Him to endure the torture that the powers of darkness were inflicting upon Him.

In the same way, God's people during the time of trouble will understand what their persecutors don't: that they are enduring a short, critical period in the universal conflict between good and evil. This will give them the courage to withstand the trial. They will know that Armageddon is just around the corner!

The end is almost here. Jesus is about to come. *Now* we are ready to talk about Armageddon!

---

1. White, *The Great Controversy*, 613–634.

2. Ibid., 613, 614.

3. Ibid., 614, 615.

4. Ibid., 615, 616.

5. White, *Early Writings*, 282, 283.

6. White, *The Great Controversy*, 616.

7. Ibid., 618, 619.

8. White, *Steps to Christ*, 62.

9. White, *The Great Controversy*, 621.

10. Ibid., 621, 622; emphasis added.

11. Ibid., 621.

12. Ibid., 623; emphasis added.

13. White, *Selected Messages*, bk. 3, 355.

14. Ibid., bk. 1, 382.

15. White, *Steps to Christ*, 62.

16. See White, *Selected Messages*, bk. 1, 382.

17. Ibid., bk. 3, 355.

18. White, *The Great Controversy*, 623.

19. Ibid., 624, 625.

20. Ibid., 625.

21. Ibid., 626.

22. Ibid., 629.

23. Ibid., 631.

24. Ibid., 634.

25. Ibid., 635.

26. Ibid., 634.

CHAPTER 28

The Battle of Armageddon–Part 1

Two terms in Revelation are familiar to most people in the Western world, including those who don't profess to be Christians. One of these is *the mark of the beast*, and the other one is *Armageddon*.* The word *Armageddon* appears only once in the Bible as part of the sixth plague in Revelation 16. Here's how Revelation describes that plague:

> The sixth angel poured out his plague on the great river Euphrates, and its water was dried up to prepare the way for the kings from the East. Then I saw three evil spirits that looked like frogs; they came out of the mouth of the dragon, out of the mouth of the beast and out of the mouth of the false prophet. They are the spirits of demons performing miraculous signs, and they go out to the kings of the whole world, to gather them for the battle on the great day of God Almighty.
>
> "Behold, I come like a thief! Blessed is he who stays awake and keeps his clothes with him, so that he may not go naked and be shamefully exposed."
>
> Then they gathered the kings together to the place that in Hebrew is called Armageddon (verses 12–16).

The sixth angel pouring out his vial on the Euphrates River to dry up its waters is reminiscent of the fall of ancient Babylon. Many readers will no doubt be familiar with the story; but for those who aren't, I will tell it here.

The fall of ancient Babylon
Cyrus became king of Persia in 559 B.C., and nine years later, in 550 B.C., he also became king of Media. The Medes and the Persians were a rising power

---

* *Armageddon* is a Greek word, *Harmageddon*, that is made up of two Hebrew words: *Har*, which means "mountain" and *Megiddo*. There was no mountain in ancient Israel named Megiddo, but there was a city by that name at the foot of Mount Carmel (*Seventh-day Adventist Encyclopedia*, 71, 700; see also 1 Kings 9:15). Megiddo is also sometimes referred to as a plain (Zechariah 12:11).

in the Middle East at the time, but there was another power that stood in the way of their total dominance of that part of the world. Babylon had ruled the Middle East for about sixty-five years (605 B.C.–539 B.C.), and Cyrus set out to conquer the Babylonian Empire. But in order to do that, he had to conquer the city of Babylon itself. Therein lay a major problem. The walls around the city were 80 feet thick and 320 feet high,[1] which made entry into the city virtually impossible for an army with the military equipment that was available at that time.

However, the city had one vulnerable feature: the Euphrates River, which ran through the city. Where the river entered and exited the city, the builders had created an opening at the base of the wall that allowed the water to pass through, but the opening was low enough that boats could not pass under it. Even if an enemy army managed to get under the wall at the entry or exit points of the city, walls along the riverbanks also protected the city. At certain places along the river, bridges had been built to connect the streets on either side. But heavy iron gates had been installed in the walls so that if an enemy army should manage to get under the outer wall, these gates could be closed, thus preventing enemies from entering the city.

This is the situation that confronted Cyrus as he anticipated conquering Babylon. However, two factors worked in his favor. First, not too far from the river's entry point into the city was a slight valley, and second, Cyrus learned that on a particular night King Belshazzar planned to host a large banquet for all the leading men of his kingdom. Cyrus hoped that in their rush to get to the banquet, the Babylonians would fail to close the river gates into the city. On the night of the banquet, the Persian general ordered his men to dig a wide ditch from the river into the low valley near where the river entered the city. This drained off enough water so that the river level dropped to the point that Cyrus's soldiers could cross under the city wall. And his hunch that the Babylonians might forget to close the gates along the river wall proved to be correct. Cyrus's army entered the city, and that night Belshazzar was killed and the Babylonian Empire fell to the Medes and Persians.

This was all part of God's plan. The seventy years of the Jews' captivity in Babylon had almost ended; the time for them to be restored to their homeland was approaching; and God used Cyrus to accomplish this purpose (Isaiah 44:28–45:4).

Now let's come back to Revelation 16:12. Keep in mind that Media and Persia lay to the northeast of the city of Babylon, so that it was "kings from the east" that conquered the city. Also bear in mind that in Revelation Babylon is used as a type, or representation, of the forces of evil in the end time. God prepared Cyrus, a king to the east of Babylon, to defeat the city, and Revelation says that in the end time "kings from the east" will defeat modern Babylon.

Now you understand the analogy between the fall of ancient Babylon and what Revelation says about Armageddon and the fall of end-time Babylon. Just as the Medes and the Persians—kings from the east of Babylon— conquered ancient Babylon and delivered God's people from Babylonian slavery, so "kings from the east"—the direction of the rising sun—will de- liver God's people who have been enslaved by modern Babylon. I will have more to say about these kings from the east in a moment. For now, let's examine Revelation 16:13, 14.

The fall of modern Babylon

John said, "Then I saw three evil spirits that looked like frogs; they came out of the mouth of the dragon, out of the mouth of the beast and out of the mouth of the false prophet. They are spirits of demons performing mi- raculous signs, and they go out to the kings of the whole world, to gather them for the battle on the great day of God Almighty" (verses 13, 14). The Kingdom of Darkness is gearing up for Earth's final battle, and Satan's de- mons are rallying the world's human leaders to join them. This is probably one reason why most interpreters view the battle of Armageddon as a con- flict between two human armies. There will definitely be two sides in this battle: the kings from the east and the kings of the whole world. And Satan will gather his earthly army "together to the place that in Hebrew is called Armageddon" (verse 16).

Let's look again at the type. God allowed the Babylonians to take Old Testament Israel captive, but He promised His people that this captivity would last only seventy years, after which time they would be restored to their homeland (Jeremiah 25:8–12; 29:10). In the antitype, modern Babylon, the Kingdom of Darkness, has held God's people captive for thousands of years on this earth, but God has promised repeatedly through His prophets that His Kingdom of Light will bring this captivity to an end at Christ's sec- ond coming. Therefore, the kings from the east in Revelation 16:12 are the armies of heaven that come down to this earth to deliver God's people. We see these armies descending from heaven in Revelation 19:11–21.

Revelation 19:11–21

John wrote, "I saw heaven standing open and there before me was a white horse, whose rider is called Faithful and True. With justice he judges and makes war" (verse 11). Notice that this Rider on the white horse is coming to Earth to make war. John went on to say that this Rider's "eyes are like blazing fire" (verse 12). In Revelation 1:14, John used almost the exact same words to describe Jesus in His heavenly sanctuary. Continuing, John wrote, "And on his head are many crowns" (Revelation 19:12). In Revelation 14:14, John described Jesus at His second coming as having "a crown of gold on his head." And lest there be any doubt about who this Rider on the white horse is, John says that "his name is the Word of God" (Revelation 19:13). That's the same title John gave to Jesus in John 1:1, 14: "In the beginning was the Word, and the Word was with God, and the Word was God. . . . The Word became flesh and made his dwelling among us." Finally, John said that this Rider on the horse had His name written on His thigh: "KING OF KINGS AND LORD OF LORDS" (Revelation 19:16).

The Rider on the white horse is none other than Jesus Christ, and He's coming out of heaven to Earth as an army general to make war! "The armies of heaven were following him, riding on white horses and dressed in fine linen, white and clean. Out of his mouth comes a sharp sword with which to strike down the nations. 'He will rule them with an iron scepter' " (verses 14, 15).

Now here's a critical point: the sixth plague is not the battle of Armageddon. It's the two sides *preparing* for Armageddon. The battle itself will take place *at* Christ's second coming. In fact, Armageddon *is* Christ's second coming. On one side will be Jesus and His heavenly angels—the kings from the east—and on the other side will be the armies of the world.

At this point, I can hear you say, "But surely human beings can't fight against Christ at His second coming. It's ridiculous for them to even think of trying!" I have a question for you: Why will "three evil spirits . . . go out to the kings of the whole world, to gather them for the battle on the great day of God Almighty" (Revelation 16:13, 14)? Whom will they fight against?

John answered this question. Let's combine Revelation 19:19 with Revelation 16:16. We'll start with Revelation 19:19 and insert the relevant part of Revelation 16:16: "The beast and the kings of the earth and their armies gathered together" (Revelation 19:19) "to the place that in Hebrew is called Armageddon" (Revelation 16:16), "to make war against the rider on the horse and his army" (Revelation 19:19).

It would have been ridiculous a hundred years ago, or even seventy-five, to think that humans would even *contemplate* trying to stop Christ and His angels from descending to Earth at His second coming. But today a number of nations around the world have nuclear warheads, with intercontinental missiles to deliver them. If these nations could put aside their differences and get all their missiles together and focus them on one common enemy, they would have an utterly formidable defense against any other human enemy army or even an alien army of the science-fiction kind. But they won't be fighting against a human army.

Here is what I propose will happen. I don't have Bible texts that state this will be the case, nor statements from Ellen White, but I believe it is probable, as I will explain. Satan has read the Bible, and as the situation described here in Revelation develops, he will understand very well that Jesus is on His way from heaven to Earth to defeat him. Satan will tell his earthly followers that an alien army from a distant galaxy in outer space is on its way to destroy the human race. In the context of today's science fiction about alien invasions from outer space, this will make perfect sense to these "kings of the whole world." Satan may even tell them to focus all of Earth's most powerful optical and radio telescopes deep into outer space to confirm what he has told them. When these nations truly believe that an "alien invasion" is about to take place, suddenly all of them that have been at war with each other will immediately put aside their differences and gather "for the battle on the great day of God Almighty" (Revelation 16:14). They will focus their intercontinental missiles with their nuclear warheads on the heavens to destroy this alien army from outer space. Satan himself will lead this army, and his demons will join wicked human beings as generals and captains and lieutenants to defeat this powerful "enemy" that is about to invade our planet.

As Jesus and His angels approach the earth, Satan will instruct his human allies to fire their missiles to destroy this "alien army" and prevent it from taking over the world. Of course, Jesus is powerful enough to disarm every single missile so that none of them can be detonated. Or Jesus could allow the missiles to be fired and even allow the nuclear warheads to explode. But against heaven's armies they would be like firecrackers on the Fourth of July.

Revelation says that "the beast was captured, and with him the false prophet who had performed miraculous signs on his behalf. . . . The two of them were thrown alive into the fiery lake of burning sulfur. The rest of them were killed with the sword that came out of the mouth of the rider on the horse, and all the birds gorged themselves on their flesh" (Revelation 19:20, 21).

That's how the battle of Armageddon will end!

Christ's second coming

We've already considered the second coming of Christ in some detail in our discussion of Revelation 19:11–21, so I won't repeat that here. However, three other passages in Revelation also describe the Second Coming, and Ellen White's chapter "God's People Delivered" in *The Great Controversy* describes Christ's second coming in dramatic language. We will consider each of these two sources in some detail. I'll begin with Revelation.

The Second Coming in Revelation. One of the three descriptions of Christ's second coming in Revelation is the seventh plague, and I'll begin with that one. It's found in Revelation 16:17–21.

Verse 17 says, "The seventh angel poured out his bowl into the air, and out of the temple came a loud voice from the throne, saying, 'It is done!' " The throne is the Most Holy Place of the heavenly sanctuary, and because the voice comes from the throne we know that it's God's voice. He says, "It is done!" Shortly before Jesus died on the cross, He bowed His head and cried out, "It is finished" (John 19:30). By this, He meant that by His death He had defeated Satan and that the plan of salvation was made secure, even though there were still many years of Earth's history yet to take place before the final act would be carried out. The words *It is done*, coming from the throne in Revelation 16, can be understood in the same way. The second coming of Christ isn't the final act in the drama of the conflict between the Kingdom of Light and the Kingdom of Darkness (that will take place at the end of the millennium), but it does mark the end of the history of sin on our planet, and that's the meaning of God's words *It is done*.

Revelation 16:18, 20 says, "Then there came flashes of lightning, rumblings, peals of thunder and a severe earthquake. No earthquake like it has ever occurred since man has been on the earth, so tremendous was the quake. . . . Every island fled away and the mountains could not be found." Picture in your imagination a global storm with deafening thunder and sheets of lightning that strike the ground all over the world. Then imagine this earthquake, which shakes the entire globe, causing mountain chains to sink into valleys and islands in the seas to collapse under the waters. That's what Christ's second coming will be like!

In verse 19, we learn about God's punishment of Babylon: "The great city split into three parts, and the cities of the nations collapsed. God remembered Babylon the Great and gave her the cup filled with the wine of the fury of his wrath." The three parts into which Babylon will split represent the three major religions that make up the city: Catholicism, Protestantism, and spiritualism.² The great earthquake will collapse the cities around the world. Imagine the massive piles of rubble that will be created when all the great, towering skyscrapers around the world crumble to the ground! God now calls Babylon to account for her persecution of His people and pours out upon her "the cup filled with the wine of the fury of his wrath" (verse 19).

Verse 21 tells us that "from the sky huge hailstones of about a hundred pounds each fell upon men. And they cursed God on account of the plague of hail, because the plague was so terrible." Can you imagine hailstones weighing one hundred pounds each? No wonder the wicked are cursing God! But that, in fact, is the problem. Just as they will curse God and refuse to repent when they suffer the fourth and fifth plagues (verses 8–11), so the wicked will curse God and refuse to repent when they are struck with these huge hailstones.

Another description of Christ's second coming is found in Revelation 6:15–17: "Then the kings of the earth, the princes, the generals, the rich, the mighty, and every slave and every free man hid in caves and among the rocks of the mountains. They called to the mountains and the rocks, 'Fall on us and hide us from the face of him who sits on the throne and from the wrath of the Lamb! For the great day of their wrath has come, and who can stand?' "

This is a vivid description of the terror that will overtake the wicked when Jesus comes. Can you imagine a fear so great that people beg to be crushed under rocks and mountains? This is mass suicide—or at least a desire to die in that way! Also notice that apparently God the Father will accompany Jesus on His journey to Earth, because verse 16 says that the wicked ask to be hidden "from the face of him who sits on the throne [God] *and* from the wrath of the Lamb [Jesus]" (emphasis added).

The fourth portrayal of Christ's second coming in Revelation is found in Revelation 14:14–20. It depicts Jesus sitting on a white cloud and holding a sharp sickle in His hand. Sickles are symbolic of harvest, and that's what the sickle Christ is holding represents. Revelation says that an angel calls to Him, "Take your sickle and reap, because the time to reap has come, for the harvest of the earth is ripe" (verse 15). You will recall that in Jesus' parable of the wheat and tares the harvest is "the end of the age" (Matthew 13:39). The same thing is true of the harvest symbol in Revelation 14.

There's also another harvest in this passage: that of the wicked. Another angel holding a sharp sickle emerges from the temple in heaven, and he reaps a great harvest of grapes, which are cast into a winepress, and "blood flowed out of the press" (verses 19, 20).

These accounts, together with John's vision of the Rider on the horse in chapter 19, are the four descriptions of Christ's second coming in Revelation. *Ellen White's description of Christ's second coming.* The chapter "God's People Delivered" in Ellen White's book *The Great Controversy* describes in vivid and dramatic language the second coming of Christ and the reaction to it by both the righteous and the wicked. I can do no better than to simply quote the most relevant passages without comment. I will begin with her description of the persecution of God's people by the wicked at the very end of the time of trouble.

As the time appointed in the [death] decree draws near, the people will conspire to root out the hated sect. It will be determined to strike in one night a decisive blow, which shall utterly silence the voice of dissent and reproof.

The people of God—some in prison cells, some hidden in solitary retreats in the forests and the mountains—still plead for divine protection, while in every quarter companies of armed men, urged on by hosts of evil angels, are preparing for the work of death. It is now, in the hour of utmost extremity, that the God of Israel will interpose for the deliverance of His chosen. . . .

With shouts of triumph, jeering, and imprecation, throngs of evil men are about to rush upon their prey, when, lo, a dense blackness, deeper than the darkness of the night, falls upon the earth. Then a rainbow, shining with the glory from the throne of God, spans the heavens and seems to encircle each praying company. The angry multitudes are suddenly arrested. Their mocking cries die away. The objects of their murderous rage are forgotten. With fearful forebodings they gaze upon the symbol of God's covenant and long to be shielded from its overpowering brightness. . . .

. . . The wicked look with terror and amazement upon the scene, while the righteous behold with solemn joy the tokens of their deliverance. . . .

. . . There is a mighty earthquake, "such as was not since men were upon the earth, so mighty an earthquake, and so great." . . . The mountains shake like a reed in the wind, and ragged rocks are scattered on every side. There is a roar as of a coming tempest. The sea is lashed into fury. There is heard the shriek of a hurricane like the voice of demons upon a mission of destruction. The whole earth heaves and swells like the waves of the sea. Its surface is breaking up. Its very foundations seem to be giving way. Mountain chains are sinking. Inhabited islands disappear. . . . Great hailstones, every one "about the weight of a talent," are doing their work of destruction. . . . The proudest cities of the earth are laid low. The lordly palaces, upon which the world's great men have lavished their wealth in order to glorify themselves, are crumbling to ruin before their eyes. Prison walls are rent asunder, and God's people, who have been held in bondage for their faith, are set free.

Graves are opened. . . . All who have died in the faith of the third angel's message come forth from the tomb glorified, to hear God's covenant of peace with those who have kept His law. . . . The most violent opposers of His truth and His people, are raised to behold Him in His glory and to see the honor placed upon the loyal and obedient. . . .

. . . Fierce lightnings leap from the heavens, enveloping the earth in a sheet of flame. Above the terrific roar of thunder, voices, mysterious and awful, declare the doom of the wicked. The words spoken are not comprehended by all; but they are distinctly understood by the false teachers. Those who a little before were so reckless, so boastful and defiant, so exultant in their cruelty to God's commandment-keeping people, are now overwhelmed with consternation and shuddering in fear. . . . Demons acknowledge the deity of Christ and tremble before His power, while men are supplicating for mercy and groveling in abject terror. . . .

. . . The clouds sweep back, and the starry heavens are seen, unspeakably glorious in contrast with the black and angry firmament on either side. . . . Then there appears against the sky a hand holding two tables of stone folded together. . . . The hand opens the tables, and there are seen the precepts of the Decalogue, traced as with a pen of fire. The words are so plain that all can read them. Memory is aroused, the darkness of superstition and heresy is swept from every mind, and God's ten words, brief, comprehensive, and authoritative, are presented to the view of all the inhabitants of the earth.

It is impossible to describe the horror and despair of those who have trampled upon God's holy requirements. . . . They have endeavored to compel God's people to profane His Sabbath. Now they are condemned by that law which they have despised. With awful distinctness they see that they are without excuse. . . .

The enemies of God's law, from the ministers down to the least among them, have a new conception of truth and duty. . . .

Soon there appears in the east a small black cloud, about half the size of a man's hand. It is the cloud which surrounds the Saviour and which seems in the distance to be shrouded in darkness. The people of God know this to be the sign of the Son of man. In solemn silence they gaze upon it as it draws nearer the earth, becoming lighter and more glorious, until it is a great white cloud, its base a glory like consuming fire, and above it the rainbow of the covenant. Jesus rides forth as a mighty conqueror. Not now a "Man of Sorrows," to drink the bitter cup of shame and woe, He comes, victor in heaven and earth, to judge the living and the dead. . . . As the living cloud comes still nearer, every eye beholds the Prince of life. No crown of thorns now mars that sacred head; but a diadem of glory rests on His holy brow. . . .

. . . The righteous cry with trembling: "Who shall be able to stand?" The angels' song is hushed, and there is a period of awful silence. Then the voice of Jesus is heard, saying: "My grace is sufficient for you." The faces of the righteous are lighted up, and joy fills every heart. And the angels strike a note higher and sing again as they draw still nearer to the earth. . . .

The derisive jests [of the wicked] have ceased. Lying lips are hushed into silence. The clash of arms, the tumult of battle, "with confused noise, and garments rolled in blood" (Isaiah 9:5), is stilled. Nought now is heard but the voice of prayer and the sound of weeping and lamentation. The cry bursts forth from lips so lately scoffing: "The great day of His wrath is come; and who shall be able to stand?" The wicked pray to be buried beneath the rocks of the mountains rather than meet the face of Him whom they have despised and rejected.

That voice which penetrates the ear of the dead, they know. How often have its plaintive, tender tones called them to repentance. How often has it been heard in the touching entreaties of a friend, a brother, a Redeemer. To the rejecters of His grace no other could be so full of condemnation, so burdened with denunciation, as that voice which has so long pleaded: "Turn ye, turn ye from your evil ways; for why will ye die?" Ezekiel 33:11. . . .

With awful distinctness do priests and rulers recall the events of Calvary. With shuddering horror they remember how, wagging their heads in satanic exultation, they exclaimed: "He saved others; Himself He cannot save. If He be the King of Israel, let Him now come down from the cross, and we will believe Him. He trusted in God; let Him deliver Him now, if He will have Him." Matthew 27:42, 43.[3]

The minister who has sacrificed truth to gain the favor of men now discerns the character and influence of his teachings. It is apparent that the omniscient eye was following him as he stood in the desk, as he walked the streets, as he mingled with men in the various scenes of life. Every emotion of the soul, every line written, every word uttered, every act that led men to rest in a refuge of falsehood, has been scattering seed; and now, in the wretched, lost souls around him, he beholds the harvest. . . .

The people see that they have been deluded. They accuse one another of having led them to destruction; but all unite in heaping their bitterest condemnation upon the ministers. Unfaithful pastors have prophesied smooth things; they have led their hearers to make void the law of God and to persecute those who would keep it holy. Now, in their despair, these teachers confess before the world their work of deception. The multitudes are filled with fury. "We are lost!" they cry, "and you are the cause of our ruin;" and they turn upon the false shepherds. The very ones that once admired them most will pronounce the most dreadful curses upon them. The very hands that once crowned them with laurels will be raised for their destruction. The swords which were to slay God's people are now employed to destroy their enemies. Everywhere there is strife and bloodshed.[4]

And now there rises a cry of mortal agony. Louder than the shout, "Crucify Him, crucify Him," which rang through the streets of Jerusalem, swells the awful, despairing wail, "He is the Son of God! He is the true Messiah!" They seek to flee from the presence of the King of kings. In the deep caverns of the earth, rent asunder by the warring of the elements, they vainly attempt to hide. . . .

Amid the reeling of the earth, the flash of lightning, and the roar of the thunder, the voice of the Son of God calls forth the sleeping saints. He looks upon the graves of the righteous, then, raising His hands to heaven, He cries: "Awake, awake, awake, ye that sleep in the dust, and arise!" Throughout the length and breadth of the earth the dead shall hear that voice, and they that hear shall live. And the whole earth shall ring with the tread of the exceeding great army of every nation, kindred, tongue, and people. From the prison house of death they come, clothed with immortal glory, crying: "O death, where is thy sting? O grave, where is thy victory?" 1 Corinthians 15:55. And the living righteous and the risen saints unite their voices in a long, glad shout of victory. . . .

. . . All arise with the freshness and vigor of eternal youth.

The living righteous are changed, "in a moment, in the twinkling of an eye." At the voice of God they were glorified; now they are made immortal and with the risen saints are caught up to meet the Lord in the air. Angels "gather together His elect from the four winds, from one end of heaven to the other." Little children are borne by holy angels to their mothers' arms. Friends long separated by death are united, nevermore to part, and with songs of gladness ascend to the City of God.[5]

That's part 1 of how the battle of Armageddon will end! It isn't a battle between nations on this earth. It isn't something to be afraid of. The battle of Armageddon is the fulfillment of the hopes and dreams of God's people since sin entered the world thousands of years ago. The battle of Armageddon is the conclusion of the struggle on this earth between the Kingdom of Light and the Kingdom of Darkness that has been going on since Adam and Eve surrendered their dominion over the world to Satan. The battle of Armageddon is the second coming of our Lord Jesus Christ, when He will forever remove His faithful people throughout the ages from the environment of sin!

If we think of the battle of Armageddon as God's entire plan to totally defeat the Kingdom of Darkness and rid the universe of this plague of evil, then it's appropriate to consider that the second coming of Christ is phase one of that battle. This phase will bring to an end the history of evil on our planet. However, it won't bring the conflict between good and evil to an end throughout the universe. That phase of the battle of Armageddon will happen a thousand years later, and it will happen on our planet, which makes it appropriate to consider it as part of the battle of Armageddon. So let's take a brief look at the millennium and the final phase of the battle of Armageddon. We will conclude with a peek at God's restored new earth.

---

1. Herodotus, *The Histories,* trans. Robin Waterfield (Oxford: Oxford University Press, 2008), 78, 79.

2. Nichol, *The Seventh-day Adventist Bible Commentary*, 7:847.

3. White, *The Great Controversy*, 635–643.

4. Ibid., 654–656.

5. Ibid., 643–645.

CHAPTER 29

The Battle of Armageddon–Part 2

S ince the battle of Armageddon is the same thing as Christ's second coming, we can say that, in one sense, it will end at the point when all the wicked have been slain and all the redeemed have gone to heaven with Christ. However, Revelation 20:7–10 informs us that one more battle between Christ and Satan will be fought at the end of the millennium, and I'm considering this battle to be a continuation of the battle of Armageddon. This will be the final battle between good and evil. When it's over, the universal conflict between the Kingdom of Light and the Kingdom of Darkness that's been going on for thousands of years will also be over. Then "there will be no more death or mourning or crying or pain, for the old order of things has passed away" (Revelation 21:4).

However, before we get to the second phase of the battle of Armageddon, let's take a few moments to reflect on the millennium. There are two aspects to consider. One is heaven, where God's people will spend the thousand years, and the other one is the earth, where Satan and his angels will spend those years.

Heaven

After the resurrected saints have all risen to "meet the Lord in the air" (1 Thessalonians 4:17), the saints living at Christ's second coming will also rise, then the cloud will ascend to heaven. In the last part of the chapter "God's People Delivered" in *The Great Controversy*, Ellen White describes the saints' journey to heaven and their initial experience there. She said that a "cloudy chariot" will transport God's people "onward toward the New Jerusalem."[1] Describing the same journey to heaven in *Early Writings*, she wrote, "We all entered the cloud together, and were seven days ascending to the sea of glass."[2] She continues,

Before entering the City of God, the Saviour bestows upon His followers the emblems of victory and invests them with the insignia of their royal state. The glittering ranks are drawn up in the form of a hollow square about their King. . . . Upon the heads of the overcomers, Jesus with His own right hand places the crown of glory. For each there is a crown bearing his own "new name." . . .

. . . Jesus opens wide the pearly gates, and the nations that have kept the truth enter in.[3]

Shortly after arriving in heaven, Christ and Adam will meet, and Jesus will extend His "outstretched arms to receive the father of our race." On seeing the nail prints in Jesus' hands, Adam "casts himself at His feet, crying: 'Worthy is the Lamb that was slain!' " Then Jesus will lead Adam to

look once more upon the Eden home from which he has so long been exiled. . . .

Transported with joy, he [Adam] beholds the trees that were once his delight—the very trees whose fruit he himself had gathered in the days of his innocence and joy. . . . The Saviour leads him to the tree of life and plucks the glorious fruit and bids him eat.[4]

Ellen White's description of our arrival in heaven is thrilling to read. I'm looking forward to being there to see it all happen, and I'm sure you are too. However, in this chapter, she presents a description of only our initial arrival in heaven. There's no description of heaven itself, and I think for a very good reason. Paul stated it well in 1 Corinthians 2:9: "No eye has seen, no ear has heard, no mind has conceived, what God has prepared for those who love him."* The reality of what heaven is like is beyond our ability, as earthly humans who have never been there, to understand.

Our activities in heaven
The Bible is largely silent about what heaven will be like. It does say that "Main Street" is made of gold and that the gates are made of pearls (Revelation 21:21). We know God's throne is there with its fiery sea of glass;

* This verse is often used to illustrate our human inability to imagine heaven. Ellen White herself used it in that way (see, e.g., *The Great Controversy*, 675), and I don't mind doing it, provided we understand that is not what Paul meant. He was writing about the ability of Christians to understand the truths of the gospel, which are incomprehensible to those who don't believe. This is apparent both from 1 Corinthians 2:6–8 and especially from what Paul said next: "But God has revealed it to us by his Spirit" (verse 10).

there's a river of life flowing from His throne; and the tree of life is planted on each side of the river (Revelation 15:2; 22:1, 2).* However, the Bible tells us about three activities we'll engage in while we're in heaven.

Singing. One activity that I believe will take up a considerable amount of our time in heaven is praising God and Christ with singing. Four passages in Revelation describe this singing: Revelation 7:10; 14:2, 3; 15:3, 4; 19:1–3, 6–8. I'll quote one of them:

> "Great and marvelous are your deeds,
>   Lord God Almighty.
> Just and true are your ways,
>   King of the ages.
> Who will not fear you, O Lord,
>   and bring glory to your name?
> For you alone are holy.
> All nations will come
>   and worship before you,
> for your righteous acts have been revealed" (Revelation 15:3, 4).

Of course, singing is an act of worship, and the context of each of these four passages in Revelation is worship of God and Christ. So God's redeemed will spend a great deal of time in heaven and on the new earth worshiping God, Christ, and the Holy Spirit.

Judging. Both Paul and John tell us of another important activity we'll carry on in heaven: judging the wicked, both angels and humans. Paul said that God's people "will judge angels" (1 Corinthians 6:3); and in his description of the millennium, John said he "saw thrones on which were seated those who had been given authority to judge" (Revelation 20:4). This means that you and I will have an opportunity to review our own life records and those of any other person we choose. We'll be able to see how God was leading us in our lives on Earth, even when we wondered why He didn't intervene to end our suffering and pain. And if someone isn't in heaven, who we were just sure would be there, we'll have the opportunity to understand why. Or if there's someone there whom we're startled to

---

* Much of what we know about heaven from the Bible comes from John's depiction of the Holy City in Revelation 21 and 22, which is a description of the city after it has descended from heaven. However, we can reasonably assume that his portrayal also applies to the city while it is still in heaven.

see, we'll be able to examine his or her life record and understand why. For example, don't you think Stephen will be shocked when he gets to heaven and sees Saul, whom we know as Paul? But when he reads about Paul's conversion—and the part he may have had in it*—don't you think he'll be thrilled?

Study. We also know that the redeemed will study the plan of salvation throughout eternity. Ellen White said,

> In this life we can only begin to understand the wonderful theme of re-demption. . . .
>
> The cross of Christ will be the science and song of the redeemed through all eternity.[5]

I have some thoughts about our activities in heaven in addition to what the Bible and Ellen White tell us. One of the things I want to learn early on is the geological history of planet Earth. Why do the geological conclusions of today's scientists suggest that life has existed on our planet for hundreds of thousands of years instead of six thousand years or so according to the biblical chronology? There has to be an answer to this question, and one of the first things I would like to do when I get to heaven is to investigate that issue. I suspect that when I ask my personal angel about this, he'll take me to a grand heavenly library where I can study the matter for myself.

Here's another question about heaven that I've pondered: We know that we'll still be physical beings when we get there, so where will we get our food? I can't imagine that God will hand out entitlements in heaven such as food stamps and subsidized housing! So will there be farmland in heaven that we can cultivate? The closest I can come to answering that question is that we know the Garden of Eden and the tree of life will be there, and Ellen White said that Adam will see "the trees that were once his delight—the very trees whose fruit he himself had gathered in the days of his innocence and joy. He sees the vines that his own hands have trained, the very flowers that he once loved to care for."[6] So maybe there will also be land in heaven that the redeemed can cultivate for food.

Finally, I also suspect that there will be some form of instruction for us

---

* Acts 7:59–8:1 says that Saul was present when Stephen was stoned, and Stephen's humble submission and his prayer, "Lord, do not hold this sin against them," may have made a deep impression on Saul. The guilt may have even driven him to persecute the saints more fiercely—until God called him on the Damascus Road.

in heaven. We'll be entering a new culture that's different from anything we could possibly have imagined before we arrived there, and the angels will need to educate us on how to get along in that new environment. And there's another kind of instruction I think we'll be given. Ellen White said that on the new earth "the grandest enterprises may be carried forward."[7] Thus, part of our time in heaven during the millennium may be spent learning how to carry out some of the grand enterprises we'll each be engaged in on the new earth after the millennium.

Satan's activities during the millennium

Revelation 20:3 says that Satan will be thrown into "the Abyss"* at the beginning of the millennium. The Septuagint, an early Greek translation of the Hebrew Old Testament, uses the word *abussos* to describe the earth in its primeval state: "formless and empty" (Genesis 1:2). John used this same word in Revelation 20:3 to describe Satan's living quarters during the millennium. In his book *Revelation of Jesus Christ*, Ranko Stefanovic writes, "In the New Testament, the abyss or the bottomless pit (Gr. *abussos*) is described as a dark and chaotic prison abode of the fallen angels, the demons, who are under God's control."[8] The abyss can be compared to the worst of the desolate deserts of the earth, such as the region around the Dead Sea in Israel or Death Valley in the United States.

Ellen White's description of Earth during the millennium is quite graphic:

The earth looked like a desolate wilderness. Cities and villages, shaken down by the earthquake, lay in heaps. Mountains had been moved out of their places, leaving large caverns. Ragged rocks, thrown out by the sea, or torn out of the earth itself, were scattered all over its surface. Large trees had been uprooted and were strewn over the land. Here is to be the home of Satan with his evil angels for a thousand years. Here he will be confined, to wander up and down over the broken surface of the earth and see the effects of his rebellion against God's law. For a thousand years he can enjoy the fruit of the curse which he has caused. Limited alone to the earth, he will not have the privilege of ranging to other planets, to tempt and annoy those who have not fallen. During this time, Satan suffers extremely. Since his fall his evil traits have been in constant exercise. But he is then to be deprived of his power, and left to reflect upon the part which he has acted since his fall, and to look forward with trembling and terror

---

* NIV. The KJV and the NKJV say "bottomless pit."

to the dreadful future, when he must suffer for all the evil that he has done and be punished for all the sins that he has caused to be committed.[9]

Having experienced significant periods of intense anxiety myself during my lifetime, I don't envy Satan for what he will have to endure during the millennium!

Now I will raise a question similar to one that I asked about God's people during the millennium: Beyond reflecting on his evil deeds during the six thousand years of Earth's history, what else will occupy Satan's time and that of his fellow angels during the millennium? The answer to this question will take us into the time after the millennium, so let's turn to that. We'll return afterward to the question of the activities of Satan and his angels during the millennium.

After the millennium

Revelation says that at the close of the millennium Satan and his angels will be released from their prison, their confinement in the abyss, and that the wicked will also be raised to life at about the same time (Revelation 20:5, 7). Satan will then "go out to deceive the nations in the four corners of the earth—Gog and Magog—to gather them for battle. In number they are like the sand on the seashore. They marched across the breadth of the earth and surrounded the camp of God's people, the city he loves" (verses 8, 9).

But why will Satan have to deceive the wicked? Keep in mind that these people will still have their memories intact, and those who were alive at Christ's second coming will remember all too well the extreme power that Christ exercised to destroy them and deliver His saints. Everyone on Earth will see the New Jerusalem, which will have descended from heaven, and Satan will have to persuade them that, in spite of the odds that seem to be against them, their vast numbers will make it possible for them to overthrow the city and take full command of the world.

Ellen White described this very thing in volume 4 of a four-volume set called *The Spirit of Prophecy*.* In a chapter titled "The Controversy Ended," she wrote,

---

* The four-volume *Spirit of Prophecy* books were a precursor to the five-volume Conflict of the Ages series: *Patriarchs and Prophets, Prophets and Kings, The Desire of Ages, The Acts of the Apostles*, and *The Great Controversy*. Selected parts of the four-volume set have been included in the book *The Story of Redemption*.

Now Satan prepares for a last mighty struggle for the supremacy. While deprived of his power, and cut off from his work of deception [during the millennium], the prince of evil was miserable and dejected; but as the wicked dead are raised, and he sees the vast multitudes upon his side, his hopes revive, and he determines not to yield the great controversy. . . . Yet, true to his early cunning, he does not acknowledge himself to be Satan. He claims to be the Prince who is the rightful owner of the world, and whose inheritance has been unlawfully wrested from him. He represents himself to his deluded subjects as a redeemer, assuring them that his power has brought them forth from their graves, and that he is about to rescue them from the most cruel tyranny. . . . Satan works wonders to support his claims. He makes the weak strong, and inspires all with his own spirit and energy. He proposes to lead them against the camp of the saints, and to take possession of the city of God. With fiendish exultation he points to the unnumbered millions who have been raised from the dead, and declares that as their leader he is well able to overthrow the city, and regain his throne and his kingdom.[10]

It's easy to suppose that the wicked will be raised to life and that very same afternoon or the next day they'll be judged and destroyed in the lake of fire. But I can assure you it won't happen that fast. Satan is smart enough to know that any hope he might have of conquering the New Jerusalem will require a well-organized army, navy, and air force, with exceedingly sophisticated weapons similar to those that were in use on the earth a thousand years earlier. In *The Great Controversy*, Ellen White wrote that in preparing for the last mighty struggle for the supremacy Satan "will marshal all the armies of the lost under his banner and through them endeavor to execute his plans."[11] And in *Early Writings*, she wrote, "Satan succeeds in deceiving them, and all immediately begin to prepare themselves for battle. There are many skillful men in that vast army, and they construct all kinds of implements of war."[12]

Back to the millennium

Now all this will take considerable time, as Satan and his followers develop their weapons and organize the military forces that will be required to take over the New Jerusalem. This brings me back to the issue of Satan's activities during the millennium. Satan is as familiar with Revelation 20 as any of us humans, and it doesn't take a genius to figure out that as he ponders his future while confined to Earth during the thousand years, he'll realize that it would be greatly to his advantage to be ready for the events following the millennium when they come.

So what kinds of preparation will Satan and his angels need to make? There will be two kinds. Their first task will be to clear away all the rubble. Cities all over the world will look like the huge piles of wreckage that were left in the wake of the terrorist attacks on the Twin Towers in New York City on September 11, 2001. Freeways, highways, and bridges all over the world will be broken up. The houses where human beings used to live will be heaps of ruins.

My point is this: I suspect that Satan and his angels will be very busy during the millennium preparing the world for the resurrection of the wicked. Why? Because I have a hard time imagining the wicked surviving very long after they're resurrected if they have to live in the world the way it was after Christ's second coming.

This brings me to the second kind of preparation that Satan and his angels will have to make for the vast multitude that will be raised from the dead at the end of the millennium. These people will need food and clothes and transportation and houses and all the other things that go with living success-fully on the earth. Stores and factories will have to be built; farms will have to be set up where the wicked can grow their food during the time they're preparing for the attack on the Holy City; cities and towns all over the world will need support infrastructure. The world will need highways and cars and freeways and airports and airplanes. They'll also need banks and money. The list goes on and on! This preparation will keep Satan and his angels very busy during the millennium.

My guess is that clearing away the rubble left over from Christ's second coming and then preparing the facilities the wicked will need after they're brought back to life will consume a major share of the time and effort of the evil angels during the millennium.

I repeat that nothing in the Bible or Ellen White's writings suggests that Satan and his evil angels will prepare the facilities that the wicked will need at the close of the millennium. But if that isn't how these things come about, I can't help but wonder where they will come from. Will God prepare these necessities for them? I have an even harder time believing that.

I've also thought of another problem that will confront Satan and his followers following the resurrection of the wicked: space to live and work in—in fact, space just to move around in! Our world today is inhabited by more than seven billion people, the majority of whom are counted among the wicked. But that's only those who are alive today. How many billions of people have lived and died in our world over the millennia since Adam and Eve were cast out of Eden? Whatever the number, let's say the wicked constitute 90 percent of all those who have ever lived on Earth. Then there are the righteous, who will also be living on Earth by then. There'll be standing room only on the planet, at least for the wicked.*

Armageddon, part 2

Revelation 20:9 says that the vast army of the wicked "marched across the breadth of the earth and surrounded the camp of God's people, the city he loves." Satan has assured his followers that with their vastly superior numbers and the firepower they've developed they can easily take the city. So they start out. Ellen White describes the scene:

> At last the order to advance is given, and the countless host moves on— an army such as was never summoned by earthly conquerors, such as the combined forces of all ages since war began on earth could never equal. Satan, the mightiest of warriors, leads the van, and his angels unite their forces for this final struggle. Kings and warriors are in his train, and the multitudes follow in vast companies, each under its appointed leader. With military precision the serried ranks advance over the earth's broken and uneven surface to the City of God. By command of Jesus, the gates of the New Jerusalem are closed, and the armies of Satan surround the city.[13]

This is part 2 of the battle of Armageddon, and, like the first part of the battle at Christ's second coming, this attack will be stopped in its tracks.

I will let Ellen White tell the rest of the story: "Now Christ again appears to the view of His enemies. Far above the city, upon a foundation of burnished gold, is a throne, high and lifted up. Upon this throne sits the Son of God, and around Him are the subjects of His kingdom. The power and majesty of Christ no language can describe, no pen portray. The glory of the Eternal Father is enshrouding His Son. The brightness of His presence fills the City of God, and flows out beyond the gates, flooding the whole earth with its radiance."[14]

Picture this in your imagination: every human being who ever lived on

---

* If the Bible's dimensions for the New Jerusalem are factual, that's fourteen hundred miles on every side (Revelation 21:16, NIV, footnote). If that's correct, there'll be plenty of room for the righteous to live in, leaving the rest of the globe for the wicked.

planet Earth will be present at this great conclave. Every eye will be fixed on Christ in His stupendous glory, and the wicked won't be able to look away.*

> In the presence of the assembled inhabitants of earth and heaven the final coronation of the Son of God takes place. And now, invested with supreme majesty and power, the King of kings pronounces sentence upon the rebels against His government and executes justice upon those who have transgressed His law and oppressed His people. . . .
>
> As soon as the books of record are opened, and the eye of Jesus looks upon the wicked, they are conscious of every sin which they have ever committed. They see just where their feet diverged from the path of purity and holiness, just how far pride and rebellion have carried them in violation of the law of God. . . . All appear as if written in letters of fire.
>
> Above the throne is revealed the cross; and like a panoramic view appear the scenes of Adam's temptation and fall, and the successive steps in the great plan of redemption. The Saviour's lowly birth; His early life of simplicity and obedience; His baptism in Jordan; the fast and temptation in the wilderness; His public ministry, unfolding to men heaven's most precious blessings. . . . All are vividly portrayed.
>
> And now before the swaying multitude are revealed the final scenes— the patient Sufferer treading the path to Calvary; the Prince of heaven hanging upon the cross; the haughty priests and the jeering rabble deriding His expiring agony; the supernatural darkness; the heaving earth, the rent rocks, the open graves, marking the moment when the world's Redeemer yielded up His life.
>
> The awful spectacle appears just as it was. Satan, his angels, and his subjects have no power to turn from the picture of their own work. Each actor recalls the part which he performed. . . .
>
> It is now evident to all that the wages of sin is not noble independence and eternal life, but slavery, ruin, and death. The wicked see what they have forfeited by their life of rebellion. . . .
>
> As if entranced, the wicked have looked upon the coronation of the Son of God. . . .
>
> Satan seems paralyzed as he beholds the glory and majesty of Christ. He who was once a covering cherub remembers whence he has fallen. . . .
>
> Satan sees that his voluntary rebellion has unfitted him for heaven. . . .

---

* This raises the interesting question of how people on all sides of the globe will be able to see Christ at the same time. That's a question we'll have to leave for God to answer.

And now Satan bows down and confesses the justice of his sentence.

Notwithstanding that Satan has been constrained to acknowledge God's justice and to bow to the supremacy of Christ, his character remains unchanged. The spirit of rebellion, like a mighty torrent, again bursts forth. Filled with frenzy, he determines not to yield the great controversy. The time has come for a last desperate struggle against the King of heaven. He rushes into the midst of his subjects and endeavors to inspire them with his own fury and arouse them to instant battle. But of all the countless millions whom he has allured into rebellion, there are none now to acknowledge his supremacy. His power is at an end. The wicked are filled with the same hatred of God that inspires Satan; but they see that their case is hopeless, that they cannot prevail against Jehovah. Their rage is kindled against Satan and those who have been his agents in deception, and with the fury of demons they turn upon them.

. . . Fire comes down from God out of heaven. The earth is broken up. The weapons concealed in its depths are drawn forth. Devouring flames burst from every yawning chasm. The very rocks are on fire. The day has come that shall burn as an oven. The elements melt with fervent heat, the earth also, and the works that are therein are burned up. Malachi 4:1; 2 Peter 3:10. The earth's surface seems one molten mass—a vast, seething lake of fire. It is the time of the judgment and perdition of ungodly men—"the day of the Lord's vengeance, and the year of recompenses for the controversy of Zion." Isaiah 34:8.

The wicked receive their recompense in the earth. . . . All are punished "according to their deeds."[15]

The Kingdom of Light has finally and forever conquered the Kingdom of Darkness! The conflict that began in heaven thousands of years earlier is over! God's wisdom and patience in not immediately destroying the work of Satan and his followers has been made manifest, and the universe is secure from ever again having to go through the terrible experiment of rebellion against God and His laws of love. While it seems incredible that any of the holy beings inhabiting the universe would ever *choose* to rebel again, theoretically it could happen, since all created intelligences have a free will. But if such an inconceivable thing should happen, this time God would immediately destroy the rebel (or rebels), because doing so would raise no questions in the minds of God's loyal followers. To the contrary, they would all, with one voice, immediately *demand* the immediate destruction of anyone rebelling against God!

The new earth

Following the destruction of Satan and his rebellious followers, God will re-create the world out of the ashes of the old one. Revelation 21 and 22 give us a snapshot of this re-created world, and Ellen White described it on pages 674–676 in *The Great Controversy*. Then she goes on to briefly describe life on this renewed planet, which, if we are there, we will enjoy throughout the ceaseless ages of eternity.

There the redeemed shall know, even as also they are known. The loves and sympathies which God Himself has planted in the soul shall there find truest and sweetest exercise. The pure communion with holy beings, the harmonious social life with the blessed angels and with the faithful ones of all ages who have washed their robes and made them white in the blood of the Lamb, the sacred ties that bind together "the whole family in heaven and earth" (Ephesians 3:15)—these help to constitute the happiness of the redeemed.

There, immortal minds will contemplate with never-failing delight the wonders of creative power, the mysteries of redeeming love. There will be no cruel, deceiving foe to tempt to forgetfulness of God. Every faculty will be developed, every capacity increased. The acquirement of knowledge will not weary the mind or exhaust the energies. There the grandest enterprises may be carried forward, the loftiest aspirations reached, the highest ambitions realized; and still there will arise new heights to surmount, new wonders to admire, new truths to comprehend, fresh objects to call forth the powers of mind and soul and body.

All the treasures of the universe will be open to the study of God's redeemed. Unfettered by mortality, they wing their tireless flight to worlds afar—worlds that thrilled with sorrow at the spectacle of human woe and rang with songs of gladness at the tidings of a ransomed soul. With unutterable delight the children of earth enter into the joy and the wisdom of unfallen beings. They share the treasures of knowledge and understanding gained through ages upon ages in contemplation of God's handiwork. With undimmed vision they gaze upon the glory of creation—suns and stars and systems, all in their appointed order circling the throne of Deity. Upon all things, from the least to the greatest, the Creator's name is written, and in all are the riches of His power displayed.

And the years of eternity, as they roll, will bring richer and still more glorious revelations of God and of Christ. As knowledge is progressive, so will love, reverence, and happiness increase. The more men learn of God, the greater will be their admiration of His character. As Jesus opens before them the riches of redemption and the amazing achievements in the great controversy with Satan, the hearts of the ransomed thrill with more fervent devotion, and with more rapturous joy they sweep the harps of gold; and ten thousand times ten thousand and thousands of thousands of voices unite to swell the mighty chorus of praise.[16]

Finally, Ellen White concludes her book *The Great Controversy* and her entire Conflict of the Ages series with these poignant words: "The great controversy is ended. Sin and sinners are no more. The entire universe is clean. One pulse of harmony and gladness beats through the vast creation. From Him who created all, flow life and light and gladness, throughout the realms of illimitable space. From the minutest atom to the greatest world, all things, animate and inanimate, in their unshadowed beauty and perfect joy, declare that God is love."[17]

Armageddon is over! God's Kingdom of Light won—not just the battle, but the war. Praise the Lord!

1. White, *The Great Controversy*, 645.

2. White, *Early Writings*, 16.

3. White, *The Great Controversy*, 645, 646.

4. Ibid., 647, 648.

5. Ibid., 651.

6. Ibid., 648.

7. Ibid., 677.

8. Stefanovic, *Revelation of Jesus Christ*, 300. See also Nichol, *The Seventh-day Adventist Commentary*, 7:791.

9. White, *Early Writings*, 290.

10. Ellen G. White, *The Spirit of Prophecy*, vol. 4 (Battle Creek, MI: Steam Press, 1884), 477, 478.

11. White, *The Great Controversy*, 663.

12. White, *Early Writings*, 293.

13. White, *The Great Controversy*, 664.

14. Ibid., 665.

15. Ibid., 666–673.

16. Ibid., 677, 678.

17. Ibid., 678.

APPENDIX

Reflections on the Wrath of God

One of the questions that often comes up in any discussion about the punishment of the wicked in the lake of fire is how that punishment can be consistent with the concept of God's love. This is a valid question, especially in the light of Ellen White's statement that Satan's "punishment is to be far greater than that of those whom he has deceived. After all have perished who fell by his deceptions, *he is still to live and suffer on.*"[1]

I can't say that I have an entirely satisfactory answer to why God will allow Satan to suffer on and on for some time in the lake of fire. Why not just destroy him and all other sinful beings instantly? The best answer I can come up with is that Satan deserves to suffer for all the suffering he's caused—and that *is* horrible to contemplate. However, I have resolved to my satisfaction the general question about God's wrath and His punishment of the wicked because of that wrath. I will share with you my thoughts regarding that wrath in this appendix.

The Bible speaks repeatedly of God's wrath. For example, Psalm 2:5 says that God rebukes the kings of the earth in His anger "and terrifies them in his wrath." God said to Jeremiah, "Take from my hand this cup filled with the wine of my wrath and make all the nations to whom I send you drink it" (Jeremiah 25:15). Revelation echoes the same theme in the New Testament. In the most vivid description of God's wrath anywhere in the Bible, Revelation says that those who accept the mark of the beast will "drink of the wine of the wrath of God, which is mixed in full strength in the cup of his anger" (Revelation 14:10, NASB). Paul also spoke several times about God's wrath in both Romans 1 and 2:

- "The wrath of God is being revealed from heaven against all the godlessness and wickedness of men who suppress the truth by their wickedness" (Romans 1:18).
- "Because of your stubbornness and your unrepentant heart, you are storing up wrath against yourself for the day of God's wrath, when his righteous judgment will be revealed" (Romans 2:5).

296

- "For those who are self-seeking and who reject the truth and follow evil, there will be wrath and anger" (verse 8).

The Bible clearly speaks of God's wrath. So what's the Adventist debate about? Why is anyone questioning what the Bible seems to teach so clearly?

Active wrath, passive wrath, or no wrath

The issue is whether God's wrath is active or passive—or whether He has no wrath at all. Each alternative has its proponents. So let's examine them.

Active wrath. The "active-wrath" model proposes that in the past God has intervened personally, intentionally, and, in some cases, forcefully (violently) to put down evil and that He will do so even more forcefully in the future. The purpose of His active exercise of wrath is either to punish evil people for their sins or to deliver His own people from their grasp, and often both purposes merge into one. An obvious example of God's active wrath in the past is His destruction of the sinful world at the time of the Flood. Another is His destruction of Sodom and Gomorrah with fire and brimstone. A third example is His deliverance of Israel from Egyptian slavery with hail and fire and storms and the slaying of the firstborn of Egyptian animals and people. The destruction of Pharaoh's army in the Red Sea is also an example of active wrath.

The Bible predicts that God will intervene actively to punish evil and deliver His people at least twice in the future. Most Christians are familiar with Revelation's description of fire coming down from heaven and devouring the wicked at the end of the millennium (Revelation 20:9). God will also intervene forcefully in human history at the beginning of the millennium with the second coming of Christ. Revelation 6:12–17 and 16:17–21 picture God destroying the earth with a violent global earthquake at Christ's second coming, and Revelation 19:11–21 shows Christ engaging the world's armies in a violent war that concludes with the destruction of the forces of evil. I'll have more to say about that war later in this appendix.

Paul also spoke of this active form of God's wrath. "Because of your stubbornness and your unrepentant heart, you are storing up wrath against yourself for *the day of God's wrath*" (Romans 2:5; emphasis added). "The day of God's wrath" is clearly a reference to the second coming of Christ, and Paul said that unrepentant Jews were preparing themselves to experience that wrath. He said essentially the same thing in verse 8: "For those who are self-seeking and who reject the truth and follow evil, there will be wrath and anger." The words "there *will be* [future tense] wrath and anger" suggest that the wrath and anger will be manifested at Christ's second coming.

Passive wrath. Active wrath has been the predominant model within the Adventist Church throughout most of our history. However, the "passive-wrath" model gained a small but resolute following during the last half of the twentieth century. This model proposes that God's wrath is primarily exercised by His abandonment of evil and evil people to the natural outworking of their choices. And here is where Romans 1 is particularly relevant: Paul says that "the wrath of God is being revealed from heaven against all the godlessness and wickedness of men who suppress the truth by their wickedness" (verse 18). This verse could be interpreted to support the active-wrath model. However, Paul phrased his words in the present tense—"the wrath of God *is being* revealed"—and there's scant evidence of God's active intervention in the lives of evil people at that time in history. Furthermore, several other statements Paul made in Romans 1 suggest that the passive-wrath model is what he had in mind:

- "Therefore God gave them [pagan sinners] over in the sinful desires of their hearts to sexual impurity for the degrading of their bodies with one another" (verse 24).
- "Because of this, God gave them over to shameful lusts," and they "received in themselves the due penalty for their perversion" (verses 26, 27).
- God "gave them over to a depraved mind, to do what ought not to be done" (verse 28).
- "Men committed indecent acts with other men, and received in themselves the due penalty for their perversion" (verse 27).

These verses support the passive-wrath model, because they state that God simply *gives sinful people over* to the natural outworking of their sins, letting nature take its course. They receive "in themselves the due penalty for their perversion."

At the beginning of this appendix, I suggested a third possibility: the "no-wrath" concept. This is actually a common theme among those who propose the passive-wrath model. They often argue for the passive-wrath model in no-wrath terms, claiming that anger is contrary to God's character of love. We'll discuss this argument in a moment. But first we need to ask, is God's wrath active or passive?

Active or passive? Provided we exclude no wrath from the passive-wrath model, I believe God's wrath is both active and passive. Romans 1 makes it clear that God's wrath is passive at times. In fact, the proponents of the passive-wrath model are close to being correct when they suggest that this is the exclusive way God expresses His wrath. In the history of our world, the incidents when God has actively intervened to put down evil with force are few and far between. And there's a reason why. Throughout nearly all of history, we humans have lived in probationary time. During this time, God has, for the most part, allowed evil to run its course as a demonstration to the universe of what evil is really like.

However, I believe it's a mistake to make the passive model the complete explanation of God's wrath. There's too much biblical evidence that God has intervened actively to stop evil in the past and that He will do so again in the future.

Anger, force, and God's love

Back in 1999 or 2000, I received a letter at *Signs of the Times®* that illustrates the objection many proponents of the passive and no-wrath models have to the idea that God's wrath can also be active. This letter was in response to an article about Armageddon that appeared in the November 1999 issue of the magazine: "I believe the view presented pictures God as arbitrary, vengeful, and severe, using His power to put down evil—the very characteristics that Satan attributes to God but that are actually characteristics of Satan himself. I do not believe that in the end God will finally resort to force to put down evil."

This letter raises a very significant question: How does the idea of God's wrath—especially the concept of His active wrath—square with the primary attribute of God's character, which is love?

The relationship of love to evil. We can safely begin by saying that any teaching about God's ultimate dealing with sin and sinners must be consistent with His love. The problem for us humans is how to bring together everything we know about God without creating unacceptable contradictions. How should love respond to evil? Does love always sit back and wait for evil to resolve itself by itself, or does love at times intervene actively to prevent evil from carrying out its harmful designs? I propose that active intervention may be the most loving thing that a loving being, divine or human, can do. Several years ago I heard a couple of stories that illustrate the point well.

The first story is about a family in which the father sexually abuses his daughter. One day he goes into the girl's bedroom, and a few minutes later the mother hears the daughter crying out, "No, Daddy, no! Please, Daddy, stop!" So the mother goes to an adjoining room, kneels down, and prays for God to intervene.

In the second story, a teenage daughter gets pregnant, but she hesitates to tell her parents because she fears that her father will kill her. Finally, however, it becomes impossible to hide the evidence. So before her father guesses the problem, she approaches him on the front porch of their house. When he learns that she's going to have a baby, he attacks her violently. In the midst of her screams, the front door to the house bursts open. The girl's mother leaps out, points a rifle at her husband, and shouts, "You strike my daughter one more time and you're a dead man!"

The question is, which mother showed the most love for her daughter—the one who prayed passively or the one who intervened actively? I think the answer is obvious. In the face of severe abuse, active intervention is the most loving thing that a loving being can do. Failing to do so would be unloving.

Is anger bad? Those who favor the no-wrath concept argue that God doesn't get angry. That's what the correspondent who wrote to *Signs of the Times*° apparently believed. He said that the active-wrath model "pictures God as arbitrary, vengeful, and severe." However, I believe this view involves a fundamental misunderstanding of anger; namely, that anger is always bad. Unfortunately, many Christians have grown up with the idea that anger is bad. I can recall being told as a child that anger was bad, but *righteous indignation* was OK. Nobody ever defined *righteous indignation*, but plain old anger was always bad. And the proponents of the passive model of God's wrath argue that, just as hot is the opposite of cold and light is the opposite of dark, so love is the opposite of anger and anger is therefore sinful, which is why a loving God will never get angry.

But let me ask you a question. What feeling would you experience if you saw a mother beating a five-year-old child on his bare back with a piece of garden hose? Name the feeling you would have if you saw a father hold the lighted end of a cigarette against his son's bare skin. Or how about the parents who keep a child tied to a bedpost or locked in a dark closet day after day for weeks on end, wallowing in his own excrement? These are extreme examples, to be sure, but they do happen. So what feeling did you get when you read about these examples of abuse?

I hope you said *anger*! Anger is our normal human response to injustice, and it's also a very loving response. Anger is bad only when we respond to it inappropriately, such as when we lose our tempers.

God's anger. God never loses His temper, but I propose that God's anger—His wrath—is a very appropriate and a very loving *divine* response to injustice. We all want an angry God from time to time. The cry "Where was God when . . . ?" is a plea for an angry God. If we can feel anger over the little bit of abuse that we observe humans perpetrating against each other, how must God feel, who sees all the abuse that ever has happened and ever will happen? I hope He feels intense anger!

I have a friend who believes that anger is contrary to God's character of love, so I asked him one day how he would feel if an intruder were to break into his house and rape one of his teenage daughters. He said, "Murderous." Then I asked him how he would want God to feel. He thought a moment, and then he said, "Murderous." I rested my case.

A number of years ago my wife and I visited the World War II concentration camp in Dachau, Germany, and we felt profound anger as we saw how Hitler treated Jews and other "undesirables." That was an entirely appropriate response.

Those who propose that God doesn't get angry are rightly concerned to avoid compromising His mercy. But mercy and justice need each other. Justice without mercy results in tyranny, abuse, and torture. But so does mercy without justice, for mercy without justice allows evil people to take charge, as in the case of the mother who prayed instead of intervening with force to protect her daughter. Justice that refuses to intervene to protect the victims of abuse is very unmerciful.

How about force? But should anger intervene with force? Our *Signs* correspondent said No. Claiming that force is a characteristic of Satan, he said, "I do not believe that in the end God will finally resort to force to put down evil." However, the stories of the two mothers that I shared with you a moment ago help us to understand that sometimes forceful intervention against evil is the most moral and the most loving thing we can do. The mother who loved her daughter the most was clearly the one who felt enough anger over the abuse her husband was inflicting on their daughter that she took strong steps to stop it. The other mother should have felt angry, and she should have intervened forcefully. In some situations, love fails if it doesn't intervene with force.

My correspondent from *Signs* said that force is a characteristic of Satan. It's true, of course, that Satan uses force—but he uses it to *impose* suffering, not to *prevent* it. Often, Satan uses force to get people to obey him. That God will never do. All who obey Him must do so by choice.

But does God ever use force? Is force ever an appropriate response from any loving being? I believe the answer has to be Yes. Force is simply the exercise of power to bring about a desired result, and situations do exist when it's absolutely essential that good people exercise force in order to prevent horrible evil from gaining control and creating chaos and suffering. I propose that, in the presence of intolerable evil, force is also an entirely appropriate response from a loving God. The Bible says that when Lucifer and his angels chose to rebel against God's law of love in heaven, Michael and His army of angels cast them out. That was force: God used His power to expel rebellion and evil from heaven. And the Bible teaches that an all-wise God will eventually exercise the same force to expel rebellion from the entire universe.

The final destruction of the wicked

What about God's wrath in the final destruction of the wicked that is described so graphically in Revelation? Those who argue for passive wrath as the exclusive way God exercises His wrath correctly point out that Revelation is highly symbolic. However, it doesn't follow that everything in Revelation is symbolic. Certainly the image of Christ riding a white horse at His second coming is symbolic. This is simply a way of stating the literal truth that His second coming will be a time of war. *And war is always an act of violent intervention.* The images of birds eating the flesh of the wicked and of beasts being thrown into a lake of fire are highly symbolic, but the idea behind these images—that Christ will destroy evil and evil people with force at His second coming—is very literal.

The proponents of the passive-wrath and the no-wrath models are quite horrified at the suggestion that God will exercise His active wrath in the final punishment and destruction of the wicked. I suspect this is because they consider all anger to be bad. But when we consider anger to be an appropriate response to evil and injustice, then it makes perfect sense for a loving God to be active as well as passive in dealing with it. And the biblical teaching about the final punishment of the wicked in the lake of fire is simply a picture—symbolic, perhaps, but true in a very real sense—of God intervening actively to put an end to evil.

Let's consider the prospect of God truly refusing to intervene with force to destroy the wicked, allowing their eternal demise to be simply the natural outworking of their choice to be evil. To do that, God would have to place them in a world by themselves long enough for them to become extinct through degeneration, disease, and the reign of "tooth and claw." They would suffer a miserable, prolonged, pathetic extinction. When I have a dog or cat with a painful terminal illness, in mercy I ask the veterinarian to put it to sleep. In the same way, I see God's forceful destruction of the wicked as a merciful alternative to truly allowing nature to take its course.

The revelation of God's glory. A common explanation suggested by those who support the passive model of God's wrath is that the wicked will be destroyed by the revelation of God's glory in the final judgment, rather than God Himself bringing fire down on them. But to absolve God of the responsibility for the death of the wicked by saying, "He'll just unveil His glory" hardly gets Him off the hook. Imagine for a moment that I have a laser beam in my forehead that will kill people if I take off my hat in their presence. If I ever did that and were hauled into court for murder, what do you think the judge and jury would say to my plea when I claimed, "I didn't kill anyone. I just took off my hat"? If it's within my power to not take off my hat, then I'm responsible for those who die when I take it off, even if I didn't strike them.

The Bible's description of the final destruction of the wicked—fire coming down from God out of heaven—sounds like a releasing of the forces of nature that heretofore God has held in check. That's pretty violent! A proponent of the passive model of God's wrath might argue that God won't personally destroy the wicked in the lake of fire. He'll simply release the forces of nature. That's like saying that I'm not responsible if my pit bull attacks and injures you, because all I did was let go of the leash. I hardly think a judge would acquit me on that basis. If it's within my power to restrain the dog, then I'm responsible for the consequences when I let it go. Similarly, if it's within God's power to restrain the forces of nature, then it's hardly an argument in favor of the passive model of His wrath to say that the destruction of the wicked in the lake of fire is simply the result of His releasing the forces of nature.

Is God vengeful and severe? My correspondent from *Signs* said that "God is not arbitrary, vengeful, or severe." It's true that God isn't arbitrary in His dealings with the wicked. An arbitrary God would destroy them with no consideration for what His loyal subjects thought. That's why God refused to eradicate sin the moment it arose in heaven many eons ago. He allowed it to continue for several thousand years so that all created beings could pass judgment against it for themselves.

Is God vengeful? No; by which I mean He isn't spiteful. Is He severe? If

303

by *severe* we mean "malicious," no; but if we mean "strict," yes. God is always strict in dealing with evil.

I propose that the life of every creature is ultimately in God's hands. Therefore, when the time comes that the wicked are permanently destroyed, God will be responsible for their deaths. Whether He takes personal action to make that happen or merely "allows" it to happen is irrelevant. I also propose that His justice is the reason He will not only allow it to happen but will actually initiate its happening. In the long-range scheme of things, that tragic event will be the most merciful thing a loving God could *do*!

---

1. White, *The Great Controversy*, 673; emphasis added.